A Sort of Utopia

A Sort of Utopia

SCARSDALE, 1891–1981

Carol A. O'Connor

State University of New York Press

ALBANY

To my mother, my father, and Clyde

Portions of Chapter Four appeared originally as "Setting a Standard for Suburbia: Innovation in the Scarsdale Schools, 1920–1930" in *History of Education Quarterly* 20 (Fall 1980), pp. 295–311. Used by permission.

Published by
State University of New York Press, Albany

For information, address State University of New York Press,
State University Plaza, Albany, N.Y., 12246

Library of Congress Cataloging in Publication Data

O'Connor, Carol A., 1946–
  A sort of utopia, Scarsdale, 1891–1981.

  Bibliography: p. 271
  Includes index.
  1. Scarsdale (N.Y.)—History. 2. Scarsdale (N.Y.)—Social conditions. I. Title.
F129.S48025 1982   974.7'277   82-5855
ISBN 0-87395-659-1   AACR2
ISBN 0-87395-660-5 (pbk.)

Contents

Preface

A cartoon in a 1936 issue of the old *Life* magazine poked fun at a scene familiar to thousands of big city commuters. A man, conservatively dressed in an overcoat, suit, hat, and tie, is sitting at a shoe-shine stand with his galoshes and briefcase off to one side. But in this scene the attendant standing in front of him is hesitating before applying wax to the commuter's argyle socks. "Good heavens," exclaims the commuter. "My shoes must be in Scarsdale."[1]

In 1979 another cartoon appeared in a major magazine. This one featured a middle-aged couple—well-dressed, overweight, and laden with suitcases. The pair has just walked beyond a sign at a crossroads, where they have avoided the paths leading to Sodom and Gomorrah. Instead, they are following the arrow to Scarsdale. The husband is saying, "Let's hope, Lucille, that our decision hasn't been too hasty."[2]

Whether as the butt of jokes about the foibles of wealthy suburbanites or as a dubious symbol of hope in a weary world, Scarsdale, New York, holds an important place in the consciousness of modern America. Although it may not have Sodom and Gomorrah's international reputation or sex appeal, it does compare to Hollywood or the White House as a goal for Americans. Indeed, the idea of acquiring a house in Scarsdale, or in a suburb like Scarsdale, is probably the most accessible version of the American dream of social mobility. What Scarsdale represents is a feasible level of material success—not a mansion on a mountain but an impressive home in a leading community.

Scarsdale has not attained this reputation accidentally. For nearly ninety years its citizens have shown a willingness to employ social pressures and legal prerogatives, not to mention their own tax dollars, in making Scarsdale a wealthy, attractive, convenient community. Moreover, success has fed their ambitions. Though at times insensitive to the interests of neighboring municipalities, the residents of Scarsdale have seen it as their special role to provide a model for the country and the world, particularly in such enterprises as planning and education. In so doing, they have acted with a degree of self-consciousness that goes beyond the usual town boosterism to assume almost nationalistic proportions.

An outsider to Scarsdale has captured the insider's sense of community pride and mission. Describing Scarsdale, in 1964, as "a sort of utopia," Millicent Carey McIntosh, the president emeritus of Barnard College, referred to its lovely houses, excellent schools, and ready access to the beauties of nature and to the culture of the city. "And," she said, "it is a place where above all others, perhaps, the problems of our times should be solved, . . . especially those problems which are fundamental to our society."[3]

From 1891 to 1981, Scarsdale's citizens have tackled many of society's problems from the most mundane, such as garbage and traffic, to the most profound, such as religion and race. Though some of their solutions have aggravated conditions beyond their own borders, they have succeeded in establishing a comfortable community for themselves. In the process they have displayed hopes, fears, and prejudices that provide an important insight into the upper-middle-class, suburban mentality as well as a special perspective on many national trends of the twentieth century.

A few words of clarification seem appropriate at this juncture. First, this book concerns the history of the coextensive town and village of Scarsdale, which should be distinguished from that more sprawling entity, the Scarsdale postal district. The latter takes in parts of the municipalities of New Rochelle, Eastchester, Yonkers, and Greenburgh in addition to the town and village of Scarsdale. Although the residents of this greater Scarsdale community often attend the same churches and clubs and patronize the same stores, they do not pay the same taxes, enjoy the same municipal services, educate their children in the same public schools, or conform to the same requirements in such matters as zoning. To write a history of this broader Scarsdale would be virtually impossible. I have not attempted it.

Second, this is an interpretive history rather than a comprehensive one. Readers familiar with Scarsdale's past will find me more interested in analyzing demographic trends and highlighting political arguments than in listing the names of prominent individuals and groups. However, while I consciously avoided making this a history of famous persons, I found I could not discuss in detail some topics in which I have a deep interest. For example, a thorough analysis of Christian-Jewish relations awaits someone who is prepared to use survey techniques or a participant-observer approach. It cannot be written on the basis of public records and selected interviews.

In the third place, this book attempts to explain why Scarsdale has become as famous as it has, not to exploit that fame. Having grown up in Scarsdale, I am sympathetic to those residents who find it hard to identify with the community's reputation for wealth. Indeed, it was such feelings of discomfort on my part that prompted me to undertake this project. But if my initial intention was to underscore the range of status among residents of the village, my research, along with ten years of living in other very different communities, has reconciled me to a couple of facts. Scarsdale's residents are as a group unusually prosperous and well informed, and they share a striking degree of agreement about the purposes of their community. While there are people equally rich and talented and dedicated in towns across the nation, rarely do they form such a dominant force. Thus, the history of Scarsdale is in some ways unique and in others quite typical. It indicates the kinds of things that can happen when the upper-middle class controls a community.

In the course of researching and writing this book, I have incurred a number of debts, one of the largest being to John Morton Blum, who guided my earliest efforts and was a great help in the establishment of this study. Sydney E. Ahlstrom, Richard W. Fox, David M. Katzman, and Arthur Zilversmit also provided advice and encouragement. My colleagues at Knox College, especially Mikiso Hane, and in recent years at Utah State University, in particular Ross Peterson, have given support in many ways.

I owe a large debt of gratitude to the people in Scarsdale who helped to make my research rewarding and pleasant. In addition to the men and women I interviewed, I would like to thank the librarians at the Scarsdale public library, especially Estelle Berman, Virginia Barnett, Sylvia Hertz, and Florence Sinsheimer; the members of the staff at the offices of the school board, especially Kathleen Connelly and Norma R. Hemer; Janet Sieck in the village manager's office; and three successive village clerks, Ethel M. Hyde, Irene C. Dalton, and Avis A. Watson. I am also grateful to Martha Chapman, Barbara Telesco Choo, Sheila Freeman, and Charles and Ruth Perera for their hospitality and friendship.

In recent weeks several people have assisted me in concrete ways. Helen Kenyon prepared the maps. Diana Brumm tracked down several pieces of information. Lori Jacobs, Carolyn Buchanan, and Connie West worked long hours typing this manuscript. Finally, I want to thank my colleague and husband, Clyde Milner II, whose love, understanding, and insight were vitally important to the completion of this work.

CAROL A. O'CONNOR

Logan, Utah
February 1982

CHAPTER 1

The Emergence of a Community Identity

In the late nineteenth and early twentieth centuries, the town of Scarsdale, New York, just twenty miles north of central Manhattan, reflected aspects of the massive transformation that the country was undergoing. As the United States changed from a predominantly rural, agricultural nation to a largely urban, industrial one, Scarsdale's adult male population, once made up almost entirely of farmers and farm workers, came to be dominated by members of the upper-middle class. Yet these business and professional men who worked in New York City, not in Scarsdale, wanted their town's transformation to stop short of that of the nation. They envisioned a community combining the advantages of urban and rural life and attracting as permanent residents people, like themselves, of good breeding, education, and talent. To bring that vision closer to reality, they began to establish new institutions and forge new alliances, but above all, the threat of annexation of a part of Scarsdale by its northern neighbor, White Plains, awakened Scarsdale's residents to the interests they shared. In their opinion, Scarsdale was different from and better than its neighbors, and in this initial stage of its suburban history, its citizens resolved that it should remain so.

At the time of the first federal census, in 1790, Scarsdale's 6½ square miles held 281 inhabitants. Fifty years later that figure had declined slightly; in 1840 Scarsdale had 255 residents, and all but four of its adult men worked as farmers or farm workers. Scarsdale's early days of fame as the birthplace of Vice-President Daniel D. Tompkins and the residence of novelist James Fenimore Cooper had passed. Lacking access to navigable waterways, Scarsdale had fallen behind the towns that bordered Long Island Sound and the Hudson River. Indeed, as the Anglo-Saxon origins of its name implied, Scarsdale had a rocky, uneven terrain that made it unsuitable for many types of farming.[1]

Nevertheless, the town's fortunes began to improve after 1846 when the New York and Harlem Railroad (later a division of the New York Central) began service in the Bronx River Valley. With daily trains to and from Manhattan, Scarsdale could not only supply the city with perishable crops and dairy products but also provide a haven to businessmen eager to escape the city's crowds. By 1860, seven merchants, two brokers, a lawyer, a clergyman, and a physician lived in Scarsdale, but although the population had more than doubled since 1840, farmers and farm laborers still headed 70 percent of local households.[2]

That pattern continued through 1890, after which a dramatic change occurred. Between that year and 1915, as the number of inhabitants increased from 633 to 2,712, the number of farms declined from approximately 35 to 12. Meanwhile, Scarsdale underwent an influx, first largely of clerks, artisans, and unskilled laborers, then of business executives, professionals, and retired men and widows of means. By 1905, members of the latter groups headed 41 percent of the households in the community. In 1915 more than 60 percent of Scarsdale's households could be categorized as upper-middle-class, and in 1925 the figure would pass 70 percent.[3]

Scarsdale grew when and as it did largely as a result of external forces. For one, as historian Robert H. Wiebe has argued, the specialized needs of urban-industrial society gave rise to a new group in America around the turn of the century. Consisting of professionals and experts in a wide variety of fields, this "new middle class"—or, more accurately, upper-middle class—shared a common faith in the ability of human beings to improve society through the instrumentality of government. Although many members of this class remained in the cities, where they provided a foundation of support for the reforms of the progressive movement, others were caught up in a second important trend of the times. As Kenneth T. Jackson has shown, ever since the development of the means for mass transportation in the mid-nineteenth century, the populations on the peripheries of America's major cities had been growing at a faster rate than those of the urban cores. This process of suburbanization occurred in

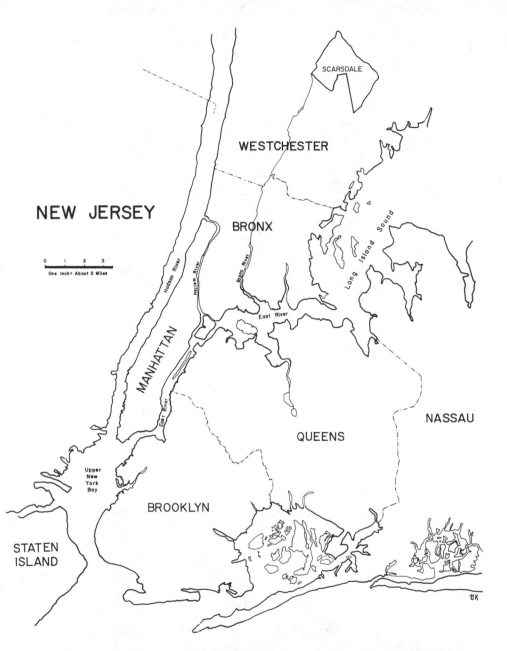

Scarsdale and the boroughs of New York City. Throughout Scarsdale's suburban history, a railroad in the Bronx River Valley has provided the vital link
between Scarsdale's houses and Manhattan's jobs. Since the 1960s, increasing
numbers of village residents have been working in Westchester County, or nearby
Connecticut, where dozens of large corporations have relocated their headquarters.

3

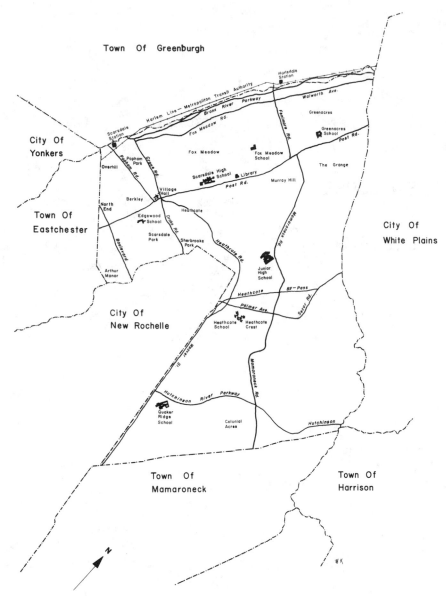

Town Of Greenburgh

City Of
Yonkers

Town Of
Eastchester

City Of
New Rochelle

City Of
White Plains

Town Of
Mamaroneck

Town Of
Harrison

Hartsdale
Station

Walworth Ave.

Greenacres

Harlem Line — Metropolitan Transit Authority

Bronx River Parkway

Fox Meadow Rd.

Greenacres
School

Post Rd.

Scarsdale
Station

Popham
Park

Overhill

Fenimore Rd.

Fox Meadow

Fox Meadow
School

The Grange

Cruse Rd.

Popham Rd.

Scarsdale High
School

Library

Post Rd.

Murray Hill

Village
Hall

Berkley

North
End

Heathcote

Edgewood
School

Drake Rd.

Scarsdale
Park

Sherbrooke
Park

Heathcote Rd.

Mamaroneck Rd.

Arthur
Manor

Boulevard

Junior
High
School

By-Pass

Secor Rd.

Heathcote

Palmer Ave.

Heathcote
School

Heathcote
Crest

Post Rd.

Mamaroneck Rd.

Hutchinson River Parkway

Quaker
Ridge
School

Colonial
Acres

Hutchinson

N

VILLAGE OF SCARSDALE

The Village of Scarsdale. The Metropolitan Transit Authority now operates
what used to be the Harlem division of the New York Central Railroad, and a
road, the Heathcote By-Pass, lies along part of the old route of the New York,
Westchester, and Boston Railroad, which ceased operation during the depression.

4

ever-lengthening spokes along the available transportation routes, with the wealthier members of society deciding either to live and work in the central city or to reside with their families in the suburbs and commute to the city for their jobs.[4]

Increasingly those residents of New York City who could afford the cost of commutation had reason to consider living elsewhere. Between 1850 and 1890 the city, officially confined to the Island of Manhattan, added close to a million inhabitants. From 515,547, the population rose to 1,515,301. As the number of its inhabitants climbed, the city's environment became increasingly impersonal, ugly, and unhealthful. Moreover, the presence of hundreds of thousands of immigrants from numerous foreign countries intensified the sense of crowding and chaos. Seeking relief from these conditions, some people employed in the city chose to commute to Manhattan from locations across the East River, the Harlem River, and upper New York Bay. Yet, by the time these areas—Brooklyn, Queens, Staten Island, and the Bronx—became parts of New York City in 1898, the process of suburbanization had begun to affect districts even farther away from Manhattan.[5]

Along with parts of Essex, Hudson, and Union Counties, in New Jersey, and part of what later became Nassau County, on Long Island, the southern half of Westchester County was one of the areas attracting new residents. As elsewhere, real estate development followed the major transportation routes, moving out along the stops on the New Haven Railroad in eastern Westchester, the Hudson division of the New York Central Railroad in western Westchester, and the Harlem line in the central part of the county. Along this central route, development had begun with the promotion of building sites in the village of Mount Vernon as early as the 1850s. Four decades later development had spread northward to the villages of Bronxville and Tuckahoe as well as to the town of Scarsdale.[6]

At the time, Scarsdale included a post office, a livery, a school, and two churches, in addition to the all-important stop on the railroad. Although several houses were located near the train station, there were no stores, no street lamps, and no paved streets. To the east and north of the station, stood the community's farms along with the estates of a few wealthy residents.[7]

Sensing the outward drift of the metropolitan population, the Arthur Suburban Home Company set out to change Scarsdale from a rural town to a residential suburb. In 1891 it purchased a 150-acre farm, which it proposed to transform into row on row of one-family houses. To that end the company drew up a map of the subdivision, plowed along the street lines, drove in stakes showing the boundaries of the lots, and advertised for clients. Its promotional material emphasized three points: the beauty and healthfulness of the location, the ease of commutation to New York City, and the protection afforded lot buyers by "judiciously worded covenants." Covenants were clauses inserted in deeds to safeguard an area's residential character. In the case of Arthur Manor, the deeds prevented the use of any lot for a store or place of business unless the owner received the written consent of the company. They also forbade the erection of any factory, slaughterhouse, forge, brewery, or "other noxious, dangerous, or offensive business or trade." With the introduction a decade later of electricity, water, and telephone service, Arthur Manor became a true suburban development: it possessed many urban conveniences in a rustic environment.[8]

Although later subdivisions resembled Arthur Manor in restricting construction to residential dwellings, within that pattern standards varied. Whereas the size of most of the lots in Arthur Manor conformed to the New York City standard of 25 feet by 100 feet, other subdivisions made more generous provisions. In Popham Park near the railroad station, lots ranged from 80 feet by 100 feet to more than half an acre. In Greenacres, in northern Scarsdale near the Hartsdale station, the smallest lots measured 75 feet by 145 feet, the largest were well over two acres, and in the Murray Hill section, lots ran from six-tenths of an acre to five acres.[9]

It was the Heathcote subdivision that earned a reputation as Scarsdale's showcase. Developed as a cooperative venture by nine New York businessmen who planned to reside there, Heathcote consisted of twenty-two lots on a 130-acre tract. The smallest lot covered roughly 1½ acres, the largest nearly 17. With its gracefully curving roads, stately trees, and beautiful pond (not to mention the impressive houses its founders built), Heathcote attracted the attention of *Country Life in America*. Describing the subdivision as "an interesting phase of the development of American suburban life," the magazine noted that the investors had succeeded in combining "the seclusion of country life" with "the companionship of [close associates]."[10]

The differences in the cost requirements of the various subdivisions, indicated in table 1, corresponded to differences in the occupational status of the people who resided in them. At the

TABLE 1. Requirements of Scarsdale's Major Subdivisions Opened before 1915

Subdivision	Year Opened	Size of Lots (Acres)	Minimum Value of Any Dwelling Constructed	Minimum Distance of Dwelling from Street
Arthur Manor	1891	0.057 to 0.114	$1,500 $2,500 for larger lots	15'
North End	1895	0.057 to 0.158	$1,500	15'
Heathcote	1902	1.374 to 16.873	$7,500	150'
The Grange	1905	1.245 to 10.101	$4,000 $5,000 for larger lots	25' 50'
Popham Park	1907	0.183 to 0.585	$4,000	35'
Overhill	1907	0.123 to 0.632	$6,000	no specification
Scarsdale Park	1907	0.061 to 0.113	$2,500 $3,500 for larger lots	15'
Murray Hill	1908	0.658 to 5.111	$7,000	75'
Greenacres	1909	0.249 to 2.324	$7,000	50'

NOTE: The information in this table was drawn from the official maps for the various subdivisions, filed in the offices of the County of Westchester, and from deeds for each of the nine subdivisions.

modest end of the spectrum stood Arthur Manor, North End, and Scarsdale Park. In 1915 the residents of the three areas included carpenters, butchers, plumbers, bookkeepers, teachers, and policemen. A live-in servant was a rarity. Residing in Overhill or Popham Park involved an important advance in status. Most of the property holders in those sections either worked as business executives or pursued careers in the professions. In addition, nearly every household included one or two servants. The men of the most luxurious subdivisions differed from the other residents of Scarsdale less in their fields of endeavor than in the degree of success they had attained. Among the buyers in Heathcote, the Grange, Murray Hill, and Greenacres were the president of a rubber company, the vice-president of a telephone company, the owner of a chain of dime stores, and the publisher of a national magazine. While some property holders in those sections may have enjoyed the advantage of a large inheritance, they

7

included few representatives of the idle rich. Typical families in Heathcote, the Grange, Murray Hill, and Greenacres employed two or three servants, though some families in Heathcote employed as many as ten.[11]

Although in the years ahead the differences in status between the residents of the various subdivisions would underlie some of the debates that occurred in Scarsdale, before 1915 the community tended to divide between the residents of the new subdivisions, on the one hand, and the owners of large properties and their employees, on the other. From the time of the establishment of Arthur Manor, nearly twenty years passed before Scarsdale's population doubled. Then, in the years 1910 through 1915, the residents of the new subdivisions came to dominate the community. Spurred by the electrification of the Harlem division of the New York Central, by the completion of a new commuter line—the New York, Westchester, and Boston Railroad, and by the promise of a highway along the banks of the Bronx River, the population rose from 1,300 to 2,712 in just five years.[12]

Many of the newcomers were urbanites. Out of a sample of 100 buyers of Scarsdale property, 56 came from New York City and 16 from other communities in the New York metropolitan area. The remaining twenty-eight sales involved people already living in Scarsdale. Some were buying lots adjacent to property they already owned. Others, like Henry H. B. Angell, Cornelius B. Fish, and Charles W. Montgomery, were engaged in large-scale speculation.[13]

The influx of urbanites throughout the period provoked discussion of an issue that was receiving attention in communities across the nation—namely, municipal improvements and their funding. Although discussion of specific proposals never resulted in a clear-cut split between the newcomers and older residents, generally the former tended to favor spending for roads, schools, and other services, while most of the latter feared measures that would effect a rise in the tax rate. Farmers had particular reason for concern. With their numbers thinned by the agricultural depression of the late 1800s, they knew an increase in taxes could destroy their margin of profit and force them out of business. People with sources of income other than farming had greater flexibility in matters affecting property taxes. They probably had enough cash to cover an initial increase in taxes. Further, they could always sell part of their land to reduce their tax base.

Still, the costs were high enough to cause the nonfarming owners of substantial property to weigh carefully each proposal for town improvements.[14]

A few long-time residents consistently supported improvements. Rich enough not to feel seriously threatened by an increase in taxes, and attracted to the new suburbanites by ties of profession, they accepted the signs of Scarsdale's growth and worked to ease its transition from rural town to suburb. To do so, they established an organization they called the Town Club. Founded in 1904, the club resembled other good-government groups of the progessive era. As had the Los Angeles Municipal League and the Pittsburgh Civic Club, the Town Club adopted a critical stance toward the existing local government. "The censorship of the conduct of town officers and a general oversight on town improvements" stood as the club's main objectives.[15] As with the Los Angeles and Pittsburgh organizations, the Town Club drew its membership from a narrow social base. Thomas F. Burgess, the heir of a farm in Scarsdale and an officer of the National Sulphur Company in New York, selected the original roster of sixteen members—nearly all, business executives and professionals. Those sixteen men admitted others, though for more than a decade they limited the number to thirty-five. Their investigations and debates set a tone of serious inquiry, previously wanting, for town affairs. Moreover, the club, though elitist, brought together residents of both the new subdivisions and the old estates. It helped create a body of leaders dedicated to the conscious development of the community.[16]

How well the average citizen, excluded from the Town Club, understood the pros and cons of specific issues was not clear. Although Scarsdale's population was growing, it was still small enough to permit information to flow freely. Thus people may have learned about the subtleties of Town Club debates despite the club's unwillingness to publish reports in its early years. One factor was certain: the people did have access to a small and biased newspaper. Begun in 1901 as an organ of the Young People's Society of Christian Endeavor of Arthur Manor, the *Scarsdale Inquirer* soon reflected the more materialistic interest of one of its founders. The son of a realtor and himself to become one, Stephen L. Angell, editor of the *Inquirer* from 1902 to 1910, supported any proposal for improvements that would give "fresh impetus . . . to building" and cause a rise in property values. Criticizing those who "bitterly sneered" at "progress," he warned that money "not spent . . . or spent too sparingly" could prove as costly to local landowners as "too great freedom in expenditures." "If we want the right kind of people to make their residences here," he said pointedly, "we must have the right kind of town to attract them."[17]

Eventually Scarsdale residents would come to share Angell's thinking, but in the years before 1915 they moved only haltingly in the direction of increased spending. In 1903 they voted to pave and light the public streets. In 1905 they agreed to spend $26,000 on the construction of a new school. A series of burglaries in 1908, along with reports that "vagrants" were harrassing female servants, prompted the provision of police protection; and a number of fires in 1913 led to the purchase of modern fire-fighting equipment and the hiring of two firemen to assist the community's volunteer force.[18] The town was spending at an unprecedented rate. Its budget had grown from $4,565 in 1890 to $88,782 in 1914. During the same years the town's total assessed valuation had increased from $605,450 to $6,744,167. The tax rate per thousand dollars of assessed valuation had risen from $7.541 to $9.433. In personal terms this meant that, while George Burgess in 1890 had paid $49.03 tax on sixty acres of land valued at $6,500, his son Thomas in 1914 paid $617.26 tax on thirty-six acres valued at $28,000. Yet, despite the dramatic increase in both taxes and property values, the people had not made adequate provision for the needs of the growing town. By 1915, Scarsdale's roads were in disrepair, the schools were overcrowded, the police and fire departments were understaffed and ill-equipped. The town lacked natural gas. It had no reliable water supply or systematic provision for waste collection. Only when the Scarsdale's residents gained a sense of community spirit would they work to establish and maintain public services of good quality.[19]

Ironically the most bitter election of this period in Scarsdale's history played a part in bringing its citizens closer together. The race, in 1909, was for the position of town supervisor, the highest official in the community and its representative to the county government. In the spring of that year, the Democratic incumbent, Chauncey Secor, announced his intention to retire from politics. The members of the Republican Town Committee were delighted. Despite a two-to-one Republican margin in most elections, it had been years since the party had fielded a candidate for town supervisor. The reason lay in Scarsdale's tradition of uncontested elections: the Republicans' single attempt to buck that tradition had ended in defeat. Even now, the Republican Town Committee proceeded with caution. Before their candidate, William C. White, announced his plan to run for supervisor, he obtained Secor's personal confirmation of the decision to retire. But Secor reversed his decision in August. The Republicans said he had succumbed to pressure from outside Democrats who wanted to retain control of the county board of supervisors.[20]

The charge that Secor had yielded to "outside interference" was only half true. Many local citizens, including some Republicans, had also urged him to run. Indeed, the split between old and new residents may have had a greater influence on the outcome of the election than the differences in party affiliation. Secor was the candidate of the old guard. He had deep family roots in Scarsdale. His father and grandfather had served as supervisor before him, and he had held the office since 1882. Moreover, with his large properties in East Scarsdale, Secor tended to oppose improvements. He stood for frugality in town affairs. White, in contrast, was not a native. Born in Nashville, Tennessee, he had settled in the New York area after law school and had moved to Scarsdale in 1903. A resident of the Heathcote subdivision, he tended to favor spending for town improvements. He represented the views and experience of the new suburban population.[21]

Although Secor and White differed on the issues confronting the growing town, the debate in the weeks before the election centered on the question of the broken promise. While White issued a sworn statement detailing his role in the matter, Secor temporized. At first Secor said that friends had induced him to change his mind. Then he denied ever promising that he would not run again. The *Inquirer* called attention to Secor's contradictory statements. "No Welching," one headline read, "Mr. Secor should be held to the situation he created." Enough voters felt differently to return Secor to office—by a margin of four votes, 146 to 142.[22]

Although the Republicans swore vengeance in the next election, the return match of 1911 never occurred. Secor retired that year; and before the two parties could select rival candidates, a number of men concerned about town affairs met to draw up a fusion slate. The slate was headed by Alexander M. Crane, a lawyer educated at Harvard and Columbia who combined a Scarsdale pedigree with Republican affiliations and business interests in New York. His willingness to serve as supervisor pleased all sides. With party politics tainted by its association with political machines, residents agreed that a man of Crane's caliber would never have run on a party ticket. With his candidacy the people of Scarsdale could resume their practice of uncontested local elections. In the years ahead, the nonpartisan—really bipartisan—nature of local politics would prove a source of community pride.[23]

More than any other factor, the threat of annexation of a part of Scarsdale's territory caused the townspeople to forget their differences. The threat first surfaced in 1908, when the leaders of the village of White Plains, Scarsdale's northern neighbor, began to consider the advisability of applying for a city charter. Since, under the law of New York, the legislature had the power to adjust town boundaries without the consent of the people involved, White Plains intended to ask that its new city limits take in adjacent areas of the community to its south.

White Plains had reason to consider the request justifiable. The affected areas of Scarsdale, Greenacres, Murray Hill, and the Grange, were physically separated from the heart of town by the 360-acre Fox Meadow estate. Many residents there were not included in the Scarsdale postal district or in the Scarsdale phone exchange. They used the Hartsdale, rather than the Scarsdale, railroad station. They did their marketing in White Plains and depended on that village for their water supply and sewage system, services for which they naturally paid. Yet some citizens of White Plains thought the residents of Scarsdale were benefiting from local improvements without bearing their share of the costs. The proponents of annexation understood that by extending their community's borders they would expand the available tax base.[24]

From the start of the White Plains city charter movement, the people of Scarsdale had protested any hint of encroachment on their territory. When the matter came up in earnest, in the summer of 1913, over 200 citizens of Scarsdale attended a meeting at which they denounced their neighbor's plans and established a committee to present their views before the authorities in White Plains.[25] Scarsdale residents opposed annexation for three reasons. Most significantly, they argued that the two municipalities were "entirely dissimilar" in character. In the words of Benjamin J. Carpenter, Scarsdale was "exclusively a residential community. Its plan of development has been unique and high class." White Plains, on the other hand, was a mixed community. It contained not only houses, many of them on small lots, but businesses, factories, and saloons. "It is not that we feel above [White Plains], . . ." said Philip W. Russell disingenuously, "but [we] want to retain our own individuality."[26] Residents of Scarsdale also argued that White Plains was acting, not out of benevolence, but greed. According to an editorial in the *Scarsdale Inquirer*, the village of White Plains looked on annexation as a means to acquire new sources of revenue "to rehabilitate its shattered fortunes." The situation recalled to Scarsdale residents the experience of the colonists in Revolutionary days. Misquoting Patrick Henry, one resident said, "Taxation under protest is tyranny." Finally, residents worried about the after-effects of annexation. Scarsdale was already the smallest town in the state. If White Plains took part of it, the rest could fall prey to the other municipalities adjoining Scarsdale—Eastchester, Greenburgh, Mamaroneck, and New Rochelle. The very existence of Scarsdale seemed to be at stake.[27]

In January 1914, the members of the Scarsdale committee spoke at a public meeting in White Plains. They warned those gathered that, if White Plains persisted in its plan of annexation, the residents of Scarsdale would boycott village stores. Further, the members of the committee reminded the audience that Scarsdale residents possessed sufficient "wealth and influence" to affect the course of events in Albany. Scarsdale would succeed in resisting annexation, "however high it may be necessary to carry [an appeal]."[28]

In the following month the White Plains City Charter Committee voted down the proposal to annex a part of Scarsdale. The danger of dismemberment had passed, at least for a time. Yet, while it lasted, the threat to Scarsdale's borders had forced its citizens to consider what the town stood for and how it differed from its neighbors. Gradually they came to realize that— whether they were life-long residents or newcomers—as relatively wealthy members of society who wanted to protect the homogeneity of their community, they had more in common with one another than they did with the residents of other towns.[29]

This new sense of unity expressed itself in a change in Scarsdale's government. During the problems of the preceding years, the Town Club had learned that, when incorporated as villages, municipalities had greater protection from annexation than they did with only a town form of government. Whereas, in New

York State, a town (usually known as a township in other states) served mainly as a unit of county government, a village had a large degree of autonomy. It could act with greater freedom in such matters as police and fire protection, highway maintenance, and municipal finance. In addition, state law permitted villages to employ a full-time engineer to supervise the technical and administrative aspects of public services. In view of the community's anticipated growth and its need for municipal services, the Town Club believed that Scarsdale should incorporate as a village having the same boundaries as those of the town. The proposal included one drawback. As a village, Scarsdale would lose $6,000 in state highway funds. In addition, some residents questioned the need for the change. They argued that Scarsdale already had honest, economical government with power equal to the community's needs. Under a village government, they feared Scarsdale would "run the risk of extravagance." Apparently, by 1915 concern over dollars and cents counted less with the majority of voters than concern for the strength and efficiency of their local government. In a referendum on the issue in March of that year, the motion to incorporate Scarsdale as a village carried by 142 votes to 39.[30]

The town board set June 15 as the date for the first village election. Leaders of the Republican, Democratic, and Progressive parties met with representatives of various sections of Scarsdale to draw up a fusion citizens' ticket. They had to choose candidates for ten positions: village president, four village trustees, village treasurer, receiver of taxes, inspector of elections, street commissioner, and police justice. Once elected, the members of the village board would have the authority to appoint other local officials, including a village clerk, counsel, and engineer.[31]

Those nominated by the committee and appointed by the trustees included several who had been working in similar capacities for the town government. A notable exception was the nominating committee's choice for village president. Instead of naming Alexander M. Crane, the incumbent supervisor, to head the village government, the committee chose Franklin H. Bethell. The committee said its decision did not indicate a lack of confidence in Crane's leadership. Rather, they believed that a businessman like Bethell would have more organizational experience of the type Scarsdale now needed than would a lawyer like Crane. The citizens respected the committee's choice. They had confidence that Bethell, who was the vice-president of the New

York Telephone Company and the president of two other Bell lines, would have the ability to serve them well.[32]

On June 26, 1915, the officers of the new village government assumed responsibility for key areas of the community's public life. Though the personnel of the local government had not much changed, the expanded power of the new government seemed to instill in its officers, and in the village as a whole, a more vigorous spirit. Henceforth, the community would act quickly to meet the needs of its growing population.[33]

Seven years later a letter to the editor of the local newspaper looked back on Scarsdale's evolution over the preceding half century. The "quiet, economical ways" of the rural town had passed, but in their place stood the prospect of "steadily increas[ing]" property values. The letter pointed to the sense of commonality that the people of Scarsdale had discovered. Although farms and great estates no longer characterized the village, it had escaped factories, tenements, and saloons. In the words of the writer, Scarsdale had become "a high class residential [suburb], . . . an almost unique community."[34] In the years ahead, its citizens would strive to protect this newly discovered sense of Scarsdale's identity.

CHAPTER 2

Progressivism for the Upper-Middle Class

In the ten years following Scarsdale's incorporation as a village, its residents acted on the *Inquirer*'s admonition of 1902. Eager to continue attracting "the right kind of people" to their community, they willingly used both public policy and private capital to assure that theirs was "the right kind of town."[1] Their endeavors in this period focused on two areas: the provision of essential services and the protection of local standards for growth. In pursuing these objectives, village residents exhibited many aspects of the progressive temperament—a willingness to experiment, an eagerness to lead, an interest in efficiency, and a desire for order. There was much worth praising in their efforts, but there were points deserving of criticism as well, for in bringing order to Scarsdale, its residents helped to exacerbate the political, economic, and social disorder of the New York metropolitan area. In the manner of residents of other wealthy suburbs, they used the progressive idea of positive government to create an island of exclusivity within the greater metropolis.

Between 1915 and 1925, Scarsdale's population grew 88 percent, from 2,712 to 5,099. The increase would have been greater had not American involvement in the First World War given rise to dislocations in the housing industry. In 1918 the federal government banned all nonessential construction, and even when the ban was lifted, the high cost of materials and labor impeded local construction. Only in 1923 did the number of housing starts in Scarsdale return to its prewar level.[2]

Although, in addition to halting private construction, American participation in the war interrupted efforts to provide public improvements, it seemed to benefit the suburb in the long run by intensifying the sense of community spirit. From the beginning of American involvement in the war in April 1917 until the end of the fighting nineteen months later, residents converted often vague directives from the federal government into mandates for carefully organized community campaigns. Although local support for the war was stronger than it would be at least initially in World War II, that support seemed, as in other communities, to be fueled in part by a hatred of the German immigrants living in the area. Moreover, as the history of Scarsdale's community farm revealed, residents liked receiving publicity for their projects, but scorned work they considered beneath their dignity.

As did so many Americans elsewhere, village leaders responded quickly to the war crisis. Only hours after Congress voted to declare war on the German Empire and it allies, the members of the village board of trustees began to carry out a three-part program. First, they issued a notice to all residents directing them to maintain "the strictest order" and "to report . . . any suspicious circumstances, conversations, or actions which indicate any disloyalty to our government." They then searched the census rolls for "alien enemies," found 102 unnaturalized immigrants from Germany, Austria, and Hungary, and sent the police to seize any firearms in their possession. Finally, they appointed twenty auxiliary policemen to prevent the outbreak of "disturbances" and ordered the purchase of "twenty riot guns . . . with ample ammunition."[3]

The strength of these actions indicated the depth of the trustees' fears, fears as frenetic as they were unwarranted. At a rally on April 22, Village President Rush Wilson, reflecting the hysteria then sweeping the nation, reminded his audience that war had unleashed "the most highly developed . . . annihilating agencies . . . ever produced" against "our own country, our own flag, our families, and our homes." Scarsdale's homes seemed especially vulnerable. Not only did most of the men leave the suburb during the day, but many families employed servants of German origin. Wilson fanned suspicion of the German immigrants living in the villagers' midst: "Every German is the enemy of every American, whether that German is in Germany or in America, and he's less dangerous and deadly over there than he is here." The village president went on to encourage local citizens to "rise in their righteous anger and place out of sight, hearing, and communication every person and thing that speaks, acts, reads, or makes signs in German."[4]

While the local government aimed to protect the village, Scarsdale's citizens contributed to the national war effort. By December 1917, sixty-eight young men had enlisted in the service, a figure that, according to the newspaper, "reckoned [Scarsdale] among the most patriotic communities in the nation." By the war's end, 135 men had served in the United States Army, Navy, or Marine Corps; seven had died in combat. Meanwhile, 100 men, "too old to serve," had enrolled in the Home Defense League. Dressed in $50 uniforms and armed with Remington rifles, they drilled twice a week to prepare "for any service that may be needed of them." In addition, village residents worked for the Red Cross and purchased more than their quota of Liberty bonds.[5]

The project that attracted the greatest attention was the community's wartime farm. The plan for the farm originated with the members of the Scarsdale Suffrage Club. Aware of the gravity of the wartime food shortage, they developed a program that would "take Scarsdale off the market" by growing the vegetables needed for local consumption. Its sponsors also hoped that, by demonstrating their dedication and talent, the farm's success would help advance the cause of woman's suffrage.[6]

The Scarsdale community farm was a cooperative enterprise run with a concern for efficiency. The plan brought under cultivation a twenty-five-acre tract near the new high school, as well as smaller plots throughout the village. An experienced farmer supervised the technical aspects of the project. He analyzed the soils, selected the proper fertilizers, and recommended what crops should be planted where and when. To finance the project, volunteers from the Suffrage Club sold $10 shares redeemable in produce at the end of the season.[7]

Coordinating the work force proved the main difficulty. The farm's directors used a postcard canvass to draw up a master schedule of available workers. Day-to-day arrangements depended on the weather and on the kind of work that needed to be done. Field workers did not donate their labor but received payment in cash or crops at an hourly rate determined by the worker's age and sex. Still, finding sufficient workers proved "an almost impossible task," according to the farm's general manager, Laura C. Burgess. In the second year of its operation, the farm's directors relied not on local workers but on a unit of "farmer-ettes," which Burgess secured from the National Land Army.[8]

It was somewhat surprising that the farm had a problem attracting workers since, from its inception, the project had received wide publicity. The Westchester County Food Supply Committee printed a bulletin on the project at the end of April 1917, and in early June the *New Republic* devoted an article to it. After that, the village government began receiving inquiries from "every part of the nation." The citizens of Scarsdale enjoyed the publicity. They liked having their community seen as one for others to emulate.[9] But although they relished the sense of community achievement, as members of the upper-middle class or aspirants to that class, they disdained the notion of engaging personally in manual labor in a public setting.

The community farm was only one of several major projects undertaken by village residents in the years between 1915 and 1925. Although as early as 1913 its citizens had spoken of Scarsdale as a "unique and high class [suburb]," it nevertheless had lacked such basic conveniences as decent roads, an adequate water supply, natural gas, and sanitation. After Scarsdale's re-organization as a village, its board of trustees provided these services in a variety of ways. For gas, the board granted a franchise to the Westchester Lighting Company, which proved to be a reliable firm. For water, it rescinded a franchise granted in 1901 and established a municipal service. For roads, it con-tracted with a private company to make major repairs and hired a village crew for routine maintenance. As for sanitation, it established a municipal service for both the collection and dis-posal of wastes.[10]

In the operation of Scarsdale's municipal services, officials said they aimed for "quality." This was a vague term which, as illustrated by the early history of Scarsdale's water and sanitation departments, referred in actual usage to three different char-acteristics. The community held in high regard services that were either extraordinarily efficient, extravagant, or experimental.

None of these attributes marked Scarsdale's water system in the first months of its operation. Established in 1922, after the Consolidated Water Company proved incapable of providing reliable service, the municipal system for a time functioned little better. One deficiency involved costs. After three months of service, the water department's expenses ran more than $6,000 ahead of estimate. Evidently the pipe system that the village had purchased from Consolidated Water contained a number of leaks. Small to begin with, the leaks became serious when the new pumping station, built by the village in the town of Greenburgh, increased water pressure by twenty-five pounds. Consumer water meters recorded only 35 percent of the water pumped; 65 percent, lost in transit, brought in no return.[11]

Rather than raise rates, the water department examined the twenty-three miles of pipe for hidden leaks and repaired them. By the end of the first year of operation, the department had turned the monthly deficit of $2,000 into a net surplus. By 1926 it had increased that surplus to a total of $90,000. Eager to use the fund to benefit those who had created it, the board of trustees reduced the charge for water service by almost one-half. The system had operated efficiently to produce that saving.[12]

The second deficiency of the water system was the lack of a reserve supply. If a break occurred in the main line between the pumping station and the village, Scarsdale would be without water, and without adequate protection against fire, until the break could be repaired. To eliminate that hazard, the village board in 1925 recommended the building of a water tower. The tower, to be located on Garden Road at the high point of the village, would hold two million gallons of water, the equivalent of two days' supply.[13]

Despite the need for the tower and the need to build it on high ground, the complaints of one resident delayed construction for nearly four years. Mrs. Alice Beavor-Webb owned the property adjoining the proposed site. Through her lawyer, she informed the board that the tower would constitute "a monstrous eyesore" visible from her house, that it would "shut off the summer winds and the winter sunlight," and that it would reduce the value of her property by $25,000, one-quarter of its worth.[14]

The members of the village board, with community support, responded sympathetically to Beavor-Webb's objections. In order to make the 100-foot tower attractive, they were willing to make a large additional expenditure. They would conceal the steel tank within a masonry structure built in the style of an English Martello tower. Trees surrounding the structure would relieve its height and further conceal it.[15]

Beavor-Webb was not appeased. In August 1926 she applied to the state court to halt the tower's construction. Judge Joseph Morschauser found for the village. The woman then appealed the decision, but before the appellate court could pass judgment, two breaks occurred in the main supply line, on each occasion leaving Scarsdale without water for hours. The two incidents, which "inconvenienced and endangered" the entire community, dramatized the need for the new tower. In December 1928 the appellate court sustained the lower court's decision, and three months later the New York State Court of Appeals, the highest court in the state, refused to hear a further appeal. Work on the tower could begin at last.[16]

By its actions in the water tower controversy, the village demonstrated a taste for extravagance that would reappear. Considerations of safety and efficiency supported the construction of the tower on Garden Road. In order to win the case, Scarsdale probably need not have spent $63,106 to conceal a tank that cost $44,704.[17] But the people of Scarsdale accepted the expense because they understood Beavor-Webb's objections, and because they wanted a tower of which they could be proud.

Scarsdale's first venture in municipal ownership of a public utility reflected the upper-middle-class nature of the community. On the one hand, the efficiency of the operation demonstrated the residents' appreciation for technical competence. On the other hand, the extravagance of the masonry tower stood as a conspicuous symbol of the community's wealth.

While efficiency and extravagance marked the operation of Scarsdale's municipal water system, extravagance and experimentation marked its sanitation system. In this, the Scarsdale service *par excellence*, two contradictory goals jostled for dominance: the residents' desire for personal convenience, as represented by their insistence on a costly method of waste collection, and their interest in the community's renown, as indicated by their approval of an experimental process of organic waste disposal. In the end, the residents' lack of cooperation would force the village government to abandon the experiment. As with Scarsdale's community farm, so with its sanitation service, residents wanted Scarsdale to be in the vanguard, but not at the risk of bother to themselves.

Scarsdale's citizens in 1923 approved the establishment of a sanitation service with two unusual features, cellar collection of residential wastes and a fermentation process of organic waste disposal. The first of these features was adopted under citizen pressure, against the recommendation of the village trustees.

In studying the sanitation service offered by sixteen suburban communities, a committee appointed by the trustees had learned that ony two cities, Yonkers and New Rochelle, provided cellar collection. There this special service doubled the per capita cost of waste removal and created such other problems as a high proportion of theft complaints. Instead of cellar collection, the trustees thought Scarsdale should have a backyard service like the one provided in Greenwich, Connecticut. Thus, in preparation for the inauguration of municipal waste collection, they proposed an amendment to the public health ordinance. The new regulation would require residents to place their household wastes in water-tight containers "outside the building but not on the street." The people of Scarsdale protested the proposal. More than 100 residents appeared before a meeting of the village board. Demanding cellar collection, they presented a petition signed by a total of 360 homeowners. With more time, they said, they would have obtained signatures from 95 percent of village voters. Faced with such a clear expression of popular feeling, the trustees revised the proposal to provide for cellar collection. One trustee explained the switch: "We believe in giving the people what they want, provided they will pay for it."[18]

At the end of one month of operation, cellar collection was taking more time than even the trustees had anticipated. The superintendent of garbage disposal blamed the homeowners for the delays. He said that more than half the residents kept their cellars locked. They expected the village employees to knock and wait, at times for as long as twenty minutes, to be admitted. Some residents asked that workers return at a more convenient time, while others who were rarely home complained about infrequent service. The trustees discussed how they might educate the public in the need for cooperation. Unwilling to use "any compelling method" to effect a change, they agreed that the people's "own comfort, convenience, and economy" would eventually lead them to work more closely with the village employees.[19] The trustees were overly optimistic. Although village records make no further reference to the difficulties encountered in cellar collection, a practice that apparently continued up to World War II, lack of cooperation on the part of residents contributed to the abandonment of Scarsdale's experimental process for disposing of organic wastes.

Scarsdale's system of waste disposal was not unusal in all regards. Along with other communities, Scarsdale used the ashes from coal-burning furnaces for land-fill and burned such combustible wastes as cardboard boxes, old clothes, and discarded furniture. But in the opinion of Arthur Boniface, the village engineer, none of the traditional methods for disposing of table wastes, such as incineration or burial in a municipal dump, seemed appropriate in "a community of uniformly high-class homes."[20]

Instead, the people of Scarsdale adopted a process little known in the United States. Called the Zymothermic Cell Method, it depended for its action on fermentation. According to its inventor, Dr. Giuseppe Beccari, the garbage would be deposited in a concrete chamber with provision for ventilation and drainage. After forty-five days, the oxidizing effect of the air on the organic waste matter would turn the garbage into a dry, odorless humus. The process appealed to Scarsdale residents in part for its novelty and in part for more practical reasons. Because the end-product, the humus, contained a high nitrogen content, the village could market it as a fertilizer. That would allow the municipality, as the *Inquirer* said, to turn "a necessary expense . . . into an investment." Further, because the process required only a series of cells, nine feet by ten feet by ten feet, it would not disfigure the landscape. As Village Engineer Boniface told a meeting of the American Society of Civil Engineers, "In communities like Scarsdale, the fact that a Beccari plant lends itself to architectural treatment is important."[21]

Yet the method did not work in Scarsdale as it had for Beccari in Italy. Since village residents failed to drain their table wastes and since they threw away whole meats, fruits, and vegetables, Scarsdale's garbage contained a high liquid content. After forty-five days in a zymothermic cell, the waste material was still an odoriferous mass, far too wet to be ground into fertilizer. When experiments with a longer cycle failed to reduce the moisture content, village officials found an alternative for drying the material. They built a drying shed on a farm in a neighboring town. After ten days in the shed, the material finally resembled the humus that Beccari had described. The use of the shed increased the cost of the process, but it enabled village officials to keep the project going.[22]

At the end of four years, village officials had managed to eliminate the need for the drying shed and reduce the length of the fermentation process to a total of thirty-five days. By constructing air ducts in the concrete cells and by using chemical additives, they had lowered the moisture content of the waste material from 45 percent to 10 percent. Members of the village board proclaimed the project a success. "Scarsdale," they said, "has taken the lead in producing a method of disposal of organic waste without any objectionable feature."[23]

Still, the process had one serious drawback. Since it worked only on organic matter, table wastes had to be kept separate from rubbish. The trustees had passed an ordinance in September 1923 requiring residents to provide separate containers for the different types of waste. From the outset, people failed to observe the ordinance, and despite repeated injunctions from the trustees, they continued to flout it. Consequently, the work of separating wastes went on at the disposal plant, where it occupied the time of several village employees.[24]

The bother and expense of separating wastes proved decisive in 1929, when the trustees had to decide how to enlarge the capacity of the village disposal plant. With the increased volume of waste from the rise in population, and the decreased capacity of the cells because of the construction of the air ducts, the village was paying to send half its waste for disposal elsewhere. To solve the problem, the trustees could have agreed to build more zymothermic cells and another rubbish burner. Instead they decided to buy an incinerator that could handle both table wastes and rubbish. Still concerned about aesthetics, they agreed to house the main part of the incinerator in an "English-type" building of stone and stucco and to conceal the forty-foot smoke-stack by the use of "careful planting." At first the trustees intended incineration to supplement the fermentation process, not supplant it. But in 1933, when they added a second incin-erator to the one already in use, they discontinued the operation of the Beccari plant.[25]

The switch in the method of waste disposal received little attention in the newspaper and public records. Having touted the process in previous years, the leaders of Scarsdale did not care to advertise their abandonment of it. Indeed, the chief reference to the change was an oblique one. The trustees' report of 1934–35, reviewing the record of the previous twenty years, stated:

> There may have been mistakes made in policies conceived, and perhaps our ambitions have sometimes led us astray, but Scarsdale is always ready to learn and willing to adopt any forward movement to better serve its citizens.[26]

The government miscalculated in undertaking the Beccari process. Instead of serving its citizens, the village had asked too much of them.

Implicit in Scarsdale's approach to essential services during the 1920s were two significant attitudes. One was a pragmatic view of the role of local government. Residents never hesitated to expect their government to undertake a service if no convenient or reliable alternative existed. There was never any suggestion that such an attitude might be socialistic, though residents did not hesitate to regard themselves as progressive. It is worth noting that they took this attitude during the business-dominated decade of the 1920s when progressivism as a national political movement was in decline.

The second attitude was a lack of concern over the issue of costs *per se*. Low costs could be praised as a sign of efficiency, an indication of the community's administrative and technical skill. High costs could be tolerated as a sign of extravagance, a symbol of the community's wealth. Uncertain costs could be risked as a part of experimentation, another sign of the community's progressiveness. According to one writer, C. Neal Barney, residents were more concerned lest Scarsdale "suffer by comparison" to other towns than they were with the size of their tax bills. They wanted essential services of which they could be proud.[27]

The majority's willingness to countenance high taxes had a predictable side-effect. As the average village tax bill, which did not include school taxes, increased from $141.73 in 1920–21 to $185.94 in 1925–26, a few residents were forced to sell their property while some would-be residents were probably prevented from buying. Although this was not a conscious goal of village policy at the time, one resident made a sarcastic prediction. In the future, he said, the trustees would use increased taxation to keep out unwanted numbers and classes of people.[28]

Although keeping out the unwanted was not a conscious aspect of village tax policy in the twenties, it was a goal of various efforts to protect local standards of development. Prior to World War I, as the newspaper noted with satisfaction, the promotion of real estate in Scarsdale had "fallen into the hands of brokers" whose actions augured "only the best kind of growth."[29] After the war, village residents were still proud of the type of development that had occurred, but they were no longer willing to let the vagaries of the real estate market determine the pattern of Scarsdale's growth. In particular, they feared that a few promoters might change the character of the village by erecting cheap stores, ugly factories, and large apartment houses. To avert that possibility, some citizens took measures to direct the growth of the community along lines they preferred. By employing local capital to finance the construction of a business district, and by establishing strict laws regulating land use and building practices, they hoped to assure for Scarsdale a high standard of development.

In early 1920 the business district of Scarsdale consisted of two small commercial buildings on the west side of the New York Central tracks. The buildings rented space for a grocery store, a meat market, a drug store, a few other shops, and some real estate offices. The Scarsdale shopping area was a convenience center. For serious shopping, most Scarsdale residents went to White Plains. The high proportion of advertising for White Plains stores that appeared in the *Scarsdale Inquirer* reflected the inadequacy of the local business district.[30]

There was, for one problem, no bank in Scarsdale. As long as Scarsdale residents did their banking elsewhere, the level of commerce within the community would remain low. No one in the community wanted Scarsdale to become a major shopping center. Yet a group of leading citizens believed that sooner or later outside profiteers would seize the opportunity to exploit Scarsdale's wealth. The group decided that a strictly local bank, conducted along conservative lines, would win community support. The bank would work for the good of the village and for the enrichment of its sponsors.

The Scarsdale National Bank opened on May 10, 1920. All its directors lived in the Scarsdale area. "Men who had given of their time and energy to the up-building of Scarsdale," they included a stock broker, three attorneys, a physician, an importer, the president of the local building supply company, the vice-president of a New York bank, the assistant to the president of the New York Central Railroad, and the vice-president of an oil company. Orion H. Cheney, president of the Pacific Bank, served as vice-president of the Scarsdale National. For bank president, the directors chose Rush Wilson, a former railroad executive who, from 1917 to 1919, had held the position of president of the village board of trustees.[31]

The bank opened with $50,000 capital and $10,000 surplus. Investments by local residents accounted for over 90 percent of the bank's capital funds. After one year of business, the bank had doubled its capital and had attracted 1,119 depositors with accounts totaling $1,022,331.14. The *Scarsdale Inquirer*, hailing the passing of the "million dollar goal," described the bank's record as "a genuine Scarsdale accomplishment, unparalleled in suburban banking history."[32]

An emphasis on safety contributed to the bank's success. After fourteen months of business, the bank advertised that it had "never lost a dollar through an ill-advised loan." Four and a half years later the bank had made 8,029 loans without a loss. A statement in the *Inquirer* helped explain how the bank had achieved that record. From time to time, the newspaper featured comments in the style of satirist Finley Peter Dunne's Mr. Dooley. One comment referred to the rumor that "ye can borry lashions iv money at th' bank in Scars-s-dale!" "Ye can," was the response, "if ye're name's in Who's Who in Ameriky."[33]

The bank continually lent the village money for local projects. For one example, it purchased the bonds that financed the construction of the water system. Using the investments and deposits of Scarsdale residents to support local improvements, the bank lent funds to the village at a lower rate than that offered by outside financial institutions. While by no means an unprofitable venture, the bank did offer responsible, community-minded service, especially when judged by the standards of the 1920s. Moreover, the bank made many indirect contributions to the well-being of Scarsdale. On the bank's first anniversary the newspaper described it as "the leading instrument in welding and uniting the community spirit." According to the *Inquirer*, the bank had become a focal point for any activity promoting the financial or physical improvement of the village.[34]

One of the activities to which the *Inquirer* referred concerned the formation in November 1920 of the Scarsdale Improvement Corporation. Although the corporation had no binding ties with the bank, seven of the sixteen members of its board of directors also served as directors of the Scarsdale National Bank, and Rush Wilson, president of the bank, headed the new corporation as well. Before publicizing its formation, the group had arranged to purchase 80,000 square feet of land east of the Scarsdale station. The directors planned to use the property as the site for a "model" small-town business center. According to Wilson, they wanted to provide all the business conveniences that the people of Scarsdale required, "with due regard for the preservation of [the community's] artistic features." The long-range plans for the center included the construction of modern apartments, a motion picture theater, and a permanent home for the Scarsdale National Bank. Above all, the corporation planned to provide space for a number of shops that together would comprise "a complete market to satisfy usual household requirements." The Scarsdale Improvement Corporation aimed to make shopping as convenient as possible, without divesting village residents of their elitist notions.[35]

Even before the corporation had drawn up specific plans, residents felt assured that Scarsdale would be spared "the usual unsightly building" found in other towns. The newspaper summed up the feelings of the people:

> Thus it is after many years of doubt and anxiety on the part of our citizens, the most prominent and valuable property in the village is to be utilized and preserved in a manner worthy of a community entitled to the best.[36]

Over the next several years the Scarsdale Improvement Corporation fulfilled its promise. In less than two years it began the construction of a four-story Tudor-style apartment house with shops on the ground level. The East Parkway Building occupied one corner of the corporation's property. Completed in April 1923, the building leased space for a pharmacy, a newsstand, a flower shop, a notions store, a delicatessen, a decorator's office, and the Scarsdale National Bank. A second unit of the building opened about a year later. Stores and offices occupied the first two floors, and apartments of three to five rooms took up the third and fourth floors. The apartments contained "the best labor-saving devices": electric dishwashers, refrigerators and ranges, folding ironing boards, built-in china cupboards with glass doors, and built-in wardrobes with sliding doors. Those who rented stores or offices included a butcher, a photographer, a doctor, a civil engineer, a dressmaker, a barber, two realtors, and the hardware branch of a local supply company.[37]

With the construction of the East Parkway Building, the Scarsdale Improvement Corporation set the precedent for a high standard of development in the business district. Between 1925 and 1928 other investors constructed three additional buildings, all of which conformed to the Tudor style of architecture. Although the depression ended plans to build a 400-room hotel resembling a castle, the business district had achieved a distinctive English aura.[38]

While residents could employ their own financial resources to safeguard the quality of development in a limited area, they had to find a different solution for establishing standards community-wide. As Americans elsewhere, the citizens of Scarsdale found a source of hope in the ideas of the city planning movement.[39]

In a sense, suburban Scarsdale "grew up" with city planning. Just two years after the Arthur Manor subdivision opened in Scarsdale, the White City of the Chicago World's Fair awakened millions of visitors to the benefits of a carefully designed environment. The construction of the mall in Washington, D.C., and the plans to rebuild the Chicago lakefront added to the interest in city planning, and in 1909 the movement passed a benchmark with the holding of the first National Conference on City Planning. Zoning was one of the key ideas discussed at the conference. It involved the establishment of separate districts for industrial and residential purposes and the regulation of the size of buildings in residential areas. Because it promised to bring sunlight and air to urban masses as it protected property values, zoning drew the support of individuals from various parts of the political spectrum. By 1916, eight municipalities, including New York City, had established zoning systems. By the late 1920s the figure exceeded 800.[40]

Zoning began as an instrument of city rather than town planning. The case for the constitutionality of zoning, for the priority of the public welfare over an individual's property rights, seemed stronger in an urban situation than in a nonurban one. Nevertheless, in May 1921, five years before the United States Supreme Court declared zoning constitutional, the State of New York empowered such villages as Scarsdale to enact zoning systems.[41]

The residents of Scarsdale had already been taking preliminary steps in that direction. In May 1920 the Town Club had appointed a committee to study the matter, and in March of the following year the committee had issued a report to the village board urging adoption of a zoning ordinance as well as of a building code. In May 1921, the village planning commission began working on the technical aspects of the ordinance. Hesitant to draw up a final map without professional guidance, the commission prevailed on the village board to approve funds for a study by the Technical Advisory Corporation. The corporation, headed by George B. Ford, chief proponent of scientific city planning, presented its report to the planning commission on March 20, 1922.[42]

Nine days later the village board held a special meeting to act on the commission's recommendations. The trustees had not announced an agenda, since their regular meeting had occurred two days earlier. They had not invited a representative from the newspaper, nor did the village clerk record the debate. Even so, on March 29, 1922, the board of trustees passed the zoning ordinance of the village of Scarsdale.[43]

The trustees recognized the irregular nature of the proceedings. Normally they would have held a public hearing before approving the ordinance. Yet they found themselves faced with what the village president called a matter of "now or never." A crisis had arisen when a Scarsdale realtor, Frederick Fox, sold a parcel of land to Horace Day, president of the Suchard chocolate interests in America. Day intended to use the land as the site for a chocolate factory. The parcel consisted of 10½ acres adjoining the tracks of the Westchester and Boston Railroad near the Heathcote station. The realtor believed that the unattractive location of the land made it unsuitable for any sort of residential purpose. He thought the Suchard factory would offer "a clean and sightly spot" as compared to "the cheap and carelessly kept places" usually found near railroad stations.[44]

The board realized that it could not restrict the area near the station to noncommercial uses, but it saw no reason to equate zoning for business with zoning for industry. Apparently the trustees believed that a business which offered goods or services to the people of Scarsdale differed greatly from an enterprise that manufactured products for a wider market. The latter would enjoy the community's resources and contribute nothing but jobs for a class of workers who at present lived elsewhere, and taxes, a negligible factor in a wealthy village like Scarsdale. In their view, granting industry a foothold would have jeopardized both the social well-being of the community—by threatening its domination by the upper-middle class—and its physical well-being—by creating such hazards as air pollution. Thus the zoning ordinance issued the general prohibition:

No building or premises shall be used for any trade, industry or purpose that is noxious or offensive by reason of the emission of

31

odor, dust, smoke, gas, or noise or that is dangerous to public health or safety.

In addition the ordinance specified fifty-two types of forbidden industries.[45]

Six days after the passage of the ordinance, the board held a special meeting to allow the Suchard Company to present its case. The meeting, however, turned into a display of community self-congratulation as prominent citizens defended the legality of the board's action and protested against the incursion of a factory of any sort. The village president said he had received resolutions of support from the Woman's Club and from the Greenacres Association, as well as thirty-eight telegrams and letters from residents of the community. Even the Suchard interests yielded to the spirit of the meeting. Horace Day, president of the company, said he would not have acquired the land in the first place if he had known that the citizens of Scarsdale would oppose the construction of a factory. He promised that the company would take no action to test the legality of Scarsdale's ordinance.[46]

One man, George W. Field, dissented. A former village president and trustee, Field spoke on this occasion as the lawyer for realtor Frederick Fox. According to Field, the location selected by the company would neither interfere with the beauty of the surroundings nor create a nuisance in any way. In his view, the village would do well to allow a company of the character of Suchard to locate near the railroad station, since some industrial enterprise would take over the property "sooner or later."[47]

The *Inquirer* opposed that argument. Urging the people of Scarsdale to beware any sign of industrialization, an editorial stated, "A community is industrialized to the degree that it makes no resistance while there is still time to resist." The newspaper used a cartoon to illustrate its message. The first picture showed a real estate agent presenting the deed of a cottage to a happy couple. In the second picture a small factory stood in the distance, but the couple, still content, seemed oblivious to it. The third picture showed the cottage overshadowed by industrial plants with smoke-belching chimneys. Predictably, the owners of the cottage looked dejected.[48] The vast majority of Scarsdale residents shared the newspaper's viewpoint. They regarded their move to Scarsdale as an attempt to escape the filth, crowds, and corruption of the industrial city. They resolved to do everything in their power to keep industry from gaining a foothold in the village. It seemed to them that, if they failed, the reason for Scarsdale's existence would have ended.

The anti-industrial attitudes of village residents contained a certain irony. They thought of Scarsdale as a haven from the industrial system, the very system that enriched them. They enjoyed an industrial income in a pastoral setting. In their opinion, others would have that option once they achieved material success.

Unlike the decision to bar industry from Scarsdale, the provisions of the zoning law that pertained to the construction of houses, businesses, and apartments did provoke controversy, particularly between the owners of large properties, on the one hand, and the owners of a basic house and lot on the other. The ordinance of March 1922 divided the land area of the village into four classes of building zones. The Residence A category, applying to approximately 93 percent of the village's land, provided mainly for single-family houses, the symbol of the upper-middle class. The category also allowed the construction of clubs, lodges, schools, and churches. It did not set minimum acreage requirements. Such requirements became part of normal zoning procedure in the years after World War II. Only 4 percent of the village was placed in the Residence B category, which permitted, in addition to Residence A uses, the construction of two-family houses, hospitals, and charitable institutions. Residence B also allowed home occupations that took up no more than one-fourth of the total floor area of a building, provided they did not create a nuisance. The law set a maximum height of two and one-half stories for buildings in the Residence A and B zones. Roughly 1 percent of Scarsdale's land area was placed in the Residence C class, which allowed the construction of hotels, provided that no building exceeded a height of four stories. The Business zone accounted for approximately 2 percent of the land area of the village. Part of the zone lay near the Scarsdale station on the New York Central line. The other adjoined the Heathcote station on the Westchester and Boston Railroad. Beyond setting a maximum height of four stories and prohibiting all "offensive" uses, the law did not limit construction in the Business zone to specifically approved purposes.[49]

On April 19, 1922, the village board held a public hearing on the zoning ordinance to consider resident grievances. Most of those who spoke at the hearing owned sizable tracts of land.

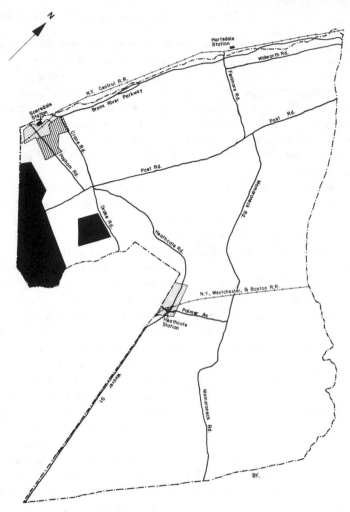

VILLAGE OF SCARSDALE

BUILDING ZONE MAP
MARCH 29, 1922

KEY

☐ RESIDENCE A   ▨ RESIDENCE C
■ RESIDENCE B   ▦ BUSINESS

    Building zone map of the Village of Scarsdale, March 29, 1922. Six months after this map was approved, the village board of trustees amended the zoning ordinance, reducing the Business zone by one-fifth and the Residence C zone by nearly half. In early 1924 they abolished the Residence B zone and placed the affected land in Residence A. Since then, about 97 percent of Scarsdale's land area has been restricted almost exclusively to the construction of single-family houses.

Since the owners would profit from intensive use of their holdings, they wanted the village board to enlarge the areas allotted for businesses, hotels, and apartments. Scarsdale's largest property holder and taxpayer, Emily O. Butler, felt that her interests should have received consideration in the establishment of the zoning law. Instead, the board had placed all 360 acres of her land in the Residence A category. According to her lawyer, Alexander M. Crane, portions of the land were not appropriate for single-family houses. A prospective buyer was planning to build a hotel and apartments, but, Crane said, the board's action had left Miss Butler "no option in the matter at all." The key holdings of the Scarsdale Improvement Corporation conveniently fell in the Business category, but Rush Wilson requested the board of trustees to shift a peripheral strip of land from the residential to commercial zone. The trustees also received a protest from Evans R. Dick, president of a New York real estate company, regarding the classification of a tract of land near the Westchester and Boston Railroad. He said the property was "manifestly unfitted" for the residential purposes to which the law had restricted it, whereas it was "particularly fitted for the erection of offices and stores." The board of trustees referred the three petitions of grievance to its committee on codes, with instructions that "any modifications should tend to the elimination, as much as possible, of the buildings for business and apartment purposes." All three petitions were denied within a month by vote of the village board.[50]

The April hearing brought under public discussion an issue that the zoning law had not made clear. The Residence C zone provided for the construction of four-story hotels, while the Business zone permitted four-story buildings not used for industry. Nowhere, however, did the law explicitly provide for the construction of apartments. One man, E.H. Klaber, said at the hearing that he feared "three-decker" tenements would overrun the Business zone because the zoning law failed to prevent their construction. Yet, while opposed to tenements, Klaber did not want to exclude apartments from Scarsdale. Instead, he asked the trustees to permit apartments in the Residence C and Business zones and at the same time to set minimum standards for their construction.[51]

Naturally the principal property holders in the Residence C zone wanted the village board to allow the use of their land for apartments. Their spokesman stressed the ambiguity of the clauses regarding the approved uses of Residence C. The zone was to act as a buffer between the commercial and residential areas. If the law permitted hotels there, they saw no reason why it should discriminate against apartments. Along with Klaber, the property holders distinguished between cheap tenements and "high class" apartments. They said they would welcome the adoption of a building code that would effectively preclude the construction of cheap tenements in Scarsdale. One man particularly urged the trustees to require fireproof construction for all multifamily houses. The requirement would rule out the construction of frame tenements, and its public safety overtones would satisfy the courts. Yet the real benefit lay in the fact that fireproof buildings would cost three times more to construct than frame buildings. The cost differential would yield a sizable tax return for the village, while the high rents would assure, he said, "a more desirable class of tenants." With such an ordinance, the speaker concluded, the people of Scarsdale would have "little to fear" from the building of apartments.[52]

Whatever merit their arguments may have had, the efforts of large property holders to change the zoning law in their self-interest caused a tightening of attitudes on the part of those Scarsdale residents whose chief investment was in their own homes. To most of the residents of the still largely undeveloped village, the thought of allowing several square blocks for apartments and shops conjured up visions of urban masses. They came to view zoning as an opportunity to exclude from the community all businesses and apartments.

Two letters appearing in the *Inquirer* on April 26 opened that line of debate. They called for amendment of the original zoning law to decrease the areas zoned for intensive use. While one writer described the law's passage as "a far-sighted and public-spirited act," he urged the village board to "go a little further." Citing the proposed construction of the East Parkway Building, he asked the board to restrict the commercial part of Scarsdale to that one block. With the stores of White Plains "so near," the writer believed that a one-block commercial zone would certainly fulfill "the present as well as the future need" of the village. The writer of the other letter stressed the changes impending for Scarsdale. He said local residents "came knowing there were no stores and preferring just the kind of community which we now have." Some people, he said, had made financial sacrifices to enjoy Scarsdale's "quiet village ways."But those who had passed the zoning ordinance obviously wanted to turn Scarsdale into a real commercial center: "Instead of stepping off the trains at once into the peaceful country, we should have to pass by the same kind of life which we gladly leave behind us in New York." The writer went on to consider the building of apartments as a special threat to the character of the community. He did not differentiate the residents of apartments from tenement dwellers. In his view all those who rented space in multifamily houses were transients who owned no property and took no real interest in the welfare of the community. Even if the zoning law confined apartment houses to "unobjectionable areas, . . . the problem of an unassimilated group of voters" would remain. The apartment population, he concluded, would act as "the leaven to change the whole atmosphere of the place."[53]

With the publication of the two anonymous letters, prominent citizens at open meetings of the village board began to speak against stores and apartments. Mrs. Burchard Dutcher, president of the Woman's Club, stated that the club's board of directors believed the building of many apartments would seriously alter the character of the village. The directors urged the village trustees to limit apartment construction as much as possible. Pliny Williamson, a lawyer who later served as town supervisor and state senator, was applauded at one meeting when he called for the exclusion of apartment houses with no exceptions. Cleveland A. Dunn, a former Town Club president, expressed the opinion that the salvation of Scarsdale lay in its homes, and its menace, in stores and business generally.[54]

Along with others, Dunn aimed some criticism at the sponsors of the Scarsdale Improvement Corporation. He said Scarsdale residents accepted the present development as inevitable because of the men who supported it. But, he continued, "We would thank God if the apartment business would stop right here. The board is faced with measuring dollars on one side, homes and family life on the other." Another critic derided the so-called improvements planned by "a few of the 'public-spirited' citizens." In the past, he said, residents had

flattered themselves . . . that Scarsdale was superior to other suburban communities in that it was strictly a community of homes and that shops and apartments would not be tolerated. Possibly, we will soon be able to boast of a new-fashioned Scarsdale which is superior to other suburban settlements on the line—with modern apartments, better shops, and a better bus service than neighboring towns.[55]

Sometimes the debate took on a bitter tone. In a long letter, Richard Edwards accused those who wanted apartments of seeking financial profit at the risk of the community's welfare. Edwards took issue with the argument that proximity of land to the railroad precluded its use for single-family dwellings. He pointed out that the station and tracks in Scarsdale were located in a gulley below the level of the area in question. Edwards thought the village could satisfactorily protect the rights of those who owned land near the railroad by uniformly restricting land use to the construction of houses. Edwards insisted that 95 percent of the people of Scarsdale opposed the construction in the future of any stores or apartments, and he accused the village board of providing for intensive use against the sentiments of an overwhelming majority of voters.[56]

The depth and bitterness of anticommercial feeling in Scarsdale surprised those property holders who believed they had always acted in the community's best interest. The Popham family had held land in Scarsdale since the eighteenth century. At private expense the Pophams had developed a park for the community. They had improved a number of roads, including the approaches to the Scarsdale station, and had ceded to the village parts of their estate for the extension of public highways. In the words of their attorney, the Pophams had never done anything "detrimental to the village or unjust to their neighbors. . . . The fact is no one has the interest of this village at heart more than they."[57]

The land owned by the Popham family lay along the two main roads to the Scarsdale station. Originally the trustees had placed a large part of the property in the Residence C zone and a small section in the Business zone, but residents of the community wanted to restrict the area to houses. One group formally petitioned the board for a change in the zoning provisions. The Pophams' attorney argued that the petition, if granted, would reduce the value of the land by 50 to 75 percent. The family had held the property for years, at great expense in taxes, with the intention of using it for business purposes, "as the interest of the village might require." The attorney insisted that the land had "never been used or intended for residences," nor was it "adaptable to residential purposes."[58]

Like the Pophams, the men who sponsored the Scarsdale Improvement Corporation found it difficult to understand the villagers' change in mood. In 1920 residents had praised the plans of the corporation. Now it had become a target for abuse. Corporation director George Field tried to regain the public's trust at an open meeting of the board of trustees. Field referred to the fact that two years earlier an outside developer held a sixty-year lease covering a narrow strip of land along Popham Road. Since at that time Scarsdale had no zoning restrictions, the developer was planning to build cheap stores. To keep central Scarsdale from becoming like Main Street in White Plains, the men of the Scarsdale Improvement Corporation had bought the lease for $5,000 and paid $125,000 for the remainder of the land. Field said, "We did it to try to do some zoning ourselves." He asked the public to allow the zoners of 1920 to continue to carry out their purpose.[59]

Somehow the village board had to appease the residents who opposed stores and apartments without embittering those who owned land near the Scarsdale station. In public statements the trustees endorsed the majority viewpoint. Their goal, they said, was to preserve Scarsdale as "a village of homes." Zoning offered the best means of protecting Scarsdale's traditions, but the trustees saw zoning as a limited instrument. They tried to educate the public regarding the legal aspects of zoning restrictions. Any plan, they said, which zoned all of Scarsdale for single-family housing would raise "legal complications," since no court would uphold a zoning law that failed to provide for different forms of land use. In order to restrict most of Scarsdale to residential development, the board had to make some provision for stores and apartments.[60]

Yet the trustees believed that the original zoning law needed adjustment. In September 1922, they approved an amendment that transferred part of the land zoned for intensive use into the Residence A category. The change reduced the Business zone by one-fifth, the Residence C zone by nearly half. When the landowners whose interests were adversely affected threatened to sue the village, the trustees carried out a long-awaited revision of the law. In November 1922, they approved the use of the Residence C zone for apartment construction.[61] Passage of the two amendments quieted all but a few diehards who continued to call for the exclusion of stores and apartments. Even the large property holders acknowledged by their silence the strength of the feeling against them. Ideally most Scarsdale residents would have preferred to restrict the village to houses, since they wanted to seal off the community from drastic change. Yet they had too much respect for property rights and too great a desire for local peace not to feel pulled both ways on some issues. Given that ambiguity, the constitutionality argument clinched the case for compromise.

Once Scarsdale residents accepted the idea of having a business district, the programs of the Scarsdale Improvement Corporation again met with favor. The corporation, which promised the village a high standard of construction, owned a part of the land zoned for intensive use. The problem was to regulate construction standards on other properties in the Business and Residence C zones. During the debate on zoning, the large property holders had suggested a means of setting general standards. Now the village as a whole supported their proposal and called for the adoption of a building code. The code took several months to prepare, since it involved technical questions regarding plumbing, electrical wiring, and the weight capacities of particular structures. In the spring of 1923, the village board completed a draft of the code, the key provisions of which set minimum standards of construction for different classes of buildings. For apartments, theaters, and hospitals, the code required the use of incombustible materials. Fire-resistant materials, such as brick or concrete, were required for the walls of schools, churches, libraries, and other public buildings. The proposed law permitted frame construction for one-family houses, but it required floors and partitions to be fire-stopped with mineral wool or mortar. The code forbade the construction of wood shingle roofs on new houses and required all houses in the village to have incombustible roofs within twelve years.[62]

A public hearing on the drafted ordinance drew only five citizens, one of whom called the code "a rich man's proposition." Though that remark came close to the truth, most residents were willing to accept its implications. A building code was constitutional because, as the trustees said, it protected the homebuyer and increased public safety.[63] If at the same time it helped to prevent members of the lower class from residing in the community, the citizens of Scarsdale were all the more satisfied. The board of trustees unanimously approved the measure on

July 11, 1923. Passage of the building code complemented the purpose of the zoning law. Zoning confined to a limited area the construction of stores and apartments. The building ordinance controlled the quality of their construction. Together the laws worked to secure Scarsdale as a bastion of the upper-middle class.

Six months later the trustees acted to further secure the character of the community. On petition from many of the affected property holders, the village board voted to change property originally placed in the Residence B zone to Residence A. The petitioners, homeowners in Arthur Manor, North End, and Scarsdale Park, opposed the construction of two-family houses in their neighborhood as well as the use of residences for home occupations. With the passage of this amendment, approximately 97 percent of the area of Scarsdale was restricted, almost exclusively, to the construction of single-family houses.[64]

Though Scarsdale's laws barred factories and precluded the construction of cheap tenements or two-family houses, they did not insulate the village from all the unpleasant aspects of industrial society. In November 1923, the Scarsdale Supply Company set up a lumber yard on the site where the Suchard Chocolate Company had planned to build its factory. The supply yard, which served primarily local needs, occupied six acres near the Westchester and Boston Railroad station. The area fell under the Business category, which permitted most nonmanufacturing activities. The board of trustees ruled that establishment of the lumber yard did not violate the zoning law.[65]

Some Scarsdale residents were outraged to learn the limits of the protection offered by zoning. Offices, shops, and restaurants they were willing to accept, but the sight of piles of building materials—lumber, bricks, sand, pipes, and shingles—repelled them. A man who lived near the yard complained that it was ruining land values in the neighborhood. He pointed out that the presence of the lumber yard created an additional nuisance, for residents had to endure the noise of heavy trucks on their quiet country roads.[66]

Those immediately affected tried to enlist others on their side. They reminded members of the community that hundreds of people passed by the Heathcote station daily. One man called the suburban station "the front doorway of all our homes from which the passing traveler or the guest gets his first impression." Sensitive to the role of the suburban station, the village had taken steps to preserve the beauty of its two stations on the New York Central line. A formal garden adjoined the station at Hartsdale, while the Scarsdale station had a pond and waterfall surrounded by trees. Heathcote residents did not call for such measures at their station. They only asked that the rest of the community support them in their attempts to eliminate the supply yard from the area.[67]

The residents' argument lost its force when the Scarsdale Supply Company offered to compromise. At a meeting of the village board in March 1924, representatives of the company presented a plan for planting their lot at the Heathcote station to screen the piles of building materials from the public. An improvement in customer relations would probably offset the cost to the company. The trustees received the plan with relief. They knew the courts would not have sustained an action against the company, yet they understood the discomfiture of the area's residents.[68] The people of Scarsdale liked to think of life in terms of finished products. They wanted to ignore the reality of laborers, materials, and machines needed to create the goods they enjoyed. So anxious were they to maintain their illusion that a screen of trees sufficed to obscure reality from them.

During the years 1915 to 1925, as the proportion of households in Scarsdale headed by members of the upper-middle class increased from 60 to 70 percent, its residents showed a readiness to use progressive concepts of the expanded role of government. As they established municipally owned and operated services and passed laws regulating land use and building practices, they strove to achieve for Scarsdale a reputation as a model suburb. Yet their version of the ideal progressive community incorporated little of the broad humanitarianism of social activist Jane Addams or the industrial democracy of philosopher John Dewey. Indeed, far from regarding the working poor as human beings from whom they had much to learn, the residents of Scarsdale tried to insulate their suburb from contact with the lower classes, except to the extent that they required the labor of municipal employees and domestic servants. This, then, was the sort of utopia the people of Scarsdale sought to create, rather than a socialistic community like that described in Thomas More's sixteenth century discourse on the subject, or any of the so-called utopian communities established since that time. Instead, they sought a capitalistic utopia in which the comforts of society's achievers would be augmented by the actions of a progressive local government.

CHAPTER 3

Resisting the Urban Tide

Although the building boom of the 1920s that struck cities and suburbs around the nation also struck the village of Scarsdale, few communities accepted construction with such mixed feelings and such determined efforts to halt the undesirable consequences of growth. On the one hand, the boom exhilarated local realtors, the owners of large properties, and others who regarded their place of residence primarily from a pecuniary point of view. On the other, it distressed those citizens who prized Scarsdale for its tranquil beauty and social exclusiveness. Such people recognized that zoning alone could not determine the final character of the village for, although the ordinance (as amended in 1922 and 1924) restricted almost 97 percent of the area of Scarsdale to the construction of one-family houses, its passage did not guarantee that developers' subdivisions would meet the expectations of village residents—expectations that exceeded the standards prescribed by the law. These people also understood that the courts might not approve an ordinance that restricted so much of the community to residential development. Beyond the issue of the type of development that might occur, some residents felt threatened by the simple fact of development, for in any form it robbed the community of open space and complicated traffic control. Thus, by the mid to late 1920s, as the implications of growth became more pressing, more and more residents resolved to resist the urban tide and fight to retain Scarsdale's distinctiveness within the expanding metropolis.

In the decade of the 1920s the population of New York City grew 21 percent, the population of Westchester County rose 51 percent, and the population of the village of Scarsdale increased 176 percent. Although these percentages are somewhat misleading in that New York City added more than 1.3 million inhabitants, whereas Scarsdale added fewer than 6,200, they underscore the extent to which the city was expanding. As buses and automobiles began to supplement trains, trolleys, and ferries as means of commuting to jobs in Manhattan, vast new tracts were opened for suburban development.[1] The upturn in Scarsdale began in 1923. More than 120 houses were built that year, 240 the following year. In 1925 the village issued permits for the construction of 300 one-family houses, as well as 2 stores, 5 churches, and 30 garages. Scarsdale was experiencing a boom— "the wonderful change," one realtor called it. "Heretofore," he said, "we have done things in a small way. Now we must learn to do them in a larger way."[2]

By late 1925 the boom psychology had spurred a marked increase in the number and size of real estate ads appearing in the *Scarsdale Inquirer*. For wider circulation, village realtors advertised in the *New York Times*, which contained more extensive real estate listings than any other New York paper. Generally their ads took a low-keyed approach, stating the facts and the asking price. One realtor explained that since Scarsdale had "no desire to attract multitudes," its promoters abstained from "clamorous publicity." Taking his cue from Emerson, he went on, "the mark of a city should be the absence of pretension. When it speaks it should take a low tone; avoid all brag; promise not at all except by virtue of its worth and perform much to fulfill its obligations to its inhabitants." A few realtors took the opposite tack. Since they believed growth was inevitable, they favored greater publicity to increase the demand for houses, raise prices, and allow Scarsdale to select a higher class of residents—and themselves to earn higher commissions. The chief practitioner of that theory was Marie D. Kling, who spent thousands informing the public of Scarsdale's attractions. Week after week her ads called attention to the fine schools, low taxes, convenient train service, and strict zoning laws. In Scarsdale, she advertised, people would find "comfort" (top-level services), "happiness" (a delightful social life), "contentment" (beautiful trees and rolling hillsides), and "health" (Catskill mountain water, high elevation). In her view it was "the finest suburban town" within 100 miles of New York City. Her claims went still further. "Scarsdale alone," she said, "more nearly approximates the perfect place to live and enjoy life than any other place."[3]

Implicit in the two styles of advertising were appeals to class attitudes. While the restrained approach attracted people who considered themselves sophisticated, the other lured prospective home-buyers with promises of comfort and status. Such ads helped to make a name for Scarsdale as an exclusive community. They were not exploiting a reputation already secure. Rather, they created that reputation; they notified the public that Scarsdale offered quality houses to those able to pay the price.

Quality, not come-ons, sold people on Scarsdale. A combination of factors worked to effect high standards of construction throughout the village. The local government exerted a major influence. As early as 1917, the trustees had set up a planning commission to review proposals for new subdivisions. The commission could make recommendations to developers regarding their plans, but until 1922 it had no power of coercion. Passage of the zoning ordinance gave the commission the power it had lacked. By establishing rules regulating land use, setbacks, and building heights, the ordinance enabled the commission to enforce minimum standards. The planning commission served as part one in a two-part process of review. After securing its approval for his general plans, a developer had to apply for a separate permit for every house he wanted to erect. The village code required that he submit two sets of blueprints to the building inspector, who studied them for violations of the zoning and building ordinances. If the plans met those criteria, the building inspector issued a permit for the construction of the house. Returning one copy of the blueprints to the developer, he kept the other on file at the village hall to guarantee that the house erected would correspond to the plans as approved.[4]

The two levels of review fostered quality construction more by publicity than by coercion. After all, the requirements set by the zoning and building ordinances were minimum standards that most developers strove to excel. Such men used the public processes as a means for advertising their plans. Having geared their proposals to an upper-middle-class market, they welcomed reactions from the upper-middle-class residents of Scarsdale.

The degree of community interest took some developers by surprise. In October 1926, a builder named Anton Stolz applied to the planning commission for permission to divide a tract of sixteen acres into 60 by 90 foot lots. The tract was located in a wealthy section on the east side of the Post Road, north of Oxford Road. Nearby residents, viewing the plan as an attempt to bring "a cheap development" into their "high class" neighborhood, pressured the commission to withhold approval. Because the project met the standards prescribed by law—indeed, Scarsdale had more modest subdivisions—the commission had no grounds for negative action; but it did name a committee to confer with the residents. Those discussions convinced the latter that "an out and out purchase of the land was the only way of stopping the undesirable development." The group formed a syndicate, the Grange Improvement Company, which in two months acquired not only Stolz's property but other vacant land in the area as well. Eighteen months later the village board agreed to buy ten acres of the company's holdings for parkland. Thus the residents achieved their threefold purpose of safeguarding property values; of earning a profit; and of increasing Scarsdale's "desirability as a place to live."[5]

The subdivisions opened in the 1920s were neither as lavish nor as modest as those established earlier. Although individual residences of exceptional quality were built in the twenties, such as Lucius Eastman's 23-room mansion on a 9½-acre estate, not one subdivision lived up to the example of Heathcote with its multiacre lots and 150-foot setbacks. Meanwhile, all the new subdivisions surpassed the standards of Arthur Manor with its lots of 25 x 100 feet.[6]

Perhaps no subdivision of the period reflected the standards of villagers better than Berkley. Organized at the end of the decade by two long-time residents, Berkley demonstrated the correlation of upper-middle-class attitudes with civic interest and professional pride. Alexander M. Crane supplied the property, and Walter Collet the expertise. The men were dealing with forty-six acres of uneven land within a mile of the Scarsdale station. To assure that Berkley's location would work to its advantage, they weighed the need for ready access against the desire for seclusion. They agreed that convenience was essential to commuters. They, therefore, provided three streets that opened onto Popham Road, the main route to the railroad station. None of the streets connected with roads from other sections. In fact, anyone wishing to travel east or south from Berkley had first to exit north or west. The arrangement had the desired consequences. People living in Berkley could quickly reach the station and shopping center; people who did not live there had no reason to drive through.[7]

The tract itself presented one obstacle to development—what to do with the six acres of low, wet land that lay in the center. Building would have required an expensive process of draining the land and adding fill, but even that would not preclude the possibility of flooding. Crane and Collet did not want such a hazard to cheapen their project. Instead of using the six acres for houses, they created a park with two brook-fed ponds. Although the park offered a place to skate in winter, the well-trimmed lawns and rustic bridges betrayed its decorative purpose. The park provided a setting for houses guaranteed to attract people of taste.[8]

Once the developers had agreed on the general layout, they began to construct three houses. These served, not as models in the usual sense, but as style-setters, which helped establish a tone of discreet wealth. Blending creativity with conformity, they offered variations on traditional themes. One house was a large colonial of seam-faced granite, another was typically Southern with tall white columns supporting a porch. The third was an English residence of stone construction with a turreted entrance tower and leaded windows. Inside, it had oak paneling in the living room and hall, a library of knotted pine, a dining room, kitchen, butler's pantry, five master bedrooms, five baths, and two rooms for the servants. Crane and Collet had held back nothing. They had commissioned respected architects, hired skilled workers, and supplied high-grade materials. The resulting houses bespoke prestige and a sound investment.[9]

Attracting buyers was the next step. In order to sell eighty-five lots at high prices, the developers advertised in the *New York Times*. Their ads described Berkley as "a notable community development," offering custom-built houses on ample lots. According to the ads, a Berkley house would give "lasting satisfaction." "Your individuality," they said, "your taste and requirements can be embodied in a real home, expertly designed, honestly constructed." The ads mentioned, but did not stress, the landscaped park and convenient location. The developers preferred to let such features work their effect when prospective buyers visited the site. Yet Crane and Collet did want the ads to make one matter clear to all who read them: in order to preserve the character of the area and to protect property values, restrictive convenants were incorporated in all Berkley deeds.[10]

While covenants operated in most subdivisions, those for Berkley were "highly restrictive." They reduced the risk of owning property by curtailing the rights of the actual owners and by limiting the range of would-be owners. The deeds forbade the use of any lot for manufacturing, business, or trade, or "in such a manner as to be a nuisance to the owners or occupants of any of the other property." They explicitly prohibited the keeping of cows, chickens, and other farm animals. They limited construction per lot to a private dwelling and garage for one family. A lot could not be sold in part, except to an adjoining owner who then could not build on the subdivided property. The deeds further required that any dwelling erected on a lot should cost a minimum of $25,000, exclusive of the value of the land and of all furnishings and equipment. Finally, they provided that the developers would retain for twenty years the right to veto plans for the construction of any dwelling, garage, fence, or other structure. To avoid confusion regarding the binding nature of the covenants, the deeds stated that the restrictions "ran with the land"—that is, they bound not only the present owners, but also the heirs and future buyers of land in Berkley. Any deed holder had the power to take legal action regarding a violation of the covenants, or to apply for an injunction to prevent a threatened violation.[11]

Such restrictions crowned the efforts of Crane and Collet to build a harmonious subdivision. Although the depression seriously slowed sales, within a few years dozens of large, traditional houses lined the roads surrounding the park.[12] In the end, Berkley succeeded because it involved a lot of money and little imagination. For the refinements society valued, its sponsors could afford to pay. They had set about building a showcase that expressed a view of the good life. Their efforts might have yielded higher profits had they been less dedicated to class prescriptions of excellence. By placing quality first, they sacrificed dollars for a sense of satisfaction and the admiration of others.

Another subdivision secured a snob image by capitalizing on its having been organized by "a small group of prominent residents." Although Rush Wilson and Walter Collet, the men who served as president and general manager, were no strangers to the trade, the *Inquirer* insisted that Sherbrooke was not an "ordinary real estate promotion." Rather, it was "a citizens' development."[13] The distinction implied that Sherbrooke's backers cared more than other developers about saving trees, building fine houses, and protecting the rights of property holders. To the extent that as citizens they risked their reputations as well as their money, that implication was probably true.

Yet Sherbrooke, with more modest requirements than Berkley, afforded only marginal prestige. The lots averaged less than one-third acre, and the deeds set $15,000 as the minimum cost for building a house. Whether the project would prove socially acceptable depended largely on who moved there. Knowing residents would not object to their own kind, the developers sought buyers from within the village. Their campaign had a positive and a negative aspect. It appealed for community support on the basis of the project's worth as a local enterprise, and it promised not to solicit buyers from the outside. Those policies were summed up in the slogan, "a Scarsdale development for Scarsdale people and their friends." The developers refrained from advertising in the *New York Times*, but they did issue progress reports for local publication. Their tactics worked as intended, for local residents bought twenty-nine of the thirty-eight lots. By giving up houses in established sections to purchase land in the new subdivision, they won early recognition of Sherbrooke's respectability.[14]

In contrast to Sherbrooke, the sales methods for Heathcote Crest drew buyers from a range of backgrounds. "Real estate operators and investors, builders, homeseekers, and lot buyers"— all were exhorted by ads in the *Times* to weigh the project's "decided advantages." Chief among these was its location over-looking a large, new Westchester park, between two parkways, on a cross-county road, with access to three commuter lines. Illustrating the area's potential for growth, the ads predicted a development similar to that which followed the opening of Man-hattan's Central Park. Such a reference appealed to urban spec-ulative interests, but those who sought large profits from apart-ment construction were disappointed. The village zoning ordinance limited use of the area to single-family dwellings. Expanding on that restriction, the deeds set the minimum size for lots at 60 x 100 feet and the minimum cost for houses at $12,500. The deeds also provided that, until 1935, the developers would retain the right to review the construction plans, "together with the exterior color scheme," for every house proposed. Between the ads and the restrictions, there existed a conflict that probably hurt sales. Although Heathcote Crest consisted of 234 lots, the county clerk, over a five-year period, recorded the sale of only 59. Thirty of those went to builders, speculators, and home-seekers from New York City; 26 to people from other communities in Westchester; 1 to a man from out-of-state; and 2 to residents of Scarsdale.[15]

Heathcote Crest was not a cheap subdivision, yet its meager success, modest requirements, and diverse clientele did not live up to Scarsdale's self-image of the 1920s. In fact, it might have elicited protest if it had stood closer to the center of population. Isolated as it was, the project was tolerated by the rest of the community, which failed to recognize the function it performed. Since social advantage was a relative matter, the existence of Heathcote Crest bolstered the reputations of other sections.

Despite their differences, Berkley, Sherbrooke, and Heathcote Crest shared a basic feature. All three conformed to the formula: one house for one family on one lot. A violation of that rule would have involved the offender in a court action, for the ordinance of 1922 had restricted nearly all the undeveloped land to single-family houses. Still, the courts had yet to uphold an ordinance as strict as Scarsdale's. The bigger the stakes, the more tempted someone would be to challenge the ordinance, and the harder the community would fight to sustain it.

The test of the zoning ordinance came in the aftermath of the largest real estate transaction in village history. In December 1924, Jacobs Brothers realtors purchased the 360-acre estate of Miss Emily O. Butler. Fox Meadow cost the company $1.5 million. In order to assure an adequate return on its investment, the company intended to build a series of apartment houses and stores on the land adjoining the Bronx River Parkway. That area, like the rest of Fox Meadow, was zoned for single-family residences. When, in February 1925, the company asked the village board to permit intensive development of the land along the parkway, the people of Scarsdale made it clear that they opposed any change in the ordinance. In letters, editorials, speeches, and petitions, they denounced the company's plans for the forty-acre strip. The result of the plans, the *Inquirer* stated, would be to "bring in a different sort of population faster than we can take care of it." Overcrowded schools, overburdened services, congested streets, a rise in crime, increased hazard to health—all threatened Scarsdale, so the protesters claimed, if it submitted to the company's demands.[16]

Representatives of the company, now incorporated as Fox Meadow Estates, tried to reason with their critics. They explained that roads would require eighty acres; another thirty needed draining. With such costs, they said, in order to show a profit, the company could either use a small portion of the tract for stores and apartments, leaving the rest to be developed in large residential plots, or it would have to divide all of Fox Meadow into small lots for cheap houses. Company spokesmen stressed the advantages of the first alternative. They promised Scarsdale "high class" apartment construction. The company would build a maximum of thirty apartment houses with no more than eighteen families in each. The buildings would be free-standing— at least eighty feet apart, handsomely designed, and soundly constructed. Anticipating the objection that apartment dwellers would have no stake in the community, Fox Meadow Estates said it planned to offer its apartments as cooperatives. Each family in a cooperative would own the apartment it lived in. Like the other families of the village, it would pay taxes and would suffer a financial loss if Scarsdale's desirability as a suburb declined.[17]

Such arguments won little sympathy from homeowners who looked first to the welfare of their own property. They pointed out that Scarsdale's residential nature would enhance the value of apartments, whereas the presence of apartments would detract from the value of houses. Was there any reason, they asked, why the financial considerations of a company should count for more than those of hundreds of citizens. Jacobs Brothers had bought Fox Meadow with full knowledge of the zoning restrictions. The people felt no obligation to change the community's ideals in order to accommodate the company's plans.[18]

As it became clear the village would not yield, the company adopted a new tactic. Citing cases in which the courts had nullified a zoning law, the company said that, if Scarsdale failed to compromise now, it would face defeat in the courts later.[19] That argument convinced the local chapter of the Westchester County Realty Board. In view of the experience of other suburbs, Scarsdale realtors decided apartments were "bound to come in one form or another." They urged citizens to accept the company's proposal on the ground that it offered a better type of development "than could ordinarily be hoped for." The realtors' stance drew criticism from prominent citizens who stressed the ambiguities of previous rulings. "It is premature," said William T. Brewster, "to suggest Scarsdale will necessarily be beaten." "Why concede defeat before your start?" asked Cleveland Dunn. "It simply arouses all my fighting spirit."[20]

Public opinion sided with the militants. "Almost 100 percent" of the voting population signed a petition opposing the company's plea to rezone a part of its property. On April 30 the village trustees unanimously denied the request of Fox Meadow Estates. Three weeks later the local appeals board reaffirmed the trustees' decision.[21] When Fox Meadow Estates failed to refer the matter to court, it seemed that Scarsdale had called the company's bluff. In fact, the company was preparing a new request on which it planned to base a strong argument against the village.

In March 1927, Fox Meadow Estates petitioned the village board to approve for apartments the use of three acres near the Hartsdale station. The company hoped that the courts would regard the denial of such a moderate request an unreasonable use of the zoning power. Then, having set the precedent for apartments, Fox Meadow Estates could win permission for further intensive development along the parkway. At an open meeting on April 22, the trustees turned down the petition. That much the company had expected. However, a group of residents at the meeting maneuvered to defeat the company's actual intentions. The residents offered to buy more than thirty-seven acres of land fronting on the Bronx River Parkway. They promised to return to Fox Meadow Estates all the money it had invested in the land and, in addition, a 50 per cent profit. To discredit the company's argument that land near the parkway was unsuited to private houses, the residents agreed to honor the restrictions against intensive use.[22]

There was some reason to believe the company would accept the residents' offer. In the time since Fox Meadow Estates had first threatened to sue the village, the courts had come to exhibit a more positive attitude toward zoning. In November 1925, the New York State Court of Appeals sustained a Mount Vernon ordinance barring apartment houses from residential districts. The court ruled that such a prohibition promoted the general welfare by lessening the dangers of fire, disease, and accident. To the argument that the zoning ordinance violated property rights, the court answered: "The general welfare of the public is superior in importance to the pecuniary profits of the individual." A year later the United States Supreme Court sustained the zoning ordinance of Euclid, Ohio, a suburb of Cleveland. That ordinance provided for six types of land use, including the establishment of zones restricted to single-family houses. Spurning the argument that zoning amounted to class segregation, the court approved the exclusion of apartments from residential zones. In an area of private houses, it said, an apartment building often acted as a "parasite," taking "advantage of the open spaces and attractive surroundings created by the residential character of the district." Sometimes the construction of an apartment house started a trend which, in the words of the court, "utterly destroyed" an area's desirability as a place for private residences.[23]

The Euclid decision improved Scarsdale's chances but did not assure victory against Fox Meadow Estates. While upholding the principle of zoning, the Supreme Court had stated that particular applications of local ordinances might prove arbitrary, unreasonable, and, therefore, invalid.[24] Believing that to be the case in Scarsdale, Fox Meadow Estates filed suit in July 1927. During the long proceedings it elaborated three charges against the village. First, it restated the argument that Scarsdale was robbing the land near the parkway of its natural economic use. The company pointed out that other towns, such as Bronxville and Mount Vernon, had revised their zoning provisions to allow for apartments along the parkway. By refusing to yield, Scarsdale worked a financial hardship on the company, which insisted that the lack of peace and privacy along a highway made it unprofitable to develop the land in question for single-family houses. Second, Fox Meadow Estates charged that personal influence, rather than a comprehensive plan, had dictated the zoning provisions. It noted that at the Scarsdale and Heathcote stations where Rush Wilson controlled the land, the trustees had provided for intensive development. At the Hartsdale station, however, the land within the village was restricted to private dwellings. That discrepancy, according to the company, proved discrimination by the trustees and indicated the possibility of collusion with Wilson. For its third charge, the company directed an attack against the operation of the building code. It showed that, while most cities required fireproof construction only on apartments taller than five stories, Scarsdale demanded fireproofing for any residence for three families or more. The village, said the company, had enacted the requirement, not for the protection of future apartment dwellers, but to make multifamily houses difficult and expensive to build.[25]

Scarsdale countered the charges with statements by citizens and sympathetic experts. Homeowners whose property bordered the parkway testified that the traffic caused little annoyance.

Wilson said he was abroad when the trustees passed the ordinance and that they had defeated the amendments he had asked for. The fireproof requirement, according to a representative of the Regional Plan of New York, saved in insurance payments what it cost in construction expenses.[26]

Central to Scarsdale's defense was the notion of zoning as "a plastic remedy" which adapted itself to local circumstances. Village counsel, former New York Governor Nathan Miller, explained that the ordinance of 1922 had been based on existing conditions with provision for growth. At that time a small number of business buildings had stood at the Scarsdale and Heathcote stations. The trustees, recognizing the business character of those districts, allowed ample space for further development. At the Hartsdale station, a business area had developed on the west side of the tracks outside the village limits. Across from the station, in Scarsdale proper, lay the Greenacres section with its one-family houses. To protect their value, the trustees took what seemed the only reasonable action: they restricted the immediate area to private residences.[27] Later Fox Meadow Estates used that provision to imply that Scarsdale had no zoning standards. As a model the company set forth the idea that every railroad station created "a half-mile zone of influence" appropriate for intensive development. Lawyers for the village attacked that notion as "a dangerous rule-of-thumb, the bane of zoning." They believed that zoning should enable an area to maintain its character. Setting hard standards like the "half-mile zone" would, in their view, tend to eradicate the differences between localities. Then, they warned, all would "succumb to brick and mortar and congestion."[28]

The village lawyers left no room for compromise. Either general traffic streets and railroad stations created districts for intensive use, or local conditions and community sentiment were the proper determinants of zoning patterns. In the first case, Scarsdale would have to undertake extensive rezoning, which would result, they said, in "the loss of its unique charm." One witness complained that applying hard standards to Scarsdale would mean "killing the goose which laid the golden egg." If, however, the court took local conditions and sentiment into account, then the village could expect to have its ordinance affirmed. As one resident, Pliny Williamson, said:

> The opportunity was to us to develop on unusual lines. No part of our territory had been given over to factories or general business.

We had nothing to tear down, no structure to regret. With practically the unanimous voice of our people, we determined that, except in two or three small areas, there should be nothing but homes and that these should be homes in the old American sense— one dwelling to a plot with a bit of green around it.[29]

Scarsdale's pleas failed to convince the lower court judge, Joseph Morschauser. On April 16, 1930, he ruled that the zoning ordinance was "unduly oppressive and confiscatory." He said that the village should have provided for apartments near the parkway and the Hartsdale station, and he suspected that "certain interests" had a part in restricting those areas to private dwellings. As for the building code, Morschauser considered it "an invasion of property rights." He showed how the code supplemented zoning in Scarsdale: by increasing building costs, it effectively limited the amount of apartment construction.[30]

Morschauser's arguments followed those of Fox Meadow Estates. He agreed with the company that zoning should rest on principles, not on sentiments. For example, he viewed as "self-evident" the idea that "proper zoning would require each area to be self-sustaining." Though he was willing to permit some flexibility, the village ordinance seemed to him to present an extreme case. He pointed out that Scarsdale had provided for apartments in less than 0.5 percent of its total area, whereas Pelham Manor had zoned 9 percent of its territory for apartments, Rye about 7 percent, and Pelham 3 percent. On the basis of those statistics, he concluded that Scarsdale was not and could not be self-sustaining under the ordinance of 1922. The Morschauser decision evoked ridicule from zoning experts in Scarsdale. One attorney dismissed it as "bad law." Another surmised that the judge had been thinking in terms of the eighteenth century, when most towns had produced their own goods. But clearly, said Herbert McKennis, no modern suburb could in that sense be self-sustaining. Such men believed Scarsdale's arguments had not received a fair hearing. They encouraged local authorities to appeal the case to higher courts.[31]

On July 22, 1931, the Appellate Division of the New York State Supreme Court reversed Morschauser's ruling. Three factors weighed heavily in that decision. First, the court said that in preserving Scarsdale's residential character, the ordinance of 1922 had accorded with the citizens' desires. Second, the ordinance had provided for intensive development on land adjacent to the existing business and apartment districts. Inasmuch as subsequent construction had not exhausted the land reserved for intensive use, the court saw no reason to compel Scarsdale to enlarge the areas already provided. Third, Jacobs Brothers had purchased Fox Meadow with full knowledge of the restrictions on its development. In attempting to have the restrictions lifted, profit, said the court, had been the company's "sole object." The court found no evidence of unreasonable or discriminatory actions on the part of the village. It considered Rush Wilson's holdings immaterial to the case and regarded as a well-founded point of law a municipality's right to regulate construction.[32]

In its decision the Appellate Court promulgated the theory of zoning set forth by Scarsdale's lawyers, namely, "There is no rule or standard found in other municipalities which may be inexorably applied to this village." Scarsdale, it said, could adopt plans suitable to its own peculiar location and needs, acting reasonably.[33] With its support of flexible zoning, the court allowed restrictions that closed an entire community to lower-class residents. Yet the lower classes would hardly have triumphed if the court had nullified Scarsdale's ordinance. The diversification of land use would first have benefited commercial interests. According to ordinary patterns of population movement, the poor would have made their way only into sections rejected by others.

To save the situation, some city planners in the twenties and thirties called for a regional approach to zoning. They argued that regional zoning would combine flexibility with comprehensiveness. Given a broad geographical base, zoning could allow the optimal use of a district, while providing for the needs of every economic group.[34] Yet in the New York metropolitan area, which embraced twenty-two counties in three states, the political obstacles to regional zoning proved insurmountable. The planners were left with a choice between local zoning or no zoning at all. They realized that when zoning operated on a community level, it served the interests of the dominant group, but they believed that removing controls over land use would cause a chaos of activity that would benefit no one. Most planners, with the notable exception of Clarence Stein and Lewis Mumford, supported local zoning as the lesser of two evils.[35]

In December 1932, at the request of Fox Meadow Estates, the New York State Court of Appeals reviewed the case. A month later it affirmed the Appellate decision, finding for the village with costs in all courts. The ruling excited little comment. Scarsdale residents, worn by the struggle, were overcome with "a sense of relief."[36]

After years of doubt, it was clear that the community had survived the most rapid growth of its history without injury to its essential purpose. Scarsdale had remained a village of homes. It had managed to do so because its citizens possessed the power of conviction, talent, and wealth to fend off threats to their self-interests. Yet the success of such efforts depended on support from the broader culture. As long as the dream of social mobility dominated the public imagination, Americans would regard exclusive practices as privileges that might some day be their own.

Although in the course of the building boom the citizens of Scarsdale managed to prevent the construction of apartments, they learned that even growth of a desirable nature had undesirable consequences. As the population of Scarsdale climbed from 3,506, in 1920, to 9,690, in 1930, and as the population of Westchester passed the half-million mark, residents voiced concern about the urbanization of their village and dedicated themselves to the principle of "keeping Scarsdale as it is." To that end they aimed to preserve some aspects of country life, such as acres of open space, resisting the incursion of highways and other effects of urban expansion.[37] These endeavors, like so many others undertaken by Scarsdale's citizens, had both a positive creative aspect and a negative elitist one. They pioneered in the uses of public policy to establish an exclusive community.

Crowding was one of the hazards residents wanted to avoid. To some extent it was a false issue, for zoning prevented serious crowding. Yet people accustomed to an earlier Scarsdale looked with apprehension at the spread of closely built areas. If all of the land in the village were used as lots for one-family houses, precious open spaces would vanish.

Understandably this attitude was stronger in the latter half of the decade than it was before residents had experienced the impact of the building boom. Although in 1920 the voters had overwhelmingly agreed to spend $70,000 for twenty-five acres near the high school, in 1922 and again in 1925 they defeated bond issues directed at the purchase of additional open spaces.[38]

Distressed by the two defeats, park advocates at first berated the public for lack of foresight in a time of change. Then they began a process of gently educating the electorate about the need for added parkland. Taking their arguments from a report submitted to the village board by a professional planner, Feruccio Vitale, they noted that in the past Scarsdale's population had been "so sparse and the residential lots so large" that the entire village had looked like a park "in the sense of broad open space." That situation still existed except in a few areas with row on row of houses. Those areas needed parks to relieve the sense of overcrowding. At the same time, their development had caused land values to rise throughout the village. Before the cost of land became prohibitive, citizens had a timely opportunity to complete the system of parks that they had wisely begun. The village already owned 57.2 acres, including the grounds of three schools, the village hall, and the waste-disposal plant. Although that land, together with the county-owned parks at Saxon Woods and the Bronx River, fulfilled most of Scarsdale's needs, park advocates recommended the purchase of seven more tracts, totaling fifty acres. Their acquisition would assure a good distribution of open land, as well as providing space for future municipal purposes.[39]

These arguments apparently struck the proper tone at the proper time. In December 1926, the voters agreed to buy two of the seven tracts the Vitale report had recommended, and in March 1927, they approved the purchase of three others. In 1928 a sixth tract of 10.89 acres was acquired for $230,000. The trustees never submitted the seventh parcel for public approval, since, in their view, the owners persisted in demanding an exorbitant sum. In all, Scarsdale acquired sixty-five acres of property at a cost of $870,000, between 1926 and 1933.[40] Some it held for future uses. In the 1950s the community would build a junior high school and a public library on sites purchased more than two decades earlier. Yet a large part of the land was intended strictly for park purposes. As more and more houses had appeared in the village, and as open land had become relatively scarce, people had learned the need to preserve a sense of spaciousness. Their perception of that need was one indication that Scarsdale was no longer rural. Their willingness to act demonstrated their deep desire that Scarsdale should never be urban.

Although in justifying the purchase of open space residents cited the inevitability of population growth and increased property costs, they spurned such arguments when it came to highway improvements. Equating highways with "the advancing ogre of business or industrial development," they argued that any attempt to supply roads for the future would only feed an insatiable demand. Moreover, whereas the purchase of parks promoted Scarsdale's homogeneity by removing from the market land of a sort often given over to inexpensive development, the provision of roads undermined that homogeneity by attracting into the community people from all over the metropolitan area.[41] Thus residents adopted a policy of resisting highway improvements as long as possible. That policy won them small concessions. It also had a lasting effect, for from that time onward the village succeeded in avoiding the construction of new commercial routes.

The clearest statement of Scarsdale's policy regarding highway construction appeared in a report drawn up by the Town Club in 1927: "Scarsdale must care for its fair share of through traffic but should not, by superior traffic facilities, attract more than its fair share of such traffic." The report went on to describe Scarsdale's "fair share" as traffic "which in the nature of things cannot be avoided." The club specifically warned against making local highways "so convenient and satisfactory" as to invite traffic which could otherwise use alternate routes outside the village.[42]

What this policy meant in practice became clear in the course of two confrontations between village and county officials. The first involved the widening of the White Plains Post Road, the principal north-south route through Scarsdale. In 1927 the county engineer announced plans to widen the Post Road from twenty-four feet to forty feet. As residents along the right-of-way wailed about their trees and hedges, the village board employed the services of George B. Ford's Technical Advisory Corporation. Armed with statistics and legal advice provided by Ford, the trustees argued that a thirty-foot width would be "ample" for the Post Road and that the county should develop Central Avenue in the neighboring town of Greenburgh as its main north-south truck route.[43]

Since Scarsdale alone resisted the proposal, construction on the forty-foot pavement began in the other communities along the route. Soon the county engineer became eager to settle the matter. He proposed that the Post Road, within the village of Scarsdale, would have a width of thirty-six feet. It would still be a four-lane highway, but each lane would be nine rather than ten feet wide. The village trustees accepted the proposal. They believed the differential in the width would call attention to Scarsdale's distinctiveness. If the narrow lane also made motorists feel uneasy, so much the better: perhaps they would take another route.[44]

The second controversy between county and village officials involved a different classification of highway. Mamaroneck Road, the principal east-west route through Scarsdale, was a "county-aid" road. Although it was under local jurisdiction, improvements of the road were liable for county funding. In 1929 Scarsdale applied for county funds to widen Mamaroneck Road by two feet to a width of twenty feet. The county engineer responded with a proposal to widen the road by an additional thirteen feet. In the months that followed each side offered alternative suggestions. Scarsdale would approve a twenty-four foot road with stone curbs, "the standard common elsewhere in the village." The county, concerned about parking on the road, would fund a twenty-foot road with turf shoulders on either side or a twenty-seven foot, curbed road. In the end the village decided to "go it alone" in order to build the kind of road it desired. Even in a time of growing depression, the lure of $100,000 in immediate aid, as well as a pledge of permanent maintenance, would not tempt the village to yield to county specifications.[45]

The controversy was important not only for showing how the wealth of Scarsdale's citizens gave the community an independence in policy matters, but also for the opinions the villagers expressed. At a public hearing concerning the county's original offer, nearly 100 citizens spoke in opposition to a thirty-three foot pavement. They believed that the construction of such a wide road would both destroy "the peace and property" of the people who lived there and reopen the question of how the area should be zoned. Since, in their view, Scarsdale did not "owe it to the world to provide a space for excess population," they saw no reason "to invite the public to make a runway of our dooryards." That attitude received support at a meeting of one of Scarsdale's neighborhood associations. Discussing the matter in general terms, the members charged that the "material changes" proposed for certain roads would "augment through traffic of both business and pleasure vehicles originating in outside territory and bringing no benefit to the village." In order to safeguard "the unique attractiveness of Scarsdale," members of the association determined to resist "the construction of any boulevard or reconstruction of any road which [would] tend to induce such objectionable traffic."[46]

The elitism implicit in the discussion of highway improvement was explicit in the discussion of two other matters related to traffic control. In 1926 the Third Avenue Railway Company applied to the village for permission to operate a bus service between the Post Road and the Heathcote railroad station. The trustees rejected the petition after village residents made it clear that they strongly opposed the presence of buses. They said buses would endanger the safety of children, pollute the clean air of the village, and bring about an undesirable level of development. One resident elaborated on the last point. "There is a direct connection," he said, "between the people who need and use buses and the prices of houses which they want to buy." He warned that Scarsdale would jeopardize its reputation as "the Elite of Suburbs" if it allowed people to live within it who could not afford to own a car.[47]

Six years later, in the midst of the depression, the village received a petition from another bus company. The company wanted to establish a service between the Scarsdale and Heathcote stations. The debate that followed repeated familiar arguments with added intensity. Those who wanted the route said the situation had changed since 1926; in particular, the economic squeeze had increased the need for public transportation. Those who opposed the plan tried to link buses to the question of zoning, then before the courts. "Would it not be as destructive," one critic asked, "to our cherished rural atmosphere to have buses running through our narrow but picturesque streets as to fill our empty spaces with apartment houses?"[48]

To air such views, the board of trustees held a public hearing, which approximately 400 people attended. In an atmosphere charged with cat-calls and heckling, one after another of Scarsdale's neighborhood associations went on record as opposing the plan. Apparently it had concentrated support only in east Scarsdale, where 104 people signed a petition requesting service.[49]

Two weeks later the board of trustees denied permission for the route. In view of the recent display of village sentiment, it was surprising the vote was not unanimous. The mayor abstained, and one trustee, William T. Brewster, dissented. Brewster noted that although "numbers and volubility" lay with opponents of the route, "the merit of fact . . . lay largely with those who wished relief from trying conditions." He pointed out that buses would help reduce personal expenses, decrease congestion in the business district, and, according to insurance statistics, cut down the number of traffic accidents. He accused opponents of the plan of disregarding the needs of "a considerable number of citizens" on the basis of fears that were "more imaginary than real." Brewster concluded by predicting that, like it or not, the village would soon have to provide more buses. A little time would prove his prediction correct. Despite the furor of 1932, the Scarsdale Bus Company obtained a franchise in 1934.[50]

In another effort to regulate traffic, ward off urban influence, and protect Scarsdale's social milieu, the trustees in 1927 passed an ordinance restricting the operations of peddlers in Scarsdale. The ordinance prohibited the use of "any vehicle except a hand-drawn vehicle in connection with hawking or peddling" on the village streets. It provided further that such vehicles could stand in one place no longer than ten minutes, nor could they stop within 1,000 feet of any school, park, or playground. The measure was directed against one man in particular, Castas Hitali-kides, who sold snacks from a motor wagon parked outside the high school. For years parents had importuned village and school officials to rid the community of "Hot Dog Joe." They said that Joe's wagon created a traffic hazard on Post Road and marred the beauty of the surrounding area. They also blamed Joe for luring children to waste their money and spoil their appetites. Yet, according to "Kitchen Opinion," a satirical column in the *Inquirer*, there was another cause for the parents' distress. While the fictional cook regarded Joe as "a real nice pelite furrin' gentleman," she knew that "Scarsdale chillun aint sposed to come in contack wid nuthin' so common."[51]

Although from the start some village officials had doubts about the need for an ordinance, little did they realize that the issue would give Scarsdale a reputation for smugness that its residents would find hard to live down. Two days after the measure was passed, the *New York Times* carried an article that highlighted the humorous elements of the trustees' debate. In the weeks that followed, as Joe was arrested, tried, and fined, other papers joined the *Times* in covering the incident. Eventually people from all over the country were hounding the village for persecuting the peddler. Their ridicule seemed well-founded when Joe, assisted by funds from a hot dog manufacturer, won the decision in an appeal. The *Inquirer* was annoyed. It thought Scarsdale merited front-page attention, not as a summertime joke, but as a model of progressive schools, quality services, and intelligent zoning.[52]

The hot-dog incident chastened Scarsdale for a time. Joe returned to his post outside the high school, and a man with a "Coney Island" truck started selling ice cream on the Post Road. Yet by 1932 residents were again clamoring for the village board to take some action. They said peddlers seemed to constitute "a privileged class" that could park where parking was prohibited and do business where businesses were not allowed. Besides, the *Inquirer* pointed out, the peddlers served, not local residents, but "passing motorists and truck-drivers, very few of whom belong in Scarsdale." The paper wondered why such "travelers . . . could not wait until they got to White Plains for refreshment."[53]

On September 8, 1931, the trustees passed an ordinance that they were satisfied could be enforced. Two weeks later the police presented a summons to one of the peddlers on the Post Road. Although the man appealed the case to the county court, his petition was denied. Scarsdale's ordinance held, freeing the village of one more threat to peace, beauty, and property values.[54]

As the population of New York City and its suburbs swelled in the latter half of the 1920s, the residents of Scarsdale redoubled their efforts to make theirs a model community. As with municipal services, the question of costs was of little concern to them. Whether the issue involved purchasing parks, improving a highway without county funds, or appealing a court decision all the way up the judicial ladder, they willingly invested their tax dollars in making Scarsdale "the right kind of town." Yet, if costs were of little concern, questions affecting the class composition of the community mattered greatly. While such considerations lay at the root of the residents' interest in the suit over zoning, they also influenced other issues. Residents purchased parks and resisted buses partly because they wanted to prevent the construction of inexpensive houses. They protested against highways and regulated vendors because they did not want outsiders even to drive through the community, much less to loiter there. More and more, they came to believe that attracting "the right kind of people" to Scarsdale meant keeping the "wrong kind" of people out. Through it all, village residents showed a remarkable degree of community consciousness. Whether they were pioneering in the preservation of open spaces or dragging their feet on highway improvement, the citizens of Scarsdale thought about what they were doing and seemed eager to impress the world at large. If more than fifty years later some of those policies seem less than impressive, it is because modern observers are too well aware of their implications for the New York metropolitan area and for American society as a whole.

CHAPTER 4

A Quality Education

During the period from 1915 through 1930, in Scarsdale as in many other suburban towns, the increase in the number of residents necessitated the building of more public schools, and here, as elsewhere, the nature of the increase in the population played a large part in determining the quality of the education students received in those schools. Because most of Scarsdale's residents were themselves well educated and affluent, they not only cared about providing a good education for their children, but they could afford the expense involved. What they sought was an educational system that prepared their children for academic achievement in college and for success in a business or professional career. If, in trying to secure such a system, they enhanced Scarsdale's reputation for progressivism, they also pointed up the limits of that progressivism. As in other matters, so in education, the residents of Scarsdale undertook experimentation largely in the interests of their social class.

Prior to World War I there was nothing remarkable about public education in Scarsdale. As had other towns in the New York metropolitan area, Scarsdale, feeling the pressure of population growth, had found it necessary to build more schools. A two-story brick building, opened in 1906 and intended to serve as the district's only public school, was already inadequate in 1915. That year the voters approved the construction of a centrally located high school for grades seven through twelve and an elementary school for the northerly Greenacres section. Two years later they supported the construction of the Edgewood School for children living in the southern half of Scarsdale. A third elementary school, Fox Meadow, would be built in the course of the 1920s, along with additions to the other school buildings, but by that time district residents, having supported more than \$3.5 million in school-related bond issues, had shifted the focus of their concern away from the question of providing adequate facilities to that of providing superior programs.[1]

The underlying reason for the shift in focus was the increasing dominance in the community of members of the upper-middle class. Between 1905 and 1925, the proportion of households in Scarsdale that were headed by business executives, professionals, and retired men and widows of means increased from 41 percent of the total to more than 70 percent. Differing from their counterparts in more socially diverse communities, the members of Scarsdale's upper-middle class did not assume that parents who wanted a quality education for their children should have to pay to send them to private school. Instead, as the citizens in wealthy Winnetka, Illinois, and Bronxville, New York, were doing, they began to demand private school results from the public school system. According to Philip W. Russell, the president of the board of education in Scarsdale, most residents thought the pupils in local schools should receive "as good a foundation as those in other high schools or preparatory schools."[2]

School officials resented what was, in their view, an unrealistic expectation. According to the supervisory principal, Ralph I. Underhill, the notion that the local schools should rival the leading boarding schools presented "one of the most constant and irritating sources of criticism." Such an expectation failed to take into account the limitations under which the public schools operated. They could not select their students for intellectual promise or discharge them for failures in courses or problems of discipline. They had to contend with the distractions of coeducation and could not control the activities of students after class hours. Further, they had to put up with such a stream of parental complaints that eventually a committee of the Town Club attributed the presumed superiority of boarding schools in part to the distance of the parents. While the parents of children in public schools learned of each other's grievances, the parents of children in boarding schools were too far away to know what was happening and too scattered to "whisper among themselves."[3]

Although school officials resented the pressure of unrealistic expectations, they recognized that the schools needed improving. In their view, two problems undermined the quality of the education offered in Scarsdale. One was the range in the students' abilities and goals. The other was the students' lack of a sense of responsibility.[4]

The concern over the range of ability stemmed in part from the rising prestige of intelligence testing. Although, as a group, Scarsdale children ranked above the national average with a median score of 112, individual results showed a wide variation, from a low score of 70 to a high of 160. Local administrators believed in the reliability of those results. In their view, the tests measured differences that were, "generally speaking, inborn and not subject to modification by the environment."[5]

The extension in the age of compulsory school attendance intensified the concern over the differences in the intellectual ability of local students. Between 1896 and 1935, the New York State legislature, under pressure from advocates of labor and child welfare, amended the compulsory education law eight times to keep children in school longer and, consequently, off the labor market. By 1913 New York State required all children between the ages of seven and fourteen to attend school full time. Those from fourteen to sixteen could obtain permission to work, provided they had completed the sixth grade. In 1920 the state required completion of a secondary school education for release from further school commitments. Minors from fourteen to eighteen who had not received a high school diploma had to go to school at least part time. Only in 1935 did the legislature extend to sixteen the age of compulsory full-time attendance, but the 1920 requirements had sufficed, in the words of Scarsdale's supervisory principal, to bring into the high school "types of pupils who formerly did not attempt a high school course."[6]

Implicit in the concern over the range of abilities were considerations of social class. The heavy majority of pupils in the Scarsdale public schools were the college-bound children of business executives and professionals. Because of "the financial and social position of their parents," they had enjoyed "unusual opportunities." But the schools also taught children from more modest backgrounds. Their fathers included tailors, carpenters, clerks, and policemen, even gardeners and chauffeurs, men who probably could not afford a college education for their children. The Scarsdale schools were too small for tracking. With the more vocal members of the community demanding private school results, officials wanted to find a way of preventing children who were not headed for college from holding back those who were.[7]

The students' passivity also undermined the quality of the schools. In the spring of 1923, a committee of the high school faculty observed that the parents who prodded their children toward long-run success often pampered them in day-to-day matters. "If one of the pupils forgot his book, his mother brought it to school in the car. If he flunked in a school subject, father was ready to pay a tutor." Even the teachers and principal were eager to come to a pupil's aid. Under such circumstances, the committee decided, Scarsdale children "took life easy." They needed to learn that they were responsible for their own education. Otherwise, they might be unable to achieve for themselves the success that their parents held so dear.[8]

In the early 1920s school officials tried to solve the problems they had identified. They made additions to the curriculum, including some advanced courses, vocational subjects, and athletics. They introduced a measure of student self-government and provided for student control of the study halls. Finally, they issued to parents weekly reports with notices of unprepared work and neglect of past failures. Those measures contributed to an improvement in school spirit and to increased communication between parents and teachers, but they failed to get at the root of the problems.[9]

That was the situation when Gary Calkins, a member of the Scarsdale school board and Professor of Protozoology at Columbia University, read about the Dalton Plan, a new program for educational reform. The plan took its name from the town of Dalton, Massachusetts, where in February 1920 a teacher named Helen Parkhurst had introduced it in the public school. The experiment caught on rapidly in England, but did not attract wide attention in the United States until the appearance in 1922 of Parkhurst's book, *Education on the Dalton Plan*. Hailed by Englishman T.P. Nunn as "a path of progress" for those "who would hasten slowly and keep on firm ground," the plan contained both conservative and radical elements. It purported to reconcile the aims of both "the old type of school," which stood for "*culture*," and "the new type of school," which stood for "*experience*," by making "the process of attaining culture . . . a method of experience." It retained the content of the traditional curriculum but abandoned the class method of instruction, which Parkhurst termed "slavery," for a method of individual instruction, which brought "ideal freedom, . . . the very reverse of [license]."

Under the Dalton Plan each pupil received a month-long assignment or "contract" in each of his subjects. Then he worked "in his own way and at his own speed." At the end of the month, he was expected to have completed at least the minimum assignment in every subject. A student had therefore to learn to "adjust means to ends"—to budget his time and to seek help, if he needed it, from teacher-specialists and his classmates. Thus, he acquired culture "through individual development and through collective cooperation. It is no longer school," Parkhurst said; "it is life."[10]

School board member Calkins saw in Parkhurst's plan a chance to instill in the students a sense of responsibility and to deal with the differences in their abilities. He discussed the plan with the board's other members—a bank president with a law degree from New York University, a senior partner of Merrill Lynch who was also a member of the bar, the officer of a fuel company with a bachelor's degree from Columbia, and two women, one married to a stock broker and the other to an attorney. They agreed the plan deserved to be tried, and together they converted Ralph Underhill, the supervisory principal, to the idea. In other words, initiative for adoption of the Dalton Plan came from informed laymen, not from members of the professional staff.[11]

It was Underhill's task to approach the teachers. In the spring of 1923, he described the plan to the fifth- and sixth-grade teachers of the Edgewood elementary school. He hoped that the group would agree to establish a core of Dalton classes when school reopened in September. The initial response was negative. The teachers thought that writing contracts and grading individual work would entail an impossible burden. But over the summer one teacher changed her mind. With "every encouragement" from Underhill and the school board, including publicity throughout the system, she placed her class on the Dalton method. A few weeks later a high school algebra teacher asked permission to use the method in one of his sections. Soon the two experiments were producing such positive results that the entire staff of the high school became eager to study the plan. Underhill took advantage of the teachers' interest. He distributed copies of Parkhurst's book, held group discussions about its contents, and arranged for a series of staff lectures, given in November by Parkhurst herself. The result was predictable. "As teacher after teacher 'saw the light,'" they converted their classes to the Dalton method. At the end of November, less than three months after the beginning of the first experiment, Underhill told the school board that the high school was "operating almost entirely upon a modified Dalton Plan." The students attended class at an appointed hour; once there, they worked on their own.[12]

With all teachers in the high school distributing contracts for individual study, the school could become "thoroughly Daltonized." Beginning in January 1924, the high school abolished the traditional schedule. The children in grades seven through twelve had no scheduled classes, except for music and physical education. In the mornings and before and after lunch, they reported to their homeroom for attendance. Otherwise, they were free to work on any subject, in the room devoted to that subject, whenever they wished and for as long as they liked. In February the fifth and sixth grades of the elementary schools went on the Dalton system for their major subjects in the mornings, but kept a class schedule for the minor subjects in the afternoon. Little more than a year had passed since Calkins had read Parkhurst's book. The Scarsdale school board and the school's professional staff had moved quickly.[13]

The board of education had authorized the preliminary steps in implementing the Dalton Plan without consulting the public. That was to be expected in a community that regarded members of the board as so "disinterested, able, and indefatigable in their zeal for the Scarsdale schools . . . [that] they should be given a perfectly free hand in solving the . . . problems that constantly arise." Along with their counterparts on the village board of trustees, members of the school board received public endorsement in uncontested elections, and until the early 1930s, both the school and village boards conducted their deliberations behind closed doors. The people could express their views to members of the school board by letter, appointment, or friendly conversation. But except on matters prescribed by law, such as the issuance of bonds or the approval of the budget, the board did not solicit the people's advice.[14]

A change as drastic as the Dalton Plan required some explanation, however. Once the favorable response of the teachers had assured the plan's implementation, the board presented the reasons for the change in a series of articles in the *Inquirer*. Written by the board's employee, principal Ralph Underhill, the articles took the view that the community had "a great deal to gain" by working out a program of individual instruction, "and, apparently, nothing to lose." Under the traditional class method, only the average child had benefited. The expectation that all members in a class would master all subjects at a given rate placed slow pupils "under constant pressure," while bright children did "less than their best." But the Dalton Plan broke "the lock-step of the class recitation" and placed "responsibility for progress squarely upon the pupil." It challenged the bright child to work to his potential and allowed the slow child to master fundamentals before proceeding. As Underhill admitted, the Dalton Plan risked the assumption that "normal children want an education and that, if conditions are made right, they will take on the job of getting an education." But the results of Scarsdale's autumn experiments seemed to justify making that assumption. Pupils who had formerly earned such titles as "an habitual dreamer" or "the star mischief maker" were now eager to succeed. Others who had "barely made the grade" were "keeping the class leaders in sight." Some good students were accelerating in courses they found easy. In Underhill's view, the most striking evidence of the plan's superiority came from an experiment in the ninth-grade algebra course. One teacher taught two sections, one using the Dalton Plan, the other by the class method. He administered the same weekly tests to both sections. From the start, the Dalton section averaged five points higher than the students taught by the class method. In the quarterly exam the results were similar. In the section using the class method, half the students failed, and only 25 percent received a grade of over 75. In the Dalton section, only 11 percent of the students failed, and 25 percent received a grade of over 94. Underhill interpreted those results at face value. He did not see in them evidence of what present-day educators would call the Hawthorne effect—that is, the tendency for any experiment to prod people to do better. Thus, while cautioning against excessive optimism, he admittedly found it "difficult to avoid giving the impression that the millenium is here, . . . and that, at last, thanks to the Dalton Plan, we have 'arrived.'"[15]

Significantly, Underhill, in describing the Dalton Plan to the people of Scarsdale, changed the tone of Parkhurst's appeal. Parkhurst had emphasized "the importance of the child's living while he [did] his work and the manner in which he act[ed] as a member of society, rather than . . . the subjects of his curriculum." In her view, "the social experience accompanying the tasks, not the tasks themselves" furthered the child's mental and emotional growth.[16] But Underhill supported the plan mainly in terms of improved academic performance. He seemed to promise that under the Dalton Plan Scarsdale's children would learn better the subjects of the traditional curriculum, that individual instructions would give them a competitive advantage over the children in other suburbs. He was advocating the use of new methods to secure conservative ends.

With the first news of the experiment, in November 1923, the residents reserved judgment. They were willing to cooperate with the school board because they trusted its members to act in the community's interest. They also respected Ralph Underhill, who was a graduate of Harvard and Columbia Teachers College, as well as a former private school teacher. Although they deferred to the experts, the residents were careful not to commit themselves to the idea of experiment for experiment's sake. They would accept the Dalton Plan, if it worked.[17]

By January, as the plan moved into full operation, some of the early reserve had given way to enthusiasm. Scarsdale's experiment was attracting notice, and the residents found that they enjoyed it. "From even the Far West," the *Inquirer* had received requests for Underhill's articles, a development its editors had "never dreamed" of. Underhill was asked to speak at conferences and to write about the Scarsdale experience for educational journals. Experts had begun to visit the schools. Between December 1923 and April 1924, 148 official visitors would tour the schools, some from as far away as California, Germany, and Japan.[18]

The Scarsdale application of the Dalton Plan attracted more attention than the school board or staff had anticipated. Unwittingly, Scarsdale had employed the plan more intensively than any public school system in the United States. On a trip to Massachusetts in April 1924, Underhill was surprised to discover that the Dalton school system used individual instruction for only two hours a day in grades nine through twelve. The Dalton schools had never accepted Parkhurst's theory *in toto*. They had merely cut down the number of class meetings to provide time for individual work suited to a pupil's needs and interests. Later Underhill learned that another so-called Dalton school, the South Philadelphia High School for Girls, had retained group instruction and a schedule of classes. No wonder Parkhurst, overlooking the differences between Underhill's reasoning and her own, described the Scarsdale experiment as the most intelligent she had seen in a public school system. Scarsdale alone had followed her advice of placing all the students' work on an individual basis.[19]

Yet problems arose soon after Scarsdale had fully implemented Parkhurst's plan. In part the problems resulted from inadequate planning. Few teachers had anticipated the degree to which individualizing instruction would throw the pupils behind. In order to work on their own, the children had to understand the fundamentals of each subject. Some had serious weaknesses in background. Others needed review, simply to have the confidence to proceed on their own. But the teachers wanted the children to move forward. Bound by the state syllabus to cover certain material in the course of the year, they distributed contracts that required more work than the children could handle and much more than the children were willing to do. The teachers were not the only group responsible for the difficulties of the transition period. The children failed to do their part. Given the freedom to choose when they would work on a particular contract, many neglected their difficult subjects and avoided the teachers of those subjects. They fell so far behind so quickly that the staff of the Scarsdale schools found it "necessary to modify the plan almost from the start."[20]

One change involved the institution of rewards and punishments. The traditional method of teaching had employed a range of external pressures to prod children to do their work. In Underhill's view, that approach had reduced education to "a game in which teachers have been trying to increase, pupils to decrease production." The Dalton Plan, on the other hand, made pressure an inherent part of the situation, closer to real life. Children who would not work could not advance. To the dismay of some children, that meant "no bluffing is possible;" "you have to do all your work instead of about a fifth as before." The pressure under the Dalton Plan quickly exceeded that under the traditional class method. Yet weeks could pass before a child experienced the anxiety of being behind. Therefore, by the end of April 1924, the Scarsdale schools had begun to borrow from the old approach to teaching. Every day, before dismissal, the teachers checked the progress of the students in their homerooms. Those children who could not report "an honest day's work" were required to remain after school for further study. In addition to punishing children who did not work, the teachers rewarded those who did. Each week they distributed "approval cards" to children who had made satisfactory progress. Except as rewards for work well-done, the school discouraged "the custom of having parties [for the children] and 'treats' over the weekend." Such devices aimed, in Underhill's words, to take up the slack in the Dalton method while "reserv[ing] the elements of self-direction and choice that are vital to the system of individual instruction."[21]

The introduction of the fifty-minute plan also modified Parkhurst's theory. Parkhurst had assumed that "by eliminating the waste time of recitations and permitting the pupil to plan his time in accordance with his needs, the pupil will be able to keep up to standard in all of his subjects." In Scarsdale, however, the teachers found that sometimes a given subject proved so difficult for a student that it retarded learning in all the other subjects and undermined the pupil's morale. The teachers decided that as long as a child who was experiencing difficulty reported to the teacher of his problem subject for fifty minutes a day, he should be permitted to proceed normally in his other subjects. The child would spend more than a year completing the work of that course, but otherwise he would advance with his peers.[22]

The introduction of detention and the fifty-minute plan helped to save the Scarsdale schools from academic disaster. In April, Underhill had considered it questionable whether "a majority of the pupils [would] complet[e] a year's work." However, on the June Regents' exams Scarsdale had a higher percentage of passing grades than ever. Of the students tested, 91.2 percent passed as compared to the previous high of 84 percent, in 1922. The results of the college plans of the Class of 1924 were less reassuring. Two were denied admission because of poor school records and low scores on their College Board examinations. Others also did poorly on the College Boards but were accepted at second-choice schools on the basis of their Regents' records.[23]

The uneven results of the school year, 1923–24, further confused the issue of the Dalton Plan. Although no one could tell how much the new method had affected those results, everyone seemed to have an opinion grounded on the performance of his or her own child and bolstered by amateur theorizing. Scarsdale's experiment had bred "an atmosphere of intellectual adventure." That was the conclusion of the eminent historian, Dixon Ryan Fox, who also served as chairman of the Town Club committee on education. The new atmosphere, he went on, was "infinitely better than the dull unquestioning repetition of old inherited life." "From dinner table to smoking car," residents discussed the ramifications of the Dalton Plan. By comparison, said Fox, the outcome of the 1924 presidential race seemed to them of "little moment."[24]

Yet the debate was marked by restraint. Residents denounced the Dalton Plan without stint, in private. Public attacks were deemed out of place. The *Inquirer* set the tone early in the experiment. Since the school board had undertaken a program that educators throughout the world were watching, "the least the rest of us can do is to boost the plan enthusiastically." By April, a housewife named Edna Hawthorne was ready to dissent. In a letter to the *Inquirer*, she complained about the frustrations that many children experienced under the Dalton Plan. Although they worked harder, they were progressing more slowly. Many faced probable failure of promotion. "Is this loss of time and the consequent discouragement worth the moral lesson [of learning to handle a job]?" She thought the taxpayers deserved more for their money; "they are entitled to have their children taught rather than experimented upon." Although Underhill was beginning to have similar misgivings (it was at this time that the schools introduced detention and the fifty-minute plan), he responded quickly by subordinating current difficulties to promises of future success. The woman wrote back, calling into question the whole Dalton philosophy. At that point the editors of the *Inquirer* intervened. They announced that for a time the newspaper would publish no letters on the subject. The experiment merited more of a trial before the community rendered judgment. "A prolonged controversy" would serve no useful purpose.[25]

On November 1, more than six months later, the *White Plains Daily Reporter* published a letter that attacked both the Dalton Plan and the *Inquirer*'s silence regarding it. The letter, written by J.F.B. Hawthorne, husband of the original critic, called on the people of Scarsdale to stop cooperating with school authorities.[26] Immediately the people closed ranks behind the board of education. In the high school, students signed a petition endorsing the Dalton program. The "entire teaching staff" concurred: "We believe in [individual instruction], . . . and should be more than loath to return to the old system." The resolution of the Parent-Teacher Association was more equivocal. Although the association expressed "perfect confidence in the public spirit, intelligence, and justice of the school board" and resolved that "the administration of the schools be left in the hands of the school board," it did not endorse the Dalton Plan. The association apparently acted out of fear that "public controversy" regarding "certain innovations in the conduct of our schools" might work "to the prejudice of good order in the schools themselves and to the reputation of the village."[27]

On November 14, 1924, the members of the school board held a special meeting to consider the advisability of answering Hawthorne's charges. Armed with resolutions of support from the students, teachers, and PTA, and content that they were moving to remedy existing difficulties, they decided that "a statement from the board of education to the parents would probably meet the situation." The statement, dated November 18, was brief and businesslike. It blamed the problems in the schools, not on the hazards of experimentation, but on "the very rapid growth of population in Scarsdale." It reminded the people that the school board was charged with the responsibility for remedying such problems and assured them that the board would "keep [them] advised of such plans and policies as may from time to time be inaugurated or adjusted to meet changing needs." Finally, the statement attempted to undercut the force of rumor. It invited parents to "inform themselves as to exact conditions" by making "direct inquiries" and arranging for "personal visits to our schools."[28]

The November statement left open the possibility for new shifts in policy. The school board, even before the publication of Hawthorne's letter, had been considering a resumption of scheduled classes. The Dalton Plan had not worked as intended. Individual instruction had accentuated the differences in the abilities of the students to such a degree that teachers were finding it "practically impossible . . . to cope." If the school board wanted to continue to cater to individual differences, it would have to hire more teachers. So far, the results of the Dalton Plan did not seem to justify that expense. Indeed, most people associated with the Scarsdale schools were beginning to appreciate the virtues of the old class method. For one reason, the class method provided an opportunity for group discussion, oral expression, and drill activities, which the Dalton Plan had largely neglected. It not only avoided the endless repetition of basic instructions, "a pure waste of a teacher's time," but helped the student "to overcome the agony of getting started." After a year's experience with the Dalton Plan, Underhill was ready

to revise the assumption that "children want an education and
. . . will take on the job of getting [one]." He now saw the need
for direct teacher supervision.

> No matter how much we . . . may choose our own jobs or enjoy
> them, . . . there are aspects of our work that are just tasks to be
> put through as thoroughly and as expeditiously as possible. Any
> theory of education which ignores this condition of real life must
> be inadequate. It is true that interest often inspires effort, but it
> is equally true that effort may and usually does arouse interest.[29]

In January 1925, grades five through twelve returned to scheduled classes, but not to the schedule that had existed before the
Dalton experiment. A new program was now in effect, which
purported to combine the "best elements of the Dalton Plan"
with group instruction. The Scarsdale Plan, as Underhill called
it, had three key features. First, it kept the idea of the Dalton
contract, a four-week assignment with a central theme. The
contract included specific work for each class meeting, supple-
mentary drills on the core material for weak students, and
optional enrichment units for those who were bright. Second,
the plan reintroduced scheduled classes but made them longer
than those in most high schools. The long classes allowed teachers
to fit a variety of activities into one meeting. Group discussion,
checking and testing the units prepared, teaching advanced sections of the assignment, and supervising individual work were
standard parts of each class meeting. Third, though classes were
long, the plan kept down the number of meetings per week in
order to provide free periods to be used in accordance with the
needs of each student. The Scarsdale Plan attempted to balance
a recognition of individual differences in ability against the need
for group activity, discipline, and teaching efficiency.[30]

Finding a satisfactory balance proved difficult. In the course
of the search, school administrators cut the length of the class
periods from seventy minutes in 1925, to sixty in 1927, to fifty-
five in 1929, and finally to fifty-three minutes in 1931. They
also increased the number of class meetings in each subject per
week, from two for courses in the humanities and three for
courses in the sciences; to three for all subjects, with an additional
class for nonhonor students; to four classes a week in each subject
for everyone. In 1925 some students had only one-half of their
time scheduled; four years later students had at least three-

quarters of their time scheduled. Such modifications brought the local school system closer to the mainstream of public education.[31]

By the end of the 1920s, the Scarsdale schools stood out more because of the quality of their program than because of its structure. The years of experimentation had left a consciousness of purpose and a sense of respect for the individuality of each child. Visitors, and there were many, remarked on the "unusual spirit of cooperation between teachers and pupils." They noted a "seriousness" about education in Scarsdale that most other systems lacked.[32]

Test results corroborated the feeling that all was well in the Scarsdale schools. Between 1923 and 1928, the Regents' scores of Scarsdale students rose dramatically. In 1923, the cut-off point for the top quartile was 83.5, the median grade was 73, and one-quarter of the students scored below 66. Five years later the cut-off point for the top quartile had risen to 89, the median grade was 83, and one-quarter of the students scored below 77. In 1923, 18 percent of the students tested had failed; in 1928, only 4 percent failed. Scarsdale was also improving its perform-ance relative to other school systems. In 1929 Scarsdale led the county and all villages in the state in the percentage of students tested who passed the Regents' exams.[33]

The college records of Scarsdale High School graduates in 1928 proved equally encouraging. Twenty-seven members of the Class of 1928 accepted entrance to sixteen colleges. Four went to Cornell; four to Dartmouth; two each to Colgate, Columbia, Mount Holyoke, Vassar, and Wellesley; and one each to Barnard, Harvard, Michigan, North Dakota, Sarah Lawrence, Syracuse, Trinity, Wells, and Yale. Most students not only attended pres-tigious schools but also performed well. The first semester grades of the Class of 1928 included 14.1 percent As, 41.6 percent Bs, 34.1 percent Cs, 7.5 percent Ds, and 2.6 percent Es.[34]

In discussing the achievements of local students, Underhill stressed, "the value of their training in organizing time, planning work, and carrying responsibility which the Scarsdale Plan had made possible for them."[35] Yet factors other than the Scarsdale Plan may better explain the improvement in student perfor-mance. For one, the taxpayers were spending more money for education than they had in the past. The amount of money budgeted per pupil for the school year 1929–30 was 179 percent higher than that allotted a decade earlier. Indeed, a study con-ducted in the 1930s for the New York Board of Regents showed that Scarsdale and Bronxville, another innovative school district in Westchester County, spent more per pupil in average daily attendance than any other villages in the state, and that, along with Garden City (a wealthy suburb on Long Island), they led the state in terms of academic achievement. "Apparently," the author, Julius Maller, concluded, "the more a community spends on education the more likely it is to produce results."[36]

Since more recent experts would quarrel with Maller's conclusion, another factor, an improvement in the quality of the teaching staff in Scarsdale, should be considered as well. In 1920, only 16 percent of the teachers in the high school and 6 percent of the entire staff held master's degrees. In 1930, master's recipients made up more than 40 percent of the high school faculty and 27 percent of the teaching staff for the entire district. During the same period, the number of staff members who held only a teacher's certificate from a normal school declined from 61 percent to 34 percent. Instead of hiring teachers from normal schools, the district employed the graduates of such colleges as Smith, Wellesley, Mount Holyoke, Middlebury, and Cornell. These people accepted offers to teach in Scarsdale's schools, not because the salaries were high—in fact, they were lower than those in neighboring districts, but because they wanted to teach in a system where a quality education was the primary goal.[37]

In the last analysis, the factor most responsible for the success of the Scarsdale schools was the one that had prompted the concern for education in the first place. Increasingly, Scarsdale was becoming a community of the upper-middle class. Many of its residents were themselves well educated. They knew the value of a good education, and they wanted such an education for their children. The demands they made on the school board, on the professional staff, and on their own tax dollars helped to improve the quality of Scarsdale's schools. But the most significant role they played may be the one least easy to measure, for upper-middle-class parents placed demands on their children as well. The example they set for their children and the expectations they held for them certainly contributed to the atmosphere of "seriousness" that observers noted in Scarsdale's classrooms.

By 1930, the residents of Scarsdale had secured the kind of school system they wanted, one that emulated the private schools by preparing their children for good colleges. In their pursuit of that goal, they had been willing to stray far from the path of conventional practice. Lulled by Parkhurst's rhetoric and their own wishful thinking, they had thought the Dalton Plan would solve the problems that affected the schools. The experiment proved disappointing, but it taught the community a valuable lesson. There were no simple solutions to the problems of education. Having a successful program required continuing effort on the part of all concerned—members of the school board, school administrators, teachers, parents, and even children.

In time the existence of outstanding suburban school districts would be taken for granted. The public schools in such communities as Bethesda, Maryland; Shaker Heights, Ohio; Evanston and Winnetka, Illinois; and Beverly Hills, California, would regularly join Scarsdale in lists of the nation's best schools.[38] Yet not all suburbs tried to provide an educational program of high quality. For example, in the late 1950s the superintendent of schools in the predominantly lower-middle-class suburb of Levittown, New Jersey, insisted that his community "would not copy Brookline and Scarsdale," which in his view overemphasized preparation for college.[39] The Scarsdale schools had helped to set a standard for suburbia, but it was a standard likely to be met only in other communities dominated by the upper-middle class.

CHAPTER 5

Power and Powerlessness
in a Nonpartisan Setting

Because the residents of Scarsdale eschewed contested elections and claimed to disdain local politics of any sort, the answer to the question of who ruled in Scarsdale indicated more about the social structure of the community and the values of its people than it did about their stance on particular issues. While the population growth of the 1920s forced an alteration in the process of selecting candidates for village office, it did not change the fact that the impact one could have on the civic life of the community varied to some extent with one's religion, sex, education, and occupation. The last of these was the most important for, while the plumbers, bookkeepers, and policemen who lived in Scarsdale would never secure a place on its governing board, there was an occupational group less powerful than they. These people lived in some of the largest and most opulent houses in the community, but they did not own the homes in which they lived. They were the domestic servants of Scarsdale, and they lived and worked in 50 percent of its houses.

For local homeowners from the upper-middle class who were interested in influencing civic affairs, two organizations existed—one open only to men, the other to women. The Town Club, the men's civic organization, helped to determine much that occurred in the suburb. Organized in 1904, the club aimed to promote "concerted and intelligent action" on all public matters. To that end its members gathered information on local questions, discussed them in "an absolutely nonpolitical" manner, and issued reports on how best to resolve them. The recommendations of the Town Club influenced decisions of the board of trustees.

Indeed, the board never defied a clear-cut expression of Town Club sentiment.[1]

Initially the club owed its power to the prominence of its members. The founder, Thomas F. Burgess, stood in the fore-front of local society. A second-generation Scarsdale man, he was clerk of the vestry of the Episcopal Church, a charter member of the tennis, golf, and gun clubs, champion of the local schools and fire department, and a senior executive with the National Sulphur Company in New York. Burgess had conceived of the Town Club as a means for Scarsdale's best citizens to censor the conduct of town officers and oversee needed improvements. After choosing the first sixteen members, he saw to it that the club remained small and selective. The constitution he proposed set a limit of thirty-five members and provided for the screening of applicants. To gain election, an applicant needed two members sponsoring him from the start of the process and not more than four voting against him at the end. With positions in the club at a premium, members took care to accept people they knew and trusted. Not surprisingly, nonmembers came to regard the club as a clique.[2]

Sensitive to such criticism, the members of the Town Club gradually opened the organization to more men in the community. In 1914 they raised the ceiling on membership to forty-five and in 1915 abolished the ceiling altogether. A few years later, as the club neared the 100-mark, those members who wanted to reimpose a ceiling were out-voted by others who thought it undemocratic. They argued that the application process, together with the club's provision for dropping those who failed to attend, sufficed to assure dedicated members; that no matter how much care was given to the members' selection, a ceiling would have the effect of keeping out good men; and that the club ought to accept all reasonable applicants because it was an excellent school that made decent citizens even better. That line of reasoning contributed to the club's growth in the following years. In 1921 the Town Club had 111 members, in 1925, 292, and in 1933, 472. While Scarsdale's population grew three times over between 1921 and 1933, the club's membership increased by a multiple of more than four. As the newspaper remarked, "Unlike the stern days of old . . . anyone can get in now and anyone does." Yet, in 1930 the Town Club included fewer than one-sixth of the men in the community. Although the selection process had become less exclusive, the club still exuded an air of superiority that convinced some residents they would never fit in.[3]

Contrary to Burgess's assumptions, the growth in membership made the club a more effective organization. Now each member could focus his energies on the concerns of one committee more or less related to his professional interests. A professor might work on the committee on education, while a banker would be assigned to the committee on village taxation and finance. Other standing committees included public buildings, grounds, and highways; public utilities; publicity; public health and safety; municipal government; local history; Boy Scouts; and civic celebrations. The club also appointed *ad hoc* committees to handle such specific problems as zoning, transit, or county government. The committees accomplished the real work of the Town Club. They kept alert for new developments, studied problems, and wrote reports. The club as a whole met four times a year to discuss the reports and to pass resolutions on matters of importance.[4]

By this time the club's power resulted from its wisdom. The village board consulted with the appropriate committee whenever a problem arose and seriously considered the Town Club's suggestions for new legislation. A team of sociologists visiting Scarsdale observed that "while the club has no legal powers, it has become in reality the legislative body of the local government." Clearly such an organization demanded the time and energy of its members, yet civic spirit was such in Scarsdale that busy men took an active part.[5]

The Woman's Club tried to parallel the Town Club in helping the community, but the sex-basis of its membership made for differences from the start. In Scarsdale men had a monopoly on the kind of technical training that made the Town Club invaluable as a source of advice to the village board. Nonetheless, women had their share of dedication and intelligence, along with something most men lacked, time in the community.

During World War I, local women had used their time well. They had led the drive for Liberty bonds, drummed up support for the Red Cross, and established the community farm that the *New Republic* praised so highly. They also worked to get the vote. In 1919, with the end of the war and the impending ratification of the Nineteenth Amendment, they wanted to continue getting together for worthwhile purposes. So, as the *New York Herald* noted, "using the sinews of war and suffrage to serve peace and community needs," the women of Scarsdale established a Woman's Club.[6]

According to the constitution, the club aimed "to bring together all women interested in the welfare of the village, . . . and to promote such welfare, and to foster a general public and democratic spirit." The club quickly set up a program to pursue those aims. As its "first gift to the community," it took over the *Scarsdale Inquirer*, which had suspended publication just as the club was getting started. It also sponsored a number of projects, such as summer playgrounds in built-up neighborhoods, classes for immigrants in English and civics, holiday baskets for the poor, and nursing assistance for the sick. Finally, it maintained a headquarters with meeting rooms and a restaurant not merely "for the use and enjoyment of its members" but as "a center for the civic life of the village." The women's program, while directed toward community purposes, in no way duplicated that of the Town Club, which required more expertise but less time.[7]

As the years went by, the differences between the clubs became greater. Growth brought added efficiency to the work of the Town Club, but the Woman's Club accepted so many members so quickly that it seemed to lose its sense of direction. In 1929, just a decade after its founding, the Woman's Club included 1,074 members. Although it still ran the newspaper and had expanded its program of "community service," the club's civic concern was now only one of many of its interests. Drama, music, art, gardening, travel, and current events vied with the newspaper and service projects for the attention of club members. Many members thought of the club as a means to enhance their social status rather than as a way to serve the village.[8] A characteristic schedule of activities revealed the bent the club had taken:

Schedule of Woman's Club Activities[9]
February 2–8, 1929

Sat., Feb. 2	Physical culture class, 9:00 A.M.
Mon., Feb. 4	Class in flower arrangement, 10:15 A.M.
	Cooking demonstration class, 1:30 P.M.
	Section social night in charge of current events section, 8:15 P.M. Subject: "Significance of the Kellogg Pact," Professor James P. Shotwell.
Tues., Feb. 5	Studio morning, 10:30 A.M. Subject: "French Furniture of the Eighteenth Century."
	French classes, 1:30–4:30 P.M.

Wed., Feb. 6   Afternoon musical, 3:00 P.M.
                 Soloists: Mrs. Hilda Brady Jones and Miss Dor-
                 othy Kendrick.
Thurs., Feb. 7   Pottery class, 9:00 A.M.
Fri., Feb. 8   Current events class, 10:30 A.M.
                 Valentine dance, 9:00 P.M.

How such activities were supposed to carry out the club's stated
purposes was not clear. One charter member recognized the
discrepancy between that kind of schedule and the club's declared
purposes. In an interview with a visiting team of sociologists,
she said,

> I do not believe that the club is fulfilling its original obligation to
> the community. We are concentrating more and more on giving
> ourselves a good time. The newer members, I think, are more
> interested in bridges, teas, social functions, and beauty culture
> courses than in helping the community.[10]

Some members had warned against that change in 1927 when
the club, grown too large for its quarters, debated the purchase
of an old estate. Rowsley was a place of "beauty and artistic
surroundings." The grounds included four acres with a tennis
court, a garden, well-kept lawns, and fine trees. A magnificent
white oak, reputed to have been "the focal point for Indian
dances," dominated the site. Placed carefully in relation to the
oak was the manor house with its veranda and mansard roof.
The house had small rooms ideal for bridge and larger rooms
for dining; the bedrooms on the second floor could serve as
offices or rooms for guests. As for the kitchen, it was in the
basement, where "members need never come in contact with
it." The estate would cost the club $99,300—a bargain in the
view of many members, too great an expense in the opinion of
others. Those who opposed the purchase argued that the club's
traditional concerns had been civic rather than social. According
to a former club president, Mrs. George H. Mayo, Rowsley had
too much space for entertaining and not enough for enterprises
like the *Inquirer*. She wanted the Woman's Club to build quarters
to order. "Let us start from the ground up and have a simpler
but a sounder club." The majority of members, however, preferred the refinement of the estate to the utility of a modern
building. Arguing that Rowsley would give the club "an air . . .
it needed," they approved its purchase by a vote of 274 to 226.[11]

The move gave the club many airs. It indicated a shift in priorities that sent the club down the path to snobbery and away from civic concern. In 1933, in an action the *Inquirer* did not publicize, the members of the Woman's Club voted to limit their numbers to 1,200. In 1946 they reduced that total to 1,000. The Woman's Club had violated the spirit of its constitution. No longer an inclusive civic organization, it had become an exclusive social group. Increasingly in the years ahead, other organizations, such as the Scarsdale branch of the League of Women Voters and, after 1967, the Village Club, would attract those women who had a special interest in the operation of Scarsdale's government.[12]

Nevertheless, as the Woman's Club changed, its publication, the *Scarsdale Inquirer*, played an increasingly important role in the community. Bought in 1919 for a dollar and a year's printing contract, the paper, by 1931, was yielding a sizable profit.[13] Other things had changed as well. The paper was longer: the weekly edition averaged eighteen pages instead of six. It went to more families, 2,220 instead of 400. And rather than relying on Woman's Club volunteers to solicit ads, subscriptions, and stories, it was run by a small professional staff. It had also gained some notice outside the village. In 1931 it won the first of a long series of prizes from the New York Press Association, and until its sale by the Woman's Club, in 1959, its position as "the country's only newspaper completely owned, operated, and staffed by women" brought occasional attention from the nonlocal press.[14]

The women of the *Inquirer*, however, were less concerned with increasing subscriptions and winning prizes than with educating their readers on local issues. The growth of the 1920s raised important questions to be decided. To help assure intelligent choices, the paper printed reports of the Town Club, covered the meetings of the village board, and offered space for discussion to anyone willing to write. Yet the *Inquirer* went beyond presenting the facts and alternative viewpoints. Aware that newcomers could change the village through their power of the vote, the paper aimed to inculcate the "ideals" and "traditions" of Scarsdale. Its strong editorial stands helped to forge the consensus for quality services, strict zoning, open space, and superior schools. The *Inquirer* believed that behind those achievements lay a spirit of cooperation between the members of both political parties. In 1928 the newspaper declared, "one of the strongest features of Scarsdale's government is the fact that 'politics' is not its basis.''[15]

If the *Inquirer* sounded as though bipartisanship went as surely with the village atmosphere as winding roads and handsome trees, it had reason. Scarsdale's tradition of uncontested local elections dated from the nineteenth century. A break with that tradition in 1909 ultimately served to confirm it. The race that year for the post of town supervisor demonstrated to many residents the desirability of avoiding partisan contests. Beginning in 1911, and continuing in every election to 1929, members of the town committees of the Republican and Democratic parties met, drew up one slate of candidates for local office, and submitted that slate to the caucuses for endorsement. On election day the voters found the same candidates listed for both parties.[16]

Proponents of bipartisanship said that the system had two main advantages. It improved the quality of the government because it allowed officials to concentrate on community problems instead of worrying about their own chances of re-election or the welfare of their party, and it improved the quality of the officials because the people best suited for the job of governing were those least likely to tolerate the hazards of campaigning.[17]

The latter point rested on assumptions that modern readers might not share. An analysis of the social and economic affiliations of members of the village board reveals the criteria for selections to that board and the characteristics of Scarsdale's leaders.[18] Between 1915 and 1933, forty persons served on the board. Most were male, born in the Northeast, college-educated, Protestant in religion, and Republican in politics. The heavy majority belonged to the Town Club; many belonged to the Scarsdale Golf Club. They also held occupations of high status that, in the eyes of villagers, demonstrated their capacity to govern.

Sometimes the exceptions to the pattern were more telling than the pattern itself. For example, with regard to birthplace, the predominance of native northeasterners was natural; yet only one trustee came originally from the Scarsdale vicinity, while several came from the Midwest, the upper South, and from as far away as South Dakota, Colorado, and England. As a group, the trustees showed a high degree of geographic mobility.

As for religion, the exceptions to the pattern, albeit few in number, were also of importance. The fact that any non-Protestants served on the board indicated that, while nativist sentiment existed in Scarsdale, as elsewhere in the United States during this period, it was not so intense as to preclude the recognition of a few Catholics and one Jew. In 1925, more than 70 percent of the heads of household in Scarsdale came from Protestant ethnoreligious backgrounds, slightly fewer than 20 percent from Catholic backgrounds, and about 10 percent from Jewish backgrounds.[19] Meanwhile, for the period 1915 to 1933, thirty-five of the forty trustees (87.5 percent) appear to have been Protestants, four (10 percent) came from Catholic backgrounds, and one (2.5 percent) was Jewish. Among the Protestants, most came from the older, larger and more prestigious Protestant denominations in the community. Specifically, eleven trustees were members of the local Episcopal Church, eight attended the Congregational Church, and six were Presbyterians; only one trustee was enrolled at the recently organized Baptist congregation, and none were members of the local Christian Science, Missouri Synod Lutheran, or American Lutheran churches. In addition, there were nine trustees who were not affiliated with any of the local congregations. Although they may have attended a church in another community, they probably belonged to the 41 percent of Westchester residents who tended to regard themselves as Protestants but did not join an organized religious group.[20] While Protestants clearly dominated the community, they did not close off to other groups all access to power.

An individual's party affiliation had a direct bearing on his or her candidacy for the village board. By the late 1920s, those "best qualified" had to include precisely five Republicans and two Democrats. The arrangement had obvious benefits for Democrats, who gained offices they would not have won in contested elections. Registration in Scarsdale was five-to-one Republican. Although the Republican margin in elections was smaller, the Republicans could have monopolized the village board if local offices had been contested. Yet, by agreeing to the five-to-two ratio, the Republicans won some subtle advantages. The agreement enhanced their reputation for fair play, simultaneously neutralizing the Democrats. With Republicans and Democrats working side by side on the village board, both parties defended the conduct of local affairs.[21]

Women accounted for only four of the forty trustees. Following the passage of the suffrage amendment, it seemed appropriate to name two women to the board. With the expiration of their terms, one woman succeeded; and when she left, another took her place. But from May 1930 to April 1943, all the positions on the board were held by men, and not until the 1970s would more than one woman serve on the board at a given time. The situation paralleled the decline in civic activity not only at the Woman's Club but among women on the national level. It also reflected the fact that the men in the community tended to have more training, status, and experience.[22]

Education helped to determine a person's selection for the board much as did sex, for a college graduate was more likely to have skills and status than a person who had not attended college. Of the thirty-two trustees about whom information was available, at least twenty-seven (84.4 percent) had received a college education, fourteen at Ivy League schools and nearly all of the others at institutions of renown. These twenty-seven trustees had attended college at a time when only one American in sixty earned a college degree. Although the proportion of college graduates in the general population was undoubtedly much larger for Scarsdale than for the nation as a whole, it certainly did not approach 84 percent even in Scarsdale.[23]

Some evidence of community service was a virtual prerequisite for village office. Before their selection as trustees, the four women had been active in the Woman's Club, and all but one of the men had served in the Town Club. Why an exception occurred in the case of lawyer Harrison Robertson is not clear. His name did not appear in the Town Club yearbooks, but neither did his nomination to the village board produce a negative response. The Scarsdale Golf Club was the only other organization to boast a large number of trustees. Since it provided the most convenient "Christian" golf course, its popularity was hardly surprising.

Other than community service, occupation was the major factor in determining the selection of trustees. Of the thirty-six men who served on the board, there were twelve attorneys, six bankers, three engineers, one architect, a professor of English, and a man who lived on an inherited income. The others were high-level business executives in fields as diverse as silk, oil, clocks, insurance, construction, and railroads. Since experience in law, finance, engineering, and management had relevance to the concerns of the village board, nearly all the trustees possessed skills that enhanced the operation of the government. Moreover, some trustees were acknowledged leaders in their professions. Robert E. Christie, Jr., a partner in Dillon, Read, and Company, was president of the Investment Bankers of America. Malcolm

Pirnie, who headed his own engineering firm, received the Hoover Medal for distinguished achievement in engineering and served as president of the American Society of Civil Engineers. With such men in its service, Scarsdale benefited from superior technical advice and experienced decision making.[24]

Yet the careers of members of the village board had more than practical importance. Their accomplishments in the world outside added to the luster of the community's self-image. The willingness of busy men to attend to local matters made Scarsdale seem important in its own right and superior to other towns. According to Harold H. Bennett, long-term secretary of the Town Club, the residents regarded their leaders as men worth emulating, for their lives, at least to some extent, exemplified the virtues of hard work and public service. Even Gail Borden, heir of the dairy-products fortune, deserved respect for taking an interest in the community rather than languishing in a life of ease.

But residents reserved their greatest admiration for those whose careers showed social mobility. Fred Lavis, a trustee and mayor of Scarsdale, was born the son of a sailor, in Torquay, England, left school at age fourteen, came to the United States two years later, and through jobs on numerous engineering projects became an expert in the field of transportation. Lavis was president of a railroad chain in Central America, a consultant to banks in New York City, and a lecturer at Princeton, Rensselaer Polytechnic Institute, and Yale. The career of Frank Bethell, the man chosen in 1915 to head the village government, also fit the Horatio Alger pattern. Starting as a messenger boy in a Newark, New Jersey, telephone office, Bethell rose to active leadership of the whole eastern group of Bell companies. At one time he was president of eight telephone companies and vice-president of several others. Equally impressive was the career of John M. Hancock, trustee and mayor in the 1930s. Born in Emerado, South Dakota, Hancock attended the state university, worked as a high school principal, joined the U.S. Navy as an ensign, and headed the purchase division of the navy's Bureau of Supplies and Accounts during World War I. After the war he entered business. He reorganized the Jewel Tea Company, became its president, accepted a partnership with Lehman Brothers, and served on the boards of twenty-one corporations. In 1942, President Franklin Roosevelt named Hancock to the War Industries Board, and later Harry Truman appointed him as alternate to Bernard Baruch on the United Nations Atomic Energy Commission. The people of Scarsdale had reason to take pride in the achievements of such leaders.[25]

Still, the individuals who served as trustees between 1915 and 1933 comprised an elite even by Scarsdale's standards. Whether, coming from wealthy families, they had received every advantage of education and connections, or coming from modest backgrounds, they had worked their way up in the business world, each had shown dedication and talent. They provided Scarsdale with honest, efficient government.

In choosing government by an elite, the people of Scarsdale de-emphasized the principle of representation. None of the trustees resided in North End or Scarsdale Park. Only one came from Arthur Manor, while several lived in Scarsdale's most luxurious sections—Heathcote, Murray Hill, Greenacres, and the Grange.[26] Further, the nomination process, controlled by the local Democratic and Republican leaders, made no provision for neighborhood representation. As Scarsdale's population grew, the elitist nature of its government created ill-feeling.

The problem first received public attention in 1924, when Fred Lavis, president of the Town Club, charged that Scarsdale was "getting away from the true democratic spirit." According to Lavis, a "very small committee" picked the candidates for village office, while "the people as a whole" had "almost nothing to say about who they should be." Although the candidates were individuals of "the highest type," the method of their selection undermined their role as representatives of the community. Besides, said Lavis, Scarsdale was not the intimate place it had been a decade earlier. Since few residents knew the candidates personally, they came to regard the government as "a thing apart." The situation bred resentment on both sides. The citizens thought the government "unmindful of their wishes," while the members of the village board felt their efforts were unappreciated. The civic harmony that had marked Scarsdale was fading.[27]

For a time residents skirted the problem of nominations by discussing stop-gap measures to improve relations between the voters and their trustees. The *Inquirer* thought the village board could change the tone of its bi-weekly meetings. Instead of holding "a meeting before the meeting" so that in public the members would pass without discussion all the business that they raised, they should take the taxpayers into their confidence by engaging in open discussions of unsettled problems. The paper recognized that the trustees had to confer privately on many issues but warned that "'many' does not mean all." In the *Inquirer*'s view, excessive openness would present "less danger to the ideals of government in Scarsdale" than would unwarranted secrecy.[28]

Yet adjustments on the part of the trustees required more participation from the people. "To make up for the loss in personal contact caused by the growth in population," the people would have to make more of an effort. It was their obligation both to keep informed by reading the newspaper and to express their opinion at public hearings and meetings of their political caucus. Most of all, the people should vote. The *Inquirer* regarded the low turnout at local elections as a sign of voter indifference. Although indifference was a predictable result of having uncontested elections, the *Inquirer* thought it inexcusable in a town of Scarsdale's quality. In 1928 when only thirty-nine voters went to the polls, the paper sought to shame the people to action. It proposed assigning one resident to cast a ritual ballot, thus "making sure that the election would be effected . . . [and] reliev[ing] all suspense as to whether anyone was going to show up at all."[29]

Such suggestions attacked the symptoms, not the problem. As Lavis had pointed out, the change in the character of the community required a change in the methods of selecting candidates. To allow the party leaders to decide on the one available slate was undemocratic. To depend on them to reach an agreement was unwise. For the likelihood was large that the leaders of one or the other party would eventually succumb to temptation and use the rhetoric of bipartisanship to achieve partisan ends.

Yet no one gave serious consideration to alternative methods of nominating candidates until a crisis occurred. In the fall of 1929, the Democrats asked the Republicans to extend to the town board the principle of joint rule that the two parties applied to the village board. The town board was little more than a relic from previllage days. Composed of the town supervisor (Scarsdale's representative to the county board) and four justices of the peace, it handled certain "routine duties," such as the administration of the election laws, the selection of jurors, and the assessment and collection of taxes for state, county, and school purposes. The village board, meanwhile, made the ordinances and directed the operation of local services. Within a few years the members of the village board would take over the functions of the town board; but as long as the two existed as separate bodies, the Democrats thought they deserved to be represented by at least one justice of the peace. The Republicans thought otherwise. When they insisted that two Republicans be named to fill the vacancies on the previously all-Republican board, the Democrats decided to contest the election.[30]

In the recriminations that followed, each side accused the other of repudiating the ideals of bipartisanship. The Democrats said that the Republicans, in order to monopolize the town board, had refused to consider well-qualified Democrats. They charged further that Republican incumbent Joseph Carter had violated judicial ethics by accepting "a purely political position" as clerk to the budget committee of the county board of supervisors while serving as village police justice and town justice of the peace. Since a grand jury was then investigating charges of corruption in the county government, the Democrats expected to profit by linking local Republicans with the machine of the county boss.[31]

Responding to the Democrats' "eleventh hour attack," the Republicans presented themselves as men of reason and defenders of the bipartisan system. They began by criticizing the Democrats for raising "irrelevant" issues. Though willing to endorse Carter in the strongest terms, the Republicans pointed out that he was not at the time up for election. As for the charges of corruption in the county government, the Republicans cautioned against rash judgments. Not only had the grand jury issued no indictments, but with a Democratic governor like Franklin Roosevelt, one had to question the grounds for an investigation of one of the state's Republican strongholds.[32]

The election of 1929 left much unsettled, for the argument over bipartisan principles seemed to divide along partisan lines. With a Republican victory and a high Democratic turnout, the leaders of both local parties could feel that, while they might not have won others to their cause, they had expressed the views of their parties' rank and file. Both sides clung to their positions in the weeks that followed. When the time came to draw up a fusion slate for the village elections to be held in March, the two parties could not reach an agreement. Another contested election seemed imminent. Yet the autumn's strife had brought a new appreciation of the political peace that Scarsdale had for years enjoyed.[33]

At the Republican caucus on February 19, 1930, the members of the party's town committee proposed a way out of the impasse. They called for the creation of an independent committee to select a slate of candidates that both parties could endorse. Since little time remained before the election, the caucus itself named the committee, directed it to consider individuals for office "without any reference to the[ir] politics," and committed the Republican organization to accept the committee's nominees.[34]

Composed of thirty-four citizens of both parties, the nominating committee met two days later. Within a few hours it had named two Republicans and a Democrat to fill the vacancies on the village board. The committee also adopted a resolution that marked the first step in the establishment of a formal nonpartisan nominating system. The resolution urged that nominations for local office be taken out of the hands of the Republican and Democratic town committees and entrusted to a nonpartisan citizens' committee. Such a committee could be headed by the president of the Town Club and the president of the Woman's Club who, at a reasonable time before an election, would appoint three members; then all five would select at least six other persons. The resolution also stated that while "fitness" was "the primary consideration" in choosing candidates for local office, "other things being equal, . . . the political parties should be given representation on the village board in proportion to their voting strength."[35]

On February 24, the two parties endorsed the committee's slate and approved the principle behind the resolution. The community was at last establishing a nominating process suited to its ideas of government. As the *Inquirer* stated, no one could blame the Republican and Democratic leaders, "chosen . . . to strengthen their particular party," for failing to agree on a fusion slate. In the future, responsibility for nominations for local office would rest where it belonged, "squarely on the shoulders of the citizens of the village . . . through the organization of a nonpartisan committee."[36]

While admirable in principle, the proposal required some practical adjustments. The Democrats thought that the nominating process should provide for some input from party leaders (so that neither party would be offended by the candidates selected) and that representation of the different areas of the village should also be assured. The Town Club spoke to those reservations in a report, issued in December 1930, that called for three revisions in the original proposal. First, the chairman of the Republican and Democratic town committees would serve as nonvoting members of the citizens committee. Second, the presidents of the Town Club and the Woman's Club and their three appointees would select two members for the committee from each of Scarsdale's seven election districts. Third, the committee would endeavor, "so far as may be practicable," to provide for representation on the village and town boards of Scarsdale's "various geographical sections" as well as of "the two political parties substantially in proportion to their voting strength."[37]

Although the revised plan was more broadly democratic, the system still contained a contradiction. Before the slate, drawn up by a nonpartisan body, could appear on the ballot, it had to earn the endorsement of partisan caucuses. The problems inherent in the situation became apparent in 1931 when a small group of Republicans spoke against the nonpartisan slate. The views of one Republican were typical. Although he had no objection to the candidates, he wanted the party to elect its own ticket to "keep itself in trim and show its strength." Such a course was hardly necessary. In the past, despite uncontested local elections, Scarsdale had piled up impressive Republican margins in county, state, and national contests. Among those attending the Democratic caucus, there was also desire to field a ticket. But most Democrats understood that if they refused to accept the committee's candidates on any grounds other than fitness for office, they would lose the community's respect.[38]

The slate passed in both caucuses, but the expression of opposition to the principle of nonpartisanship aroused indignation from some citizens. Cleveland A. Dunn, a long-time resident, asked, "Is the village here to serve the party, or is the party to serve the village?" He blamed the dissent on newcomers who came from communities where politics flourished and who had "not fully grasped the [Scarsdale] ideal." The *Inquirer* also blamed the problem on people new to the village. "Those who have lived long enough in Scarsdale . . . know it is wholeheartedly behind the nonpartisan scheme." The paper advised newcomers who wanted to involve themselves in politics to concentrate on county, state, and national campaigns and keep their "hands off of Scarsdale." When two voters violated that stricture in the March election by writing in the names of candidates not listed on the ballot, the *Inquirer* took a shrill tone. It accused the two of not acting in an "honest way." "We have no sympathy with the endeavor to project politics into a community which wishes its government to be non-political."[39]

While some attacked the protesters, others worked to strengthen the system. In January 1933, the Town Club passed an amendment that made two improvements in the nominating procedure. It provided for a more representative committee by increasing the number of members from nineteen to thirty-seven and by directing the neighborhood associations to nominate delegates to the committee. The amendment also moved to end the contradiction in Scarsdale's nonpartisan practice by instructing the committee to file its candidates with the board of elections, independent of the action of the two parties. The future of the nonpartisan system would no longer depend on the endorsement of political caucuses. The *Inquirer* called the amendment "a wise step," and the citizens registered their approval by showing up in record numbers at the election of that year.[40]

Scarsdale had now laid the groundwork for a nonpartisan system that would satisfy the overwhelming majority of its residents for the next three decades. The new system bore a resemblance to others that were evolving in such places as Lake Forest and Winnetka, Illinois, and Garden City, New York.[41] Yet, although nonpartisanship in Scarsdale was not idiosyncratic, it did differ from the more typical application of that concept to municipal government. In most localities nonpartisanship did not preclude the holding of contested elections. It simply meant that candidates ran for office, independent of party affiliation, obligation, or support. There was no convoluted process for selecting the members of the nominating committee, as there was in Scarsdale; no prearranged division of seats based on party, sex, or neighborhood; no prohibition against candidates expressing their views. But whereas the usual purpose of nonpartisan politics was to rid local government of major party control, in Scarsdale that aim was ancillary to another—ridding local government of open competition and conflict. Time and again residents repeated the following formula: only because the village of Scarsdale avoided contested elections and, most of the time, divisive disputes, did the best qualified individuals agree to serve on its board of trustees, and only because they served, did Scarsdale enjoy honest, efficient, progressive government.

Despite the assertions of its proponents, the mechanics of the system may have had less to do with the success of Scarsdale's government than a deeper reality. By the time of the formalization of the nonpartisan nominating procedure, the efforts of policy makers, developers, and private citizens had combined to make Scarsdale, in the words of one resident, "an unusually affluent and homogeneous [village] with none [or at least few] of the major problems that afflict other communities." Statistics collected for the federal census bore out that observation. Of the 1,977 dwellings in Scarsdale in 1930, 1,951 were single-family residences. Only 21 dwellings were built for two families, 5 for three families or more. In the same year, 82.7 percent of the families in Scarsdale owned their own houses, compared to 43.4 percent in Westchester County, 36.6 percent in New York State, and 46.7 percent in the United States. Of the owned nonfarm houses in Scarsdale, 92.6 percent fell into the most expensive category listed by the federal census, those valued at $10,000 or more. Meanwhile, 70.1 percent of the owned houses in Westchester were worth at least $10,000, compared to only 33 percent of the houses in New York State, and 17 percent of the houses throughout the United States. No wonder one woman ascribed "the charm of suburban life" in Scarsdale to "that identity of community interests which a permanent group of home builders naturally develop. . . . Our neighbors are our friends with common interests, mutual ambitions, and worthy ideals."[42]

This commonality of interests seemed to win out despite the differences between the financial circumstances of the families who lived, for example, in Arthur Manor and those who lived in Scarsdale's more expensive subdivisions. The property holders in Arthur Manor were at one with their wealthier neighbors in wanting Scarsdale to remain a village of homes, and they worked to change the zoning of their district from Residence B to Residence A. They too recognized that many of the services they paid for in higher taxes accrued to their long-term benefit in the form of increased property values. If occasionally they disagreed with the majority viewpoint—as when, in 1926, they supported a petition for bus service in their neighborhood, or when, in 1930, they criticized the go-it-alone policy on highway improvement—they did not long sustain such independence. Perhaps the residents of Arthur Manor did not care to advertise, by dissent, their inferior position in the community, or perhaps they genuinely identified with the goals and policies of the majority and found little reason to dissent. In any case the differences in social status that existed among the residents of the various subdivisions had no profound impact on the content of political discussion in the 1920s and 1930s.[43]

Similarly, differences in religion, while greatly affecting the private associations of village residents, did not affect public discussion in the village during this period. Although Catholics and especially Jews had reason to feel restive, they were more intent on winning acceptance from the Protestant majority than in broadcasting their grievances within the community.

To some degree the problems encountered by Roman Catholics resulted from prejudices of social class rather than religion. An Arthur Driscoll, who was a graduate of Brown University and Harvard Law School, lawyer to celebrities Mary Pickford and George M. Cohan, and owner of a $175,000 Italian Renaissance mansion, could win election as Scarsdale's first Catholic mayor and serve as president of the Town Club, Scarsdale Golf Club, and Fox Meadow Tennis Club. Even so, a disproportionate number of Catholics lived in Scarsdale's more modest neighborhoods, and many of the community's servants attended the local Catholic Church. Religious prejudice may have compounded the discomfort that less affluent Catholics felt in Scarsdale, but it was not the only cause of their discomfort.[44]

Still, even upper-middle-class Catholics encountered some indications of prejudice on the part of non-Catholics. When Margaret M. Treacy moved to the village in 1928 with her husband, a chemical engineer, many of the Protestants she met assumed all Catholics were "foul-mouthed and vulgar." Although some of the same Protestants would accept individual Catholics, she noted their surprise when people they considered "nice" proved to be Catholic. Scarsdale was "definitely a WASP area," she said, with "an undercurrent of anti-Catholicism," but to her knowledge no clear-cut cases of discrimination occurred against members of the Catholic Church.[45]

While the anti-Catholicism that existed in Scarsdale in the twenties and thirties was partly a function of class bias, anti-Semitism flourished in spite of the wealth of the community's Jews. Regardless of whether they practiced Judaism, people who came from a Jewish family found it difficult to buy property in many parts of Scarsdale, and impossible in some. The small number of Jews who moved into the village discovered that non-Jews refused to associate with them socially. Although they could join the local civic organizations, they were not admitted to the Scarsdale Golf Club, nor were they included among the guests at the parties described in the *Inquirer*. No matter how wealthy and cultured a Jewish family was, its members, until recent years, could not gain full acceptance within the community. Scarsdale mirrored the anti-Semitic attitudes of America's elite.[46]

Local real estate practices demonstrated the community's hostility to Jews. Realtors, normally eager for clients, tried to discourage Jewish couples from buying property in Scarsdale. If dissuasion failed, the realtors had an agreement whereby they refused to show Jews the houses in certain areas. Although these "restricted" areas took in broad sections of the community, from luxurious subdivisions in the northern part of town to modest subdivisions in the south, Jewish families with sufficient money and persistence could succeed in finding property. They did so disproportionately in Scarsdale's wealthiest sections—Heathcote, Murray Hill, Greenacres, the Grange, and later Fox Meadow. Although the residents of wealthy areas may have been more secure in their sense of their own status and, therefore, more willing to tolerate having Jews as their neighbors, other factors also influenced Jewish families' places of residence. Although in no area did Jews constitute a majority of the homeowners during the mid-twenties, their presence probably helped to attract other Jewish families. Moreover, the development of Fox Meadow by two New York Jews opened a large new tract to Jewish settlement.[47]

The Jewish families in Scarsdale represented an impressive collection of wealth. Al Jolson, the entertainer, lived in Scarsdale; so did Sidney Weinberg, a partner in the investment firm of Goldman, Sachs; and Jacob Aronson, head of the legal division of the New York Central Railroad. Non-Jewish residents could not overlook the achievements of such individuals, but most were sufficiently imbued with the anti-Semitism of the era to look on Jews with a degree of distrust. Thus Jews came to hold an anomalous position in the civic life of the community. They were too prominent to be excluded from the men's and women's civic organizations. Aronson even served a term on the village board of trustees. Yet they could rise only so high in local government. Until the late 1950s (in spite of the fact that their numbers grew rapidly after World War II), Jews in Scarsdale had to content themselves with an occasional seat on the school and village boards. The presidency of the Town Club, the office of mayor, and the presidency of the board of education in school district number one, all remained in Christian—and, with the exception of Arthur Driscoll, Protestant—hands.[48]

While Jews and Catholics served as out-groups in the predominantly Protestant, upper-middle-class society of Scarsdale, domestic servants, regardless of religion, faced another kind of ostracism. Because they were the employees of taxpayers and not themselves taxpayers, the local government all but ignored them. Scarsdale was, as its residents said time and again, a village of homes. Home ownership entitled an individual, regardless of background, to some sense of belonging within the community. Living and working in Scarsdale brought no such guarantee.

Scarsdale, especially in the years before World War II, included a sizable population of lower-class residents, virtually all of whom were servants. They did not own homes in part because the zoning law and building code worked together to prevent the construction of lower cost housing. But in general servants were not expected to own homes or rent apartments, if they lived in Scarsdale. Instead, many of Scarsdale's single-family houses had quarters for one or more servants. The servants provided the labor that freed local property holders for social events and civic ventures. The tone of community life depended on their presence, but they enjoyed few of Scarsdale's benefits. Cut off from relatives and friends who lived outside the village, they were the objects of scorn and suspicion within.

In 1925, out of a total of 5,099 residents in Scarsdale, 910 were servants who resided with their employers. Nearly two-thirds of these were immigrants, representing thirty foreign countries. Irish, Germans, and West Indians were the most numerous, but there were also fifteen Japanese, seven Italians, and one Filipino. The remaining servants were native-born, 155 whites and 176 blacks. More than three-fourths of all Scarsdale's servants were women who worked as maids, cooks, and nurses for children. Men were employed, mainly in the wealthier households, as butlers, chauffeurs, and gardeners.[49]

With 910 servants in Scarsdale and 1,021 households, there could have been one servant for nearly nine-tenths of the households. The actual distribution was more complicated. Approximately half the households had no live-in help, although they may have hired workers by the day. Two hundred eighty-seven households employed one live-in servant, typically a woman to do the cooking and general cleaning; 125 households hired two servants, sometimes a husband and wife; 80 households employed three or four servants; and 19 employed five or more. In 1925 the New York State census reported that one household in Scarsdale included ten full-time, live-in domestics. Their employer was a female head of household with one seven-year-old son.[50]

The relations between employers and servants, while varying from household to household, existed within the context of what employers called the "servant problem." That term summed up the employers' perennial complaints that servants were hard to acquire, hard to keep, inefficient, expensive, and bothersome. During the 1920s, at least some of those complaints appeared to have substance. The immigration restriction laws of 1921 and 1924 reduced the supply of potential servants, while the high wages offered by industry lured workers away from domestic employment.[51] Conditions in Scarsdale aggravated the difficulty of finding servants, at least white servants. Although the village attracted lots of families who wanted to hire servants, few servants were willing to trade a job in an urban center for a position in Scarsdale, which lacked ethnic subcommunities. Those who were willing came either on a short-term basis or at the promise of higher wages.[52]

The servant shortage hit families where they were most vulnerable, in their sense of their own status. Not only did the act of employing servants indicate that a family possessed the means to do so, but even with the introduction of household appliances, the lady of the house could hardly keep up with the demands of her children, maintain a clean and comfortable residence, entertain in the style expected, and participate in civic, church, and club affairs—all without the assistance of one or more servants. A family had to have servants to meet the standards of respectability that prevailed in Scarsdale. Accordingly, both the constriction in the supply of servants and the rise in wages threatened the social positions of some families and thwarted the aspirations of others.

For a time the community dealt with the servant problem as with other delicate matters. Individuals may have joked about it. Close friends may have discussed it in earnest. But it was not considered a topic suitable for polite conversation. Women were particularly sensitive on the subject. Since they were responsible for managing the household, they felt that any difficulty they encountered in dealing with servants reflected on their competence as housewives. Even women with good servants preferred to avoid discussing them for fear they might lose them to "unscrupulous listener[s]." And, according to the *Inquirer*, no woman cared to engage in a conversation that might cause her "to reveal the exact extent of [her] household budget." Thus, women exerted pressure on each other to keep quiet about servants. Anyone who broached the subject risked being snubbed as an "old fashioned bore."[53]

Skirting the issue had drawbacks. It meant that individual employers lacked basic information about the wages and benefits servants were receiving in other households. Employers did not know how much work to demand from their servants and whether to insist upon high standards of performance. Because they lacked a sense of the market, many felt apprehensive in dealing with servants. That apprehension undermined their ability to function as efficient household managers, and it made life uncomfortable for all members of the household, including the servants.[54]

In the fall of 1929, the editors of the *Inquirer* broke through the silence on the subject of servants. Regarding the issue as one too "vital" to be ignored, they mailed questionnaires to their 1,600 subscribers. The questionnaires requested data on servants' wages, hours, and workloads and solicited employers' opinions regarding mistress-servant relations. Since some of the questions were admittedly "personal," the editors promised to keep the names of their sources in "strictest confidence." A few women still objected to the plan, but nearly 500 others cooperated.[55] Their responses became the basis for a four-part series, which inspired additional contributions. Letters on servants appeared in the paper, as well as an article by Mrs. L. M. Moore, proprietor of the Scarsdale Employment Agency, and a long statement by Anna Filak, a maid employed by a Scarsdale family. The *Inquirer* had succeeded in opening the subject of mistress-servant relations for consideration by the public.

As expected, the survey showed that most employers thought their servants were "not worth the pay." One woman expressed the opinion that "real servants" no longer existed, that only "help" was available now and "mighty inefficient [help] at that." "I keep my servants," another said, "because I give them privileges out of all proportion to their ability and service to me."[56]

The facts showed that those views did not tell the whole story. According to the data received by the paper, the wages paid in one-servant households varied from $50 to $150 a month. While top wages went only to men, suggesting the existence of sex discrimination, the editors found "no particular connection between the scale of wages and length of service." They also found that employers who thought their servants worth praising often paid wages below the average. One maid who, in the opinion of her mistress, did "everything" and "well" received $60 a month, compared to the average of $75. Another maid, described as "an excellent cook" who could serve dinner for eight "with no apparent effort," received $65. In other words, some mistresses were paying low rates for highly regarded servants while others paid much more for servants they distrusted.[57]

The discrepancy in the quality and cost of servants led a number of women to call for the organization of a "Housekeepers' Union." They reasoned that, if all the domestic employers in Scarsdale adhered to strict standards of wages and efficiency, then all would receive value relative to the wages they paid. The scheme implied that a few of Scarsdale's "wealthier" women were ruining the system for others. Instead of following the common sense rule, "adequate pay for decent work," the wealthy offered "exorbitant wages for help who were really incompetent." One resident described her reaction: "When some people give their servants such high wages—$90 to $100 a month—it makes other girls [i.e., maids] dissatisfied, and I can't afford any higher wages." The proponents of an employers' union did not say how they planned to win the support of the wealthy. They kept their appeal on the level of platitudes. "Cooperation" among employers would work to the benefit of all.[58]

If housewives favored cooperation among members of their own class, they feared any signs of it among their servants. They felt that, since the turn of the century, the behavior of servants had changed completely. Instead of respecting their employers and depending on them, servants resented their employers and appeared to conspire against them. They kept alert to conditions in other households, insisted on raises in pay for limited work, and threatened to resign if their employers did not grant their demands. From the employers' point of view, such behavior suggested the influence of sinister forces. According to one woman, "[The domestics here] seem to be banded together and are apparently coached as to what and what not to do. Sometimes I think they will form a union."[59]

Despite their employers' suspicions, domestics did not have to be "coached" to know what constituted their own best interest. They wanted a share in the prosperity of the times. Writing in the *Inquirer*, a maid named Anna Filak reasoned that if other workers were receiving higher pay for lighter workloads, then so should servants. "Haven't domestics the same ambitions as the others?" she asked. "Doesn't the march of progress affect [them] as much as it does other workers?" Statistics collected for the National Bureau of Economic Research demonstrated the essential modesty of Filak's proposal. Between 1899 and 1939 the wages paid domestic servants rose 130 percent. That rise closely paralleled the increase in national income per member of the labor force. Domestics had improved their situation, but no more than the workers in other fields. In terms of wages, status, and freedom, they still lagged behind the workers in industry.[60]

The housewives in Scarsdale in the late 1920s had a different perspective. They thought they treated their servants generously, perhaps too generously. Responding to the *Inquirer*'s survey, employers spoke of providing their servants with good food ("the same as we have"), comfortable lodging (usually in a private room in a distinct section of the house), and prompt medical attention (by the employer's doctor and at the employer's expense). Most servants had time off during the day, "when work [was] not pressing," as well as the equivalent of one free day a week, usually consisting of every Thursday after lunch and every Sunday after the midday meal. Some servants enjoyed paid vacations. Many received gifts for birthdays and holidays. One family even treated their maids to a supper party with a live band and sixty guests of the maids' own choosing. The *Inquirer* saw something ludicrous in the measures residents were willing to take to keep their servants. In its feature "Kitchen Wisdom," a character called Miss Washin'ton boasted, "Cooks ain't so easy to git in Scarsdale. Dey treats 'em heaps more respeckful den school teachers."[61]

That joke measured the distance between the attitude of Scarsdale's mistresses and the experience of its servants. Far from feeling respected, most servants thought they were treated as "drudges." According to Anna Filak, it often seemed that each member of an employer's family was "working against what she was hired to accomplish," that each had set out to prove that Anna did not "know a thing." Children wrecked her housework. Teen-agers chose their own time for meals. One mistress, who would not perform the smallest task herself, required Anna to do the work she had formerly expected of five servants, and then reproached her if all was not perfect. Even a kind gesture could prove insulting. One young employer, on the advice of her mother, exchanged the gift she had planned to give Anna for something less expensive. The woman's mother had written, "[A clock worth $7.50] is too much to give help. They don't appreciate it anyway."[62]

The loneliness many servants experienced in Scarsdale made it harder for them to bear their employers' contempt. Immigrants from various countries and blacks from north and south, they were alienated not only from the upper-middle-class culture of Scarsdale, but also, to a degree, from each other. They spoke with different accents, and had different cultural heritages; and the whites among them looked down on the blacks. Those differences were especially important in view of the other obstacles to their making and cultivating friends. Servants worked long hours, most of them in separate households. They could not comfortably invite other servants to the homes of their employers. The Episcopal Church sponsored special groups for black servants, but the community provided no place where servants could gather informally, and because of the limited availability of public transportation, few could participate in the working-class groups of other towns. As a result, some servants literally had "no one to talk to except to say, 'Yes, Mrs. So-and-So' or 'No, Madame.'" For them, life consisted of a constant round of hard work, of meals eaten in silence, and of nights spent alone.[63]

Employers were not completely indifferent to their servants' isolation. After all, it affected their own self-interest. As one employer said, "the lack of church and companionship" kept some servants from Scarsdale and drove others away within a short time. To counter the problem of loneliness, housewives who could afford the expense hired more than one servant. They found that their servants worked better and stayed longer than servants who worked alone in a household. Other employers relied on the Scarsdale night school to provide their servants with an outlet for social contact. Directed by the Woman's Club, the school gave servants a chance to make some acquaintances while improving their English and learning the fundamentals of good citizenship. Yet, in view of the number of servants employed in Scarsdale, attendance at the school was relatively low. In 1927, in a community with close to 1,000 servants, an average of 22 persons attended the school. Either employers were loath to release their domestics for the one-night-a-week class, or servants preferred to use differently the small amount of leisure they had. According to Mrs. L. M. Moore, proprietor of the Scarsdale Employment Agency, what servants needed was a centrally located club room where they could gather when they were free. She thought that the establishment of such a club would work to the benefit of employers by making their servants "more contented." That suggestion drew no public response. Perhaps it sounded too unstructured, too unsupervised, arousing employers' fears of a servants' union. In any case, the people of Scarsdale never implemented Moore's proposal or anything like it. Their efforts to enhance their servants' happiness stopped short of measures that would reduce their own control.[64]

According to the evidence published by the *Inquirer*, the relations between employers and servants represented a source of strain within the community. Considerations of status and self-esteem on the part of employers and problems of loneliness on the part of the servants complicated basic differences in economic self-interest. In view of those differences, a polite but distant relationship was probably the best the two groups could achieve. The advice offered by women considered successful household managers showed how carefully they maintained a distance from their servants. The women urged housewives like themselves to "master the calm, sure touch in dealing with [servants];" to "be definite about their work, their time off, their pay;" to "know what good work should be, to expect [it]," and "to show an appreciation of [it];" to make "no apologies" about the work demanded, and to "promis[e] nothing" for the future. Anna Filak had a degree of respect for such standards. She loathed hypocrisy in an employer and preferred an efficient household to "an easy place." But Anna longed for something more than a good working system of management. She thought employers should treat their servants with patience, consideration, and tact. Above all, she looked forward to the day when "mutual understanding and friendship" would replace the "mutual hatred" that flourished in the domestic field. Judging from the remarks of Scarsdale's mistresses, that day was unlikely ever to come.[65]

All servants in Scarsdale suffered indignities, but those who were black endured the added burden of racial prejudice. Denied jobs by many employers and segregated socially from white servants, they were the most oppressed members of the community's lower class. Their oppression held a special irony. In view of the existence of black neighborhoods in several communities close to Scarsdale, black servants might have been better able to overcome the problems of loneliness of which servants in Scarsdale generally complained.

In 1925 blacks comprised less than 30 percent of the total number of domestic servants in Scarsdale. The proportion of blacks might have been larger had employers not made efforts to secure the services of whites. While housewives preferred servants of German or Scandinavian origin, they thought whites of any national group made better servants than blacks. In their opinion, white servants were "cleaner," "quicker," "more responsible," and "certainly more loyal" than black servants. Many of those who held such views had had no experience as employers of blacks. As long as they could find whites to fill whatever vacancies occurred in their households, they refused to interview blacks, much less to hire them.[66]

The help-wanted columns in the *Scarsdale Inquirer* showed the existence of discrimination against black servants. Of the sixty-two positions advertised during September, October, and November of 1927, twenty required that applicants be white. During the same period, eighteen of the thirty-six ads requesting positions came from persons who identified themselves as "colored." The proprietor of the Scarsdale Employment Agency presented stronger evidence of discrimination. She found it "impossible" to meet the demands for white servants although she traveled throughout the metropolitan area trying to attract white workers to Scarsdale. On the other hand, she found she could not place all the blacks who applied at her office, despite the fact that most expected lower wages than whites. Apparently the servant shortage was primarily a shortage of white servants.[67]

Those blacks who did secure employment in Scarsdale faced a degree of segregation within the community. They were allowed to sing and pray in the company of other blacks, but not to attend the night school with servants who were white. As has already been noted, the Episcopal Church assumed responsibility for the spiritual and social well-being of at least some of the village's black servants. During the 1920s it sponsored a group known as the St. Mary's Guild "for the colored women of the parish." The Guild, which held meetings on every other Monday night, assisted in the work of the Episcopal missions "at home and abroad." In addition, the church provided practice space for the "Scarsdale unit of the county chorus of all-Negro voices."

Although domestic employers had no objection to either of those programs, they blocked a proposal submitted by Ralph I. Underhill, the superintendent of schools. Underhill wanted the board of education to take over the night school run by the Woman's Club. He considered it improper for a private club to operate "a service which really belong[ed] to the community as a whole." Moreover, the change in supervision would make the night school eligible for funds from New York State which, according to Underhill, would cover up to one-third the cost of the program. Members of the Woman's Club showed little interest in a possible saving of money. They were concerned that the board of education, in operating the night school, might encounter "certain problems . . . which had not troubled the Woman's Club." For example, the club had avoided admitting blacks to the school on the grounds that it was "a class for foreigners." But the school board could not make that distinction. It would have to include all residents, regardless of race, who wanted to improve their ability to read and write English. In the judgment of a committee of the Woman's Club, the inclusion of blacks would undermine the entire program. Their presence would make the school less desirable to the other pupils, "who represent[ed] a much higher level of intelligence." Convinced by the committee's arguments, the members of the board of education decided to allow the Woman's Club to operate the night school as before.[68]

The housewives of Scarsdale shared the racial prejudices of other Americans. They discriminated against blacks in large part because they feared them. In a letter to the *Inquirer*, one resident wrote, "I think you are making a mistake in publishing all the facts regarding the servant problem. . . . It gives too much information to a certain class of the colored maids." Another woman, who for twenty years had "imported" her servants from her "old home" in Virginia, said that her servants were "fine until contaminated by association with their Northern friends." A third woman, alarmed at the increase in the size of the area's black population, made a statement which even the *Inquirer* regarded as "drastic." She said that blacks were "swarming into White Plains . . . attracted from New York and the South by reports of high wages." Soon, she thought, part of White Plains would become "a little Harlem." As for Scarsdale, residents employed "too many colored servants." Their numbers were so great as to give Scarsdale "almost the appearance of a colored community on days off."[69]

Although such a perception was obviously distorted, it served, much as the employers' fears of a servants' union, to point up the contradictions of the mistress-servant relationship. The housewives of Scarsdale needed the help of domestic employees to meet the social expectations of the community. At the same time, they resented not only the cost and complications involved in having servants but also the contact with foreigners and blacks. Consequently, dealing with servants troubled women caught up in the goals and prejudices of the community. Still, the realities of being a servant were far worse.

In the politics of the community, as well as those of the household, upper-middle-class homeowners clearly held control. Their domination of the community helped to explain why the nonpartisan system succeeded as well as it did. But although the system functioned smoothly, it ignored the interests of the 18 percent of village residents who were servants. Their social condition as much as their economic class put these servants in a virtually powerless position within Scarsdale. Many were un-naturalized immigrants who had no voting rights. While others could have voted, probably few did because their vote would have meant so little. Thus, since most servants conformed to the expectation that they play an invisible role, the presence of a lower class in Scarsdale had almost no impact on its politics. Instead of class strife, a consensus prevailed in the community. What rumblings occurred among the community's powers concerned subtle distinctions of neighborhood and religion, not major differences in occupational point of view.

A view of Crane Road, taken at the turn of the century, near the present entrance to the Bronx River Parkway. The lack of paving and streetlights indicates how rural Scarsdale was at the time. (Courtesy of the Scarsdale Public Library)

The Scarsdale station of the New York Central Railroad in 1896. A new station, in the Tudor style of architecture, was erected in the early 1900s. (Photo, Hal Costain; courtesy of the Scarsdale Public Library)

The opening of real estate offices was one indication of the changes ahead for Scarsdale. This photograph of the North End Land Improvement Company was taken in about 1900. (Courtesy of the Scarsdale Public Library)

These three houses, all built by the Collet Construction Company in the 1920s, illustrate the different levels of status that existed in Scarsdale. The first house (*right*) was erected in the Arthur Manor section for Henry Szaniawski, a Polish immigrant who operated a tailor shop in the local business district (from the uncopyrighted pamphlet, "Construction by Collet"). The second (*p. 114, top*), a demonstration home in the Berkley subdivision, was later purchased by Charles A. Perera, an eye surgeon and member of the medical faculty of Columbia University (from "Construction by Collet"). The third (*p. 114, bottom*) is the garden view of the Lucius R. Eastman residence, a 23-room mansion on 9½ acres bordering Mamaroneck Road. Eastman was the president and chairman of the board of The Hills Brothers Company, importers of dried fruits and coffee. Although his heirs tried to keep the property intact, the opposition of neighboring property owners in 1962 convinced the zoning board of appeals to prevent its use for a music school. Since there were no other buyers, the property was subdivided and the mansion demolished in 1968. (Courtesy of the Scarsdale Public Library.)

Two views of the Scarsdale business district in the 1920s. The construction of the East Parkway Building (*to the right in top photograph*) set the standard for the rest of the district. For a time, even Scarsdale's gasoline stations conformed to the Tudor style of architecture. While the buildings in these pictures look very similar today, a memorial to those who served in World War II takes up most of the land at Boniface Circle (*bottom photograph*). This is also the site where the village board used to permit a committee, representing eight area churches, to display a crèche every holiday season.

The water tower on Garden Road. Its construction was delayed for four years in the 1920s while a neighboring property owner opposed it in court. The steel water tank cost $44,704; the decorative masonry work, $63,106. (Photo, John Gass; courtesy of the Scarsdale Public Library)

Rowsley, the home of the Scarsdale Woman's Club. The club's proposed purchase of this small estate divided its members in 1927. While opponents thought its acquisition would detract from the club's original emphasis on civic action, advocates said that Roswley would give the club "an air . . . it needed." The advocates won the vote, but the opponents' concerns proved to be well founded. (Photo, Hal Costain; courtesy of the Scarsdale Public Library)

Increased village taxes prompted this wry comment from a local cartoonist in September 1925. (Courtesy of the Scarsdale Inquirer)

The Scarsdale Inquirer

"Entered as second class matter November 18, 1919, at the Post Office at Scarsdale, N. Y., under the Act of March 3, 1879."

Published every Friday by The Scarsdale Inquirer, Inc.

Mrs. Robert R. Updegraff
President

Mrs. Guy Wellman
Treasurer

Mrs. Allan Richardson
Secretary

Ruth Nash Chalmers
Editor

Ruth Gardner McClare
Associate Editor

Harriette Mason Chalmers
Advertising Manager

Owned by the Scarsdale Woman's Club

Subscription per year, $3.00; single copy, Seven Cents

Office: 201-203 Harwood Building
Telephone Scarsdale 624

Communications and Advertising Copy must reach us not later than Wednesday noon. All communications should be sent direct to the office of The Scarsdale Inquirer, Scarsdale, N. Y.

The familiar masthead of the *Scarsdale Inquirer* appeared with a telling addition, from September 8, 1933, to May 24, 1935. By displaying the blue eagle, the *Inquirer* indicated that it was cooperating with the efforts of the National Recovery Administration to bring the country out of the depression. The *Inquirer*, and the people of Scarsdale, became increasingly critical of the New Deal in the late 1930s. (Courtesy of the Scarsdale Inquirer)

WITH *your* COMPLIMENTS

You send Hitler or Hirohito a bomb with your compliments when you buy a Defense Bond.

SCARSDALE NATIONAL BANK AND TRUST COMPANY

Scarsdale's Oldest Bank

Member Federal Deposit Insurance Corporation — Federal Reserve System — Westchester County Clearing House Association

This dramatic advertisement was only one of many that encouraged the purchase of war bonds in the early months of World War II. (Courtesy of the Scarsdale Inquirer)

118

During the second bond drive held during the war, Scarsdale residents began applying the proceeds of local bond sales toward the purchase of Thunderbolt fighter planes. By 1945 residents had contributed to the acquisition of 125 planes, all of which bore the name of Scarsdale. (Courtesy of the Scarsdale Inquirer)

"OH MY GOSH! — THE TIRES AND THE SUGAR!"

This cartoon comments on a less positive aspect of the behavior of village residents during World War II. According to the *Inquirer* many residents engaged in black market activities and the hoarding of goods in short supply. (Courtesy of the Scarsdale Inquirer)

Scarsdale High School as it appeared in the 1950s. The process of selecting books for the high school library and for choosing speakers at programs held in the high school became the subjects of an intense campaign in the late 1940s and early fifties, spearheaded by a group of local anticommunists. (Courtesy of the Scarsdale Public Library)

These two cartoons (*right*), the top from the original *Life* mazagine, the bottom from the *New Yorker*, illustrate Scarsdale's notoriety among the general public.

120

"Good Heavens. My shoes must be in Scarsdale."

By permission of Henry T. Rockwell

"Let's hope, Lucille, that our decision hasn't been too hasty."

Drawing by Ziegler; © 1979. The New Yorker Magazine, Inc.

121

CHAPTER 6

The Press of National Events

Although in the history of many communities the year of the stock market crash, 1929, marked a decisive turning point, in Scarsdale 1933 appeared to be an even more pivotal year. Before that time, discussions of zoning, traffic planning, education, and the nonpartisan system preoccupied the public. The local newspaper and public records alluded infrequently to the depression, and then often to remark that Scarsdale was faring comparatively well. By 1933, however, the depression had begun to have a significant impact, not so much in displacing residents from their jobs and houses as in causing a rethinking of municipal spending. Moreover, the inauguration of Franklin D. Roosevelt as president and the passage of his New Deal legislation brought about changes that members of the community came to resent, changes in the relationships between the national and local governments and between government and business leaders. Scarsdale, the progressive suburb of the 1920s, the model of what wise planning and willing spending could accomplish, became a naysayer to the national planning and spending of the 1930s. Only gradually, in the course of World War II, would residents of the community put aside their partisan rancor and develop a sense of civic spirit more in accord with the national mood. There was evidence of both selfishness and sacrifice in Scarsdale during the war, as there was in other towns, but in the end the organizational abilities and financial resources of community residents would help to make Scarsdale's contributions to the war effort stand out.

Between 1929 and 1933, as unemployment in the United States increased from 3.2 percent to 24.9 percent, as the gross national product fell from $103.1 billion to $55.6 billion, and as disposable income in the nation dropped from $683 per capita to $362, only a small percentage of Scarsdale families suffered financial calamity. To be sure, there were signs of an economic downturn. The cost of houses declined, and so did the amount of new construction in Scarsdale. Residents, experiencing reductions in salaries and lower profits from dividends, cut back on expenditures for entertainment and travel. Some families faced serious hardship and needed charity or welfare to get through the hard times. But, observers agreed, Scarsdale was surviving the depression relatively unharmed.[1]

Perhaps the housing market best reflected both the fall-off in the local economy and its continuing strength. In fiscal 1925–26, at the height of the building boom, the village government issued 300 permits for the construction of new houses. In 1932–33, in the depths of the depression, that figure was down to 13. Yet, over the course of the eleven years from 1930 through 1940, 781 new residences were completed, along with 16 business buildings and 8 apartment houses. These new buildings were not sitting vacant, but were purchased by buyers whose presence in the community helped to increase the population from 9,690, in 1930, to 12,966, in 1940. Most people welcomed such signs of growth. Reflecting a change in mood from the 1920s, the *Scarsdale Inquirer* labeled even the building of stores and apartments "a welcome sight, . . . however much we may prize our rural scene." In the opinion of the *New York Times*, building in Scarsdale only made sense. Repeatedly in the 1930s the *Times* lamented the "shortage of homes" in the Scarsdale area and the need for investment in what was clearly a stable market.[2]

Just as the decline in construction signaled a downturn in the local economy, so did the new concern for unemployment. Although a temporary committee, organized in November 1930, found unemployment in the Scarsdale area "little worse than ordinary around this time," a survey conducted sixteen months later came up with different, but not particularly grim, results. Out of the 1,249 households responding to the questionnaire, eighty-six people were unemployed, and twelve families were in urgent need. The survey, sponsored by the local American Legion Post, also uncovered twenty-one unfilled permanent jobs and ninety-three temporary jobs with pledges of short-term job expenditures amounting to $34,200. Yet the jobs did not always suit the skills of the men who needed them. To counter that problem, the American Legion secured space in the *Scarsdale*

Inquirer. Under the caption, "These Scarsdale Men NEED JOBS," it listed the qualifications of six residents: an accountant, a draftsman, a chemist, a textile salesman, a personnel manager, and an advertising executive who had been out of work for eighteen months. The advertisement also listed two telephone numbers, one in New York City, the other in Scarsdale, and urged readers to "pass along any 'tip' or 'lead.' "[3]

Although the Legion's ad did not identify the unemployed men by name, the curious could easily have surmised who they were. Indeed, the description of the advertising "idea man" concluded, "Advertising men of Scarsdale should know this neighbor."[4] Yet, in a community where success was so highly valued, some individuals would have done whatever they could to obscure their financial misfortune. In other words, the Legion's survey probably undercounted the number of unemployed, but by how much was uncertain.

The need for discretion in dealing with victims of the depression was a point emphasized by the community service committee of the Scarsdale Woman's Club. The committee aimed to help those "who have never known want before, who are temporarily out of funds, those who do not want charity and yet do not know where to turn." By and large, in Scarsdale, such individuals were white-collar workers with sufficient financial assets to disqualify them for welfare. Still, they needed money to pay for their mortgage, for medical expenses, or for food. In every case, community service, as a private organization, could adjust the amount of assistance to "particular needs." For example, families accustomed to a high standard of living would be taught how to get by on a more modest level of expenditure, but in the process of adjustment, the committee could support the family on "a higher minimum standard" than that generally permitted on public welfare.[5]

In fiscal year 1933–34, community service had a budget of $3,044.37 and aided twenty-six families consisting of 101 individuals. No one, it emphasized, aside from the chairman of the group and its social worker, knew which residents received assistance. As a result, community service achieved "the maintenance of morale through a minimum of humiliation." A spokeswoman explained, "It is certainly far less humiliating for a family to receive help in this way than when friends meaning to be kind raise private funds." This, she continued, caused "a spread of the news of the financial upheaval and the good intentions become the messengers of misfortune." The community service committee lived up to its name, helping people in Scarsdale in a way that was sensitive to the suburb's standards and values— and its fears.[6]

Community service did not meet all the community's financial needs during the depression. Some Scarsdale residents sought and received public welfare. Up to 1947, welfare payments in New York State were primarily the concern of the local and county governments, with the state government providing partial subsidies and setting general standards to determine eligibility. In the mid-1930s, in order to qualify for welfare, a person had to have exhausted all his or her cash resources, including the ability to borrow on any insurance. In addition, the state required an investigator to visit the applicant's residence, to inquire about the value of the home and its contents, and to determine the ability of family, friends, churches, and other organizations to assist. In fiscal 1935–36, approximately thirty families in Scarsdale convinced local authorities of the propriety of granting them home relief. That year the town government spent $6,176 on such relief, more than in any other year of the decade, and the state reimbursed the community for over half of its expense. Clearly, relief costs were not draining the municipal budget. During the same year Scarsdale spent $12,904 on snow removal and $55,925 to collect and dispose of garbage and trash. The net expenditure for home relief and institutional care amounted to 0.6 percent of the combined village, town, and school board budgets, while at the same time neighboring communities were spending a larger proportion of their budgets on welfare. In White Plains, welfare expenditures amounted to 20 percent of the total budget, and in New Rochelle, 10 percent. Those statistics provided one more indication that, although some Scarsdale families endured hardship during the depression, the community as a whole fared relatively well.[7]

With less than one household in sixty-seven thrown on the local welfare rolls, compared to one in six for the state, it was not surprising that village residents supported President Herbert Hoover's approach to ending the depression. Hoover believed in voluntary, cooperative efforts to find jobs for the unemployed and in the use of private charity to complement local welfare spending. In Scarsdale, the American Legion's unemployment survey, which was undertaken with the blessing of the village board, and the activities of the community service committee, which were supported by bridge games, mite box collections, jewelry sales, and fund-raising drives, followed through on Hoover's principles. In Scarsdale such programs succeeded in alleviating the worst of the suffering, but in other towns with higher rates of unemployment and lower levels of income, Hoover's emphasis on local self-help did not meet the people's needs, and the depression grew far worse.[8]

As president, Hoover also wanted to curtail public expenditures in order to permit a reduction in taxes while achieving a balanced budget. Coming under increasing pressure from Congress and the nation to provide federal loans to big business and to localities for public works and relief, he found it necessary in 1932 to abandon the goal of retrenchment.[9] Yet the budget-tightening he and most traditional economists advocated was applied in Scarsdale with one difference. There, the village and school boards reduced the salaries and wages they paid their employees, not the services they rendered to residents.

The question of the level of government costs had preoccupied local voters back in the early 1900s when Scarsdale was beginning to change from a predominantly rural community to a suburban one. By the 1920s residents had come to accept demands for more village services, more expenditures, and more taxes. Although they joked and philosophized about their high taxes, they seemed to agree that what they paid to the local government came back to them in both the quality of the services they received and the value of the real estate they owned.[10]

With the onset of the depression, residents no longer viewed the high cost of their government with equanimity. They wanted lower taxes, but they refused to accept a curtailment of municipal services and even refused to rule out new expenditures. They thought a substantial cut in the tax rate could come from reducing the wages of village employees. In 1932–33, the same year the village spent $35,000 on a second incinerator, the trustees cut the wages of all employees by 5 percent. For the following fiscal year, they proposed further reductions in wages: 19 percent for administrators, 10 percent for laborers, 5 percent for police and firemen. Those reductions would produce a $70,000 saving, and permit a drop in the tax rate from $7.209 to $6.02.[11]

Some residents considered that decrease insufficient. In April 1933, a self-appointed citizens' budget committee, consisting of two former village presidents, a former town supervisor, and fourteen other prominent citizens, appeared before the village board. They demanded wage cuts to reduce the budget an additional $24,000. Mayor Malcolm Pirnie asked the committee to clarify one point: did its members want "the same services, . . . including the same waste disposal service, the same fire and police protection, and similar services with the reduced budget?" William Walker Orr spoke for the committee. Pointing to the cuts occurring in business, he said that a reduction in wages could be made "without impairing the efficiency of our village in any way."[12]

In the debate during the weeks that followed, most residents opposed further reductions in the budget. In a letter to the newspaper, a former mayor, Warren W. Cunningham, underscored the enormity of the cuts proposed by the committee. The village engineer would face a 36 percent reduction in salary, while laborers employed by the village would receive little more than they would on relief. The newspaper focused on the issue of justice. In an editorial on the subject it asked, "Is it entirely fair for the citizens of Scarsdale to continue to demand exactly the same services which they had in times of prosperity and then to pay substantially less for them?" Citing the salaries paid to police and firemen, the newspaper continued, further reductions would be appropriate only if village workers had received "boom wages" in "boom times." At the end of April, the trustees rejected the proposals made by the citizens' budget committee. They were defeated on the basis of arguments that could have been made, though to a lesser degree, against the original budget. The taxpayers sought a reduction in costs without any reduction in their own comfort. They agreed that the village should reduce the salaries of its employees. They disagreed about the amount of the cut.[13]

During the depression the desire to reduce expenditures also affected educational spending, although for only a couple of years. The school board cut the budget from $702,661.58 in 1931–32 to $679,026.23 in 1932–33. The following year the board trimmed an additional $7,300, though after that the budget rose consistently until 1939–40, when it reached $921,391.08.[14]

Throughout the depression, members of the school board tried to balance the immediate need for tax relief against the long-term goal of maintaining high standards. They went ahead with a program to build additions to the schools to take advantage of the "present low costs of construction." They purchased needed equipment and maintained proper care of the buildings to prevent "a disproportionate increase" in future expenses. They were also generous toward Scarsdale's own. Residents who for "financial reasons" had to leave the school district and lease their property to others were allowed to let their children remain in the schools without paying the usual fees.[15]

It was the teachers who bore the brunt of the cutbacks. Their relationship to the community had never been close. In 1920 a member of the school board said that residents paid more attention to athletics and architecture than to cooperating with the teachers. Throughout the twenties and early thirties, the budget reflected those priorities. Although Scarsdale spent more per pupil than other communities on total educational costs, including the construction and maintenance of school buildings, support for student activities, the provision of books and classroom supplies, as well as the cost of instruction, the salary scale for teachers was comparatively low. In 1928 the teachers in Scarsdale earned an average $2,276, about $800 less than the teachers in Bronxville. After repeated pleas from Supervisory Principal Ralph Underhill, who was finding it hard to secure good teachers, the school board lifted teachers' salaries. When jobs were scarce a few years later, however, the board had the teachers at its mercy. In 1932 it approved a wage cut of close to 10 percent. It then increased the rents for Maple Lawn, a boarding house established for teachers because of the scarcity of rooms in Scarsdale and the high cost of commuting. When the teachers protested, the board of education closed the house.

The teachers had not seen the end of their troubles, for the budget cuts of 1932 had failed to satisfy a number of voters. According to Cleveland A. Dunn, the vice-president of a silver firm, since most residents had suffered reductions in salary of 25 to 50 percent, "why not the teachers whose jobs are firm?" The teachers pointed out that many of them were already living with sizable deficits and that their salaries were lower than those of teachers in comparable suburbs. But popular pressure triumphed. Again in 1933 the board cut salaries by 5 percent. The taxpayers had in their own view secured "a real saving" without curtailing the quality of the education they provided for their children.[16]

Scarsdale's reliance on Hooverian principles in the policies of its school and village boards underscored the obvious: that local voters would continue to support the Republican Party in the presidential election of 1932. Scarsdale had sided with the Republican nominee in every presidential election in the twentieth century, except for the three-way race of 1912. That year the Republican incumbent, William Howard Taft, had gained the endorsement of the *Inquirer* but received only 90 votes in Scarsdale, compared to 141 for former President Theodore Roosevelt, now the candidate of the Progressive Party, and 121 for the Democrat Woodrow Wilson. In 1916 Scarsdale had returned to the Republican fold and, in the presidential elections of the 1920s, nearly three-fourths of the voters in the community had successively cast their ballots for Warren G. Harding, Calvin Coolidge, and Herbert Hoover. By 1932, the nation that had elected those Republicans president was in a different situation and mood, but the voters of Scarsdale did not change their political loyalties. While people across the country gave Franklin D. Roosevelt 57.4 percent of the popular vote and people in New York State as a whole gave him 54.6 percent of the vote, people in Scarsdale gave Hoover 76.6 percent of their votes. Specifically a total of 3,440 village residents cast ballots for Hoover, whereas only 1,065 voted for the man who became the thirty-second president of the United States.[17]

Nevertheless, residents of the village seemed willing to give Roosevelt the opportunity to show what he could accomplish. From 1933 through early 1935, they cooperated with his programs. After that they grew increasingly critical of the programs and increasingly bitter toward the president himself. Eventually the people's negative views of the New Deal would color their feelings concerning the administration of local matters. Residents had reduced municipal salaries in the early 1930s. In the late 1930s they adopted a conservative policy toward municipal spending in general.

After Franklin Roosevelt became president on March 4, 1933, he worked with Congress to establish programs aimed at fighting a number of economic problems. Some of these programs, for example, the Agricultural Adjustment Administration, the Civilian Conservation Corps, and the Tennessee Valley Authority, had little impact on Scarsdale. Others, including the bank holiday, the National Recovery Administration, the Federal Housing Administration, and the public works programs, affected the community in varying ways.

The bank holiday caused a minimum of inconvenience and commotion for the people of the village. Since the new governor of New York, Herbert Lehman, had suspended banking operations in the state on March 4, Roosevelt's order of March 5 simply carried out nationwide what Lehman and thirty-seven other governors were already trying to accomplish. Their aim was to prevent further runs on banks by closing them until the hysteria had subsided and by providing them with government assistance and guidelines.[18]

Although the three banks in the Scarsdale area—the Scarsdale National Bank, the Caleb Heathcote Trust Company, and the Hartsdale National Bank—had not been subject to panicked withdrawals, they abided by the orders of their governor and president. They accepted no deposits in regular accounts, permitted no withdrawals except for the purchase of necessities, and negotiated no new loans. Yet their doors remained open during most of their normal hours, and they performed such useful functions for their patrons as cashing small checks for food and medicine, furnishing change, and accepting cash from stores and businesses in special trust accounts. On Sunday night, March 12, after Congress had passed an emergency banking measure, Roosevelt announced that all banks with sufficient liquid assets could resume normal business, and three days later the banks in the Scarsdale area did just that. Yet, although they had not been in danger of failing, they seemed to have benefited from the president's policy. Shortly thereafter all three banks could report that their deposits had substantially increased.[19]

The bank holiday lasted less than two weeks, but the National Recovery Administration survived for nearly two years. Approved by Congress in 1933, the NRA was supposed to bring order to the nation's troubled economy. Under the NRA, representatives of management, labor, and consumer groups for each of the nation's manufacturing and service industries met to draw up a code for that industry. The codes established production quotas, set prices, determined wages and hours, and presumably had the force of law.

Although the NRA represented a major departure from classical views of free enterprise, its establishment did not bring protests in Scarsdale. No doubt, some skeptics were reassured when prominent citizens became active in various aspects of NRA operations. For example, Orion H. Cheney, a founder of the Scarsdale National Bank, directed the drafting of the code for the contractors' industry; Scarsdale's Republican mayor, Malcolm Pirnie, was an assistant deputy administrator for construction and building materials, and John M. Hancock, also a Republican and a member of the village board of trustees, served as a personal aide to General Hugh Johnson, the man in charge of the NRA. In any case, local businessmen were quick to pledge to cooperate with the president in shortening working hours while shoring up wages. Within two weeks of the program's inception, the proprietors of 106 local business firms had signed the blanket recovery pledge and had received a blue eagle to display in their windows. They quickly began featuring the eagle in their advertisements as well. Grocers, car dealers, tailors, printers, milk distributors, and clothing store managers—all seemed eager to prove "We do our part."[20]

The drive to enlist local merchants had already begun when the Scarsdale Rotary Club called a meeting to organize a support committee for the recovery campaign. Representatives of the Town Club, the Woman's Club, and other civic organizations as well as the local clergy, were included on the committee. The committee intended to complete the recruitment of local businesses in the NRA program, to elicit pledges of support from consumers, and to investigate charges of code violations.[21]

For a few months the committee performed its task with enthusiasm. It found some signs that the program was succeeding, that some of the unemployed were acquiring jobs as a result of the emphasis on spreading work. It also heard rumors of code violations—presumably some businesses were dismissing workers rather than raising their wages to the $14.00 weekly minimum. Most of all, its role was one of exhortation. "Let's All Share— To Bring Back Prosperity!" said one committee-sponsored advertisement. Another read, "President Roosevelt has done his part. . . . Now YOU DO SOMETHING! Buy Something—buy Anything . . . This old world is starting to MOVE!"[22]

When, despite the haranguing, economic conditions did not improve dramatically, the committee and the community seemed to tire of the NRA campaign. Although the presence of the blue eagle in ads and store windows stood witness to the official continuation of the program, merchants were again appealing to customers on the basis of the quality and price of their products, not on the basis of one's patriotic duty to buy.

On May 24, 1935, the blue eagle made its last appearance in the ads on the pages of the *Scarsdale Inquirer*. Three days later in an unanimous decision, the Supreme Court declared that the establishment of industrial codes involved an unconstitutional delegation of the law-making powers of Congress. The court stated further that the interstate commerce clause did not allow federal regulation over all aspects of the nation's economy, that some businesses were limited to intrastate operation and thus were not subject to federal control. The NRA was dead; and given the Court's interpretation of the commerce clause, other aspects of Roosevelt's New Deal seemed threatened. In a mild editorial, the *Scarsdale Inquirer* endorsed the court's decision. If the court's action produced any stronger displays of emotion in the community, those displays went unrecorded.[23]

Although the bank holiday and the NRA required the participation of banks and businesses, other New Deal programs enlisted voluntary support. For example, the Federal Housing Administration made long-term, low-interest loans available through private lending institutions to people who wanted to purchase new houses or to remodel old ones. The *Scarsdale Inquirer* noted approvingly that the plan did not undermine the free enterprise system. "It merely gives the individual a chance to borrow money . . . in order to give his family the house which they need." As in the case of the NRA, a local committee was established to help bring the program to the attention of the community. This committee proved to be quite active, conducting a canvass of the community in order to gauge the demand for construction funds and providing free consultation with an architect to residents planning to remodel their houses. Between July 1, 1934, and March 15, 1935, individual homeowners and contractors spent $1,066,870.91 on construction work in Scarsdale. According to the *Inquirer*, that figure put Scarsdale "far ahead of any other Westchester community in the revival of the building industry." Yet only a small part of the money, specifically $28,529.54 of the $222,170.91 spent on remodeling, was guaranteed through the FHA. Either local homeowners wanted to avoid paying the commission charged on FHA remodeling loans (a maximum of $5 per $100 borrowed), or they needed more money than the $2,000 ceiling on such loans permitted.[24]

During the course of the New Deal, the federal government also made combinations of grants and loans available to localities for public works. Because participation in most of the public works programs was a voluntary matter, requiring an application for each project from the local government, this issue elicited more debate in Scarsdale than any of Roosevelt's other economic programs. Moreover, the debate changed in tone as the attitudes of village residents toward the president changed. In 1933, most residents were willing to accept federal funding, five years later they were not.

Shortly after the establishment of the Public Works Administration, in June 1933, the mayor of Scarsdale, Malcolm Pirnie, announced that the village board had been studying "needed public improvements," including the construction of a new village hall, a library, another firehouse, a hospital building, and additions to the schools, "with a view to recommending an appropriate public works program." The mayor pointed out that, while on the basis of local need or even population Scarsdale would not be eligible for large amounts of funding, its location near centers of heavy unemployment made it likely that the village would receive the funds it applied for. In his opinion, village residents ought to agree on an ambitious public building program, in part to provide employment for people outside the village, but mostly to provide improvements at little expense to themselves. With the federal government paying 30 percent of the cost of labor and materials and with a low-interest loan to cover the remaining expenses, Scarsdale could acquire needed facilities at half their cost in the years ahead.[25]

Residents differed in their response to the mayor's announcement. Surprisingly, William Walker Orr, who had led the citizens' fight for budget reductions, supported Scarsdale's participation in the public works program. In doing so, he emphasized not the short-term saving to the community, but the long-term impact on the nation's economy. Stimulating the construction industry through federally subsidized local projects would increase the demand for materials used in construction. It would give more men jobs and therefore more money to spend. Most of all, it would help to produce a change in the mood of the people of the nation and eventually cause an increase in private investment. "This industry if started would exert more surely than any other the psychological effect necessary for a foreward movement. . . . If we get that," said Orr, "all Scarsdale citizens, whether living by salary, rentals, dividends, or interest payments, will benefit."[26]

Other residents expressed a more conservative view. A former mayor, Fred Lavis, attacked the national government's "orgy of spending borrowed money" and urged the village to renounce the chance to acquire some "easy" cash. He reminded residents of the recent efforts of their village board "to cut the budget to the bone as we saw it" and questioned the logic of adding up to a million dollars "to our funded debt and future taxes." Cleveland A. Dunn agreed. He denounced "'improvements' . . . as mere luxuries . . . which do nobody any good except those who live at the taxpayers' expense." "The way to help bring back normal times," he added, "is to do everything possible to reduce taxes, so that instead of the authorities spending our money, we can get a chance to spend our money our own way."[27]

In 1933, Lavis and Dunn expressed a minority viewpoint. When the leaders of Scarsdale's civic associations and the members of the village board met to agree on a list of public works projects, there were questions raised concerning the practicality of certain projects, but only one of the twenty-seven residents present questioned the idea of using federal funds. On September 30, 1933, the village board voted to apply to the PWA for $74,000 to support the construction of some sanitary sewers, storm drains, and culverts. Slightly more than one year later, Scarsdale formally received the combination grant and loan.[28]

During the course of the 1930s, the village board applied for and received both additional funds and free labor to build more sewers and drains and to conduct some miscellaneous road work. In 1939 the board estimated the total cost of the projects at $736,203, of which $377,455 had come from federal or state coffers.[29] Yet the village board never applied for federal funding to support the building of the items first mentioned—a village hall, a public library, a firehouse, a hospital, or a school. The board never spelled out its reasoning in the matter, but it appeared that the projects funded had two advantages over the projects that were initially considered. Sewers, drains, and roads were essential to the preservation of public health and to the protection of private property. They had to be built and maintained—the sooner the better—and it was wise to do so at the lowest possible cost to local taxpayers. In addition to being essential, such projects had a second advantage. Once built, they were inconspicuous. Consequently, they would not stand as lasting reminders to the public at large that Scarsdale had deigned to accept funds from the federal government. That consideration grew more important as local residents grew more disaffected from the Roosevelt New Deal.

Up to 1936, the local newspaper and public records contained only occasional indications of anti-Roosevelt feeling. An Independence Day editorial, in 1934, calling for a return to America's traditional individualism, objected to the "regimentation of society by governmental forces" and described the United States as the most "restricted . . . country in the world which is not controlled by a dictator." The following year, the *Inquirer* printed a long story featuring a resident named George W. Baekeland, a vice-president of the Bakelite Corporation and chairman of the New York organizing committee for a group called the Crusaders. The Crusaders aimed to preserve the Constitution of the United States and to oppose the New Deal and other "radical and communistic tendencies." Appealing particularly to businessmen, Baekeland charged that the New Deal was causing the depression to continue. Because of Roosevelt's unpredictable efforts "to control business, bankers, and everyone else," business was "naturally . . . repressed and discouraged."[30]

The kind of statement that appeared occasionally before 1936 became habitual from that year on through the outbreak of the war. During the course of the 1936 presidential campaign, Herbert McKennis—a former chairman of the Scarsdale Democratic Town Committee, a former vice-chairman of the County Democratic Committee, a member of the village board from 1932 through 1935, and the current police justice for Scarsdale—publicly proclaimed his intention to vote for the Republican candidate, Alfred M. Landon. "My Democratic philosophy," McKennis explained, "is entirely opposed to the New Deal philosophy. The argument that the New Deal has helped the common man is a sham and a delusion." Another resident, Albert Reese, said that creating "a supermonopoly called the state" would not solve the problems of corporate abuse. In colorful language he predicted that Roosevelt's re-election would lead to more regulation, more coercion, and eventually totalitarianism. "For then we shall goose-step to orders from Washington. We shall march in seven-league boots to the same tragic destiny that has overtaken Italy, Russia, Germany, Austria, and is about to overtake Spain." The heavy majority of local residents agreed with Reese that a second term for Roosevelt was "the wrong road to take." On November 3, only 23.7 percent of village voters cast their ballots for the president. His margin in New York State was 60.7 percent, and in the country at large it was 60.8.[31]

Three months after his re-election, Roosevelt proposed a piece of legislation that his opponents in Scarsdale interpreted as confirming their worst fears. Using the argument that some Supreme Court justices were too old to deal expeditiously with the cases before the court, the president asked Congress for the power to appoint a new justice, up to a maximum of fifteen, for every member of the court whose age exceeded seventy. Roosevelt described the measure as "court reform." His critics, bringing forth evidence that the court was not behind in its work, labeled it "court-packing." To residents of Scarsdale the lesson was plain. As a former village trustee put it, "The president wants more power, he wants all the power of control over us that he can get, and he will try to gain that power by whatever means."[32]

On February 15, 1937, fifty-seven prominent citizens, including six Democrats, called a mass meeting "to consider and take appropriate action on the recent proposal of the president of the United States to enlarge the Supreme Court." By the margin of 548 to 18, those who attended the meeting voted to "record their emphatic opposition to the content and method of the president's proposal . . . and [to] urge and entreat their representatives in the Congress vigorously to oppose by all fair means in their power the passage of the president's program or any compromise on it."[33]

Although Congress blocked the proposal, its introduction by the president succeeded in hardening opinion in Scarsdale against him. Indeed, it was after the confrontation over the composition of the court that village residents began viewing any use of federal monies with suspicion. For example, in 1938 a man who signed himself "An Old-Fashioned American" condemned Scarsdale's reliance on the Roosevelt administration for its sewer-building project. "Can't we see," he asked rhetorically, "that when as a well-to-do community, we join the hand-out line, we are actually supporting the very bureaucracy we individually condemn?"[34] The village government was already committed to building more sewers with federal assistance, but when a local organization proposed using federal monies for a new project, the debate became intense.

The incident that brought the issue to the fore was the decision of the Scarsdale Girl Scout Council, with the support of the village board, to apply to the Works Progress Administration for workers to build a central meeting place for the Girl Scouts. The members of the council explained that the use of WPA labor would lower the cost of the project by $6,000, a sum that would otherwise have to be raised through private donations. Council members assured village residents that they had "no desire to take sides on any question of national policy or politics" and agreed to abide by community sentiment.[35]

Such sentiment was not long in coming. In a letter filled with allusions to "the hardy, independent, and courageous men and women" who had settled Scarsdale, Gertrude Torrey asked the Girl Scouts to dedicate their lives to the pioneer tradition. "Build only as you can with your own efforts and those of your many friends. Give service to your country rather than receive from it at the fountain of tax-paid plenty. . . . Be American—independent and unafraid." Another letter, titled "Goose-Step, Girl Scouts," said, "Some one must break this vicious spiral . . . toward complete regimentation. Why not Scarsdale, Scout House or no Scout House?" A third resident was more direct: "I am in favor of the Girl Scout House if it is built without WPA funds. I won't give it a cent, however, if they use the WPA." Less than a week after the controversy had arisen, the members of the Girl Scout Council reversed their earlier decision. They agreed to raise the funds for the building entirely through private subscriptions.[36]

A few months later the village was prepared to view the affair in a humorous light. The annual Town Club show included a skit entitled "Little Red Girlie Scout." Complete with a woodsman who slew the wolf to save Girlie Scout as well as her grandmother, the skit came to a climax with a song to a tune from "The Wizard of Oz":

> Ding Dong the Wolf is dead.
> Which old Wolf?
> The federal Wolf.
> Down with the WPA!
> We won't take a cent
> From the old government.
> But double taxes we will pay.[37]

As residents renounced the use of federal grants, they began to mull over the local implications of public spending. For a time they were willing to countenance large-scale spending for civic improvements. In early 1937, by a margin of 184 to 32, the voters approved a bond issue of $875,000 to build an addition to the high school. The new wing would house an auditorium, cafeteria, gymnasium, and school library and provide rooms for biology, home economics, and music.[38]

Around the same time residents began seriously to consider building a new library and village hall. In the opinion of the

Scarsdale Inquirer, the need for both facilities was "self-evident." Since its establishment in 1928, Scarsdale's library had been "temporarily" located at Wayside Cottage. A clapboard building dating back to around 1717, the cottage was a charming example of colonial architecture but too small and too much of a firetrap to house a public library. Similarly the village offices had been lodged in a building never intended for that purpose. The existing hall had been built as a school, back in 1905. A plain, box-like structure, it seemed satisfactory when the village acquired it in 1919, but by 1937 it no longer suited village needs or standards.[39]

Mindful of those and other village requirements, the members of the board of trustees brought forth a plan, in April 1937, for the construction of a large civic center that would include not only a village hall and a library but a police headquarters as well. By combining all these facilities within one structure, the board intended to save the taxpayers a minimum of $75,000. Furthermore, they proposed to build the center on property already owned by the village, the northwest side of Butler Field, near the Boy Scout House and the high school athletic grounds.[40]

Property holders both in and outside the area fiercely objected to the proposed location. They argued that the village hall and police headquarters served largely business functions and did not belong in an area zoned for single-family residences. Although they admitted that proximity to the high school made the location suitable for a public library, they preferred to preserve the field strictly for park purposes.[41]

Members of the village board decided that the matter deserved further study. On May 11 they voted to retain two architects and two landscape architects to study possible sites for all the needed facilities. Later that year the experts presented their findings to the village board, which printed the report in a 26-page supplement to the *Scarsdale Inquirer*. The report called for a $452,000 building program with the village hall and library to be housed in separate structures on Butler Field, and the police building to be located on the southwestern corner of the intersection of Post and Fenimore Roads. In addition, the report called for the construction of a firehouse in the eastern part of Scarsdale. It recommended that all the buildings be constructed of brick in the Georgian architectural style.[42]

That report touched off one of the most intense debates in village history. Between December 24, 1937, when Mayor Manvel

Whittemore announced that the board would submit the program to the voters, and March 15, 1938, when the referendum was held, the *Scarsdale Inquirer* devoted 978 inches of space to letters on the subject. Although some of the debate still focused on the location of the buildings, the key issue was an economic one: specifically, should Scarsdale's taxpayers take on twenty more years of bonded indebtedness.[43]

Those who responded affirmatively included John M. Hancock, an investment banker and sometime adviser to the federal government, who had recently served as village mayor. Hancock pointed out that, despite the depression during the preceding eight years, Scarsdale had paid $655,000 on its municipal bonds while enjoying the lowest tax rate in Westchester County. Even if the voters approved the additional $450,000 bond issue, the average debt retirement over the next twenty years would be smaller than it had been over the past ten years. The voters, he implied, should base their decision on rational calculations and not on exaggerated fears for the future.[44]

Four out of five members of the Town Club's special committee on the village building program took a view similar to Hancock's. They calculated that the bond issue in its most costly year would add only 46.4 cents in taxes per $1,000 of assessed valuation. In other words, the average property holder with a $15,000 assessment would pay a maximum of $7.41 a year as his share of the cost for all four buildings.[45]

The dissenting member of the Town Club committee did not find those figures so comforting. Arthur F. Hebard reminded the taxpayers that they had recently committed themselves to another larger bond issue for the addition to the high school. Although the bills for school and village taxes arrived separately, he urged the taxpayers to consider them jointly because "the same purses pay the same bills." Hebard went on to stress that economic conditions had worsened in recent months (a phenomenon historians call the Roosevelt recession) and concluded by labeling the program as "rash and ill-considered in these days of uncertainty." Richard R. Hunter, a vice-president of Chase National Bank and a former village president, agreed. "The general economic structure, village-wise, county-wise, state-wise, and nation-wise," he said, "demands the utmost caution in any spending program."[46]

Inevitably a few residents drew a comparison between the proposed bond issue and the deficit spending of Franklin D.

Roosevelt. One writer said he joined most residents in condemning "the useless spending . . . being indulged in by the current administration in Washington." However, he felt compelled to point out that Scarsdale's own administration had proposed "improvements fully 75 percent of which could be eliminated by utilizing the things we now have." Another resident likened Scarsdale's plan both to Roosevelt's program and to the schemes of the decade's demagogues. He asked the community to

> set an example of economy to those who have been induced to regard the "Huey" plan, the Roosevelt (F.D.) plan, the Townsend plan, the Coughlin plan, and the installment plan as a legitimate method of getting what you want but cannot pay for.[47]

On March 15, 1938, 1,276 owners of assessed property cast ballots in the largest village referendum up to that time. Although the mayor reminded the voters that the costs of construction were currently low, only one aspect of the program, the firehouse, won their approval. The library, police headquarters, and village hall, including three possible sites for the latter, went down to defeat. The margins were stunning. The library bond issue lost by a ratio of 2 to 1, the police building by 4 to 1, while the various sites for the village hall were rejected by margins of 6 to 1 (Butler Field), 10 to 1 (Harwood Park), and 3 to 1 (Post Road and Crane Road). Ever since Scarsdale had incorporated as a village, the voters had never so firmly defeated a measure supported by their board of trustees.[48]

A letter that had appeared in the newspaper before the vote was held indicated the significance of that outcome. Responding to the view that Scarsdale was fine the way it was and that the trustees were forcing the village to change, a former mayor, long active in village matters, made the following statement:

> There's been a lot of talk about preserving Scarsdale, preserving this, preserving that, preserving what makes Scarsdale Scarsdale. I suppose we should have preserved the unpaved roads, preserved the lack of sewers, preserved the private collection and disposal of garbage, preserved the inadequate water supply, preserved the single school house. . . . Scarsdale hasn't been preserved, it has been created, created in the past twenty years.[49]

The comprehensive building program of 1938 was a belated expression of the boldness that had marked village policy during the 1920s. Its rejection by the voters ended an era of creativity in municipal affairs and ushered in an era of fiscal conservatism. Not until 1967 would the village board again seek to finance a community project by calling on the voters to authorize the sale of long-term municipal bonds. Improvements built before that time, the police headquarters and library among them, would be financed largely on the basis of current taxation.

In rejecting the sale of municipal bonds, local residents acted partly for political reasons. They wanted their community to serve as an example of fiscal restraint to counter the alleged squandering of funds occurring in Washington. Yet residents did not limit their political offensive to avoiding further municipal debt and renouncing future federal funds. They established an anti-Roosevelt campaign, which they called the Village Movement.

The Village Movement began in late 1939 with the blessing of the community's most prominent citizens of both parties. Its objectives included a familiar litany of anti-Roosevelt phrases. Members pledged themselves to support individual freedom, the free-enterprise system, local home rule, and governmental simplicity and to resist "governmental encroachments upon legitimate business," "the coercive tactics of all pressure groups," and efforts to destroy "the division of powers which the Constitution of the United States ordains." The movement advertised itself as "an appeal to independent thinkers." By February 1940, it had spawned a similar organization in the Westchester community of Tarrytown and captured the attention of such national figures as Michigan Senator Arthur H. Vandenburg.[50]

In the late spring the movement's efforts were beginning to coincide with those of another political campaign. Ever since 1936, a local resident named Harold Whitcomb had forwarded the name of Wendell L. Willkie, the president of a utilities corporation, as a candidate for president of the United States. Willkie was not a politician. In 1936 he had not even been a Republican. But according to Whitcomb, he was "the best speaker in American business . . . [with] one of the finest records in American business. . . . He is just the kind of mind the country needs." In 1940, Whitcomb's neighbors in Scarsdale agreed. Before the Republican convention met in Philadelphia, at a time when Thomas E. Dewey and Robert A. Taft were considered the frontrunners for the party's nomination, nearly 75 percent of the registered voters in Scarsdale had signed petitions endorsing Willkie. When Willkie won the nomination, Scarsdale's citizens congratulated themselves on their foresight.[51]

If residents were exhilarated by Willkie's nomination, they were appalled by Roosevelt's bid for an unprecedented third term. Local Democrats outdid each other trying to detach themselves from the Roosevelt candidacy. According to William T. Brewster, the president's ease in securing his party's nomination would turn Mussolini and Hitler "green with envy." Arthur F. Driscoll declared, "I do not believe there is any indispensable man." To most local citizens the issue was clear: "traditional Americanism with Willkie or self-perpetuating one-man rule with Roosevelt." They thought they were riding at the forefront of a huge Willkie bandwagon. In Scarsdale, of course, they were. On November 5, 1940, Wendell Willkie won a larger percentage of the vote in Scarsdale, 82.1 percent, than any candidate before or since. Roosevelt received 17.6 percent of the vote in the village. He also lost in Westchester County with 35.1 percent of the vote. Yet he defeated Willkie in New York State by capturing a slim majority of the ballots, and on the national level he was re-elected by a margin of 54.8 percent of the popular vote to 44.8 percent for Willkie. The fact that Willkie had done better than Landon, in 1936, or Hoover, in 1932, was no consolation to village residents who, in the words of the *Inquirer*, were still "breathing hate and destruction against the government."[52]

The bitterness residents felt toward the Roosevelt administration helped to explain part of their ambivalence toward United States participation in the Second World War. Villagers were not more isolationist than other Americans; their support for the internationalist Willkie disproved that. Yet despite their concern for world events, it was not until 1943 that the residents of Scarsdale developed a level of commitment to the war effort equal to the dedication and ability they had displayed in other pursuits. Once extended, that commitment was remarkable, at least in the area of raising funds for the war. By 1945, residents could take satisfaction in the fact that they had lived up to their own high standards of achievement and that, as a result, the nation's victory was in a special way their own.

Between 1934 and 1941, public opinion in Scarsdale, as in much of the United States, shifted from a profound desire to avoid any war that might occur to a willingness to accept United States participation in the war that had begun in Europe and Asia. In the mid-1930s a group of women, marching in the local Memorial Day parade, carried a banner inscribed, "There Shall Be No More War"; and Scarsdale's delegates to the County American Legion Convention encouraged the federal government to adopt measures, like those included in the Neutrality Acts of 1935 through 1937, that aimed to prevent American involvement in a foreign war. But after the outbreak of war over Poland in September 1939, and with Nazi successes in Denmark, Norway, Holland, and Belgium in the spring of 1940, villagers began to express a different view. An editorial entitled "Thinking Peace Through" approvingly quoted the dean of Vassar College:

> If peace means to us nothing but "keeping out of war," then we may expect of life nothing more than a succession of Munich appeasements. . . . Peace, sought just for itself, just to avoid war, may lose the chance of making a fairer and more decent world and in the end prove to be the surest path to war.[53]

Still, most residents wanted to influence the course of the war in behalf of the Allies without sending American troops to fight. In January 1941, six months after the fall of France, thirty-three community leaders sponsored an advertisement in the *Scarsdale Inquirer* calling Congress to approve Lend-Lease assistance "to those countries now holding the Axis tyrants at bay." By "turning our whole production resources and ingenuity" to the task of aiding the Allies, they said, "the Axis powers *will* be defeated." In July 1941, with the Germans on the attack against Russia and the Japanese about to move into southern Indochina, the *Inquirer* reported that most members of Scarsdale's college generation did not want the United States to declare war against the Axis. They agreed on the desirability of sending economic aid and military supplies, especially to Britain, but they did not want the country to send any troops.[54]

During the fall of 1941, village residents seemed to resign themselves to the likelihood of full-scale American intervention. Audiences in the community heard Henry C. Wolfe, author of *The German Octopus*, predict that Japan would strike by mid-December, and William L. Shirer, then a CBS news correspondent, say that Britain and Russia needed American supplies and troops. On November 28, 1941, a number of old and new organizations, including the American Legion, the American Red Cross, the Boy and Girl Scouts, the Daughters of the American Revolution, Bundles for Britain, the Life Line to China, and the Free French, sponsored "a patriotic preparedness rally." The rally was held in the high school auditorium where a gigantic American flag hung stretched across the back of the entire stage. There, nearly 1,000 citizens of Scarsdale listened to John A. Krout, a Columbia professor and a fellow resident. Krout spoke to them about the growth of the United States and how it had depended on the existence of a balance of power to Europe. He discussed the views of Thomas Jefferson, usually the idol of isolationists, and revealed how Jefferson had feared for American interests were Napoleon to be victorious. He then turned to the Napoleons of the present day, Hitler, Mussolini, and the Japanese. "The time is running out," he said. Nine days later, Japanese planes attacked American forces in the Pacific. The United States had entered the war.[55]

In the aftermath of Pearl Harbor, the *Scarsdale Inquirer*, as did newspapers everywhere in the United States, noted that a sense of unity had developed in the village and the nation. "As members of a family draw together in times of trouble, America has drawn together as never before." In the area of home defense, village residents followed through on that sense of common purpose by taking precautions against air raids and acts of sabotage. Some participated in the national air alert system by building and manning a watchtower in the Fort Hill section of the Scarsdale postal district. Others agreed to serve as auxiliary policemen, volunteer firemen, medical assistants, and air raid wardens. All residents became involved to a certain degree. They prepared their houses for use during blackouts by darkening windows and screening lights. They purchased oilcloth hoods to cover the lights on their automobiles. They guarded against the spread of fires by cleaning their attics and cellars and bringing in supplies of sand. They learned where to turn off the gas if the bombs started falling. On a grimmer note, many placed the fingerprints of their children in public files for identification in case of disaster.[56]

In January 1942, six weeks after Pearl Harbor, the numerous wartime drills began. There were simple blackout drills and full-scale air raid drills, night drills, and day drills, announced and unannounced. Most proceeded smoothly, but not with perfect compliance. When a surprise blackout occurred on Tuesday evening, April 7, four homes were left vacant with lights blazing, and three families refused to go along with the drill. When another blackout occurred in December, those in their houses cooperated, but twenty houses were empty, lighted, and locked.[57]

Sometimes the drills included mock incidents requiring the coordination of several volunteer units. The incidents in one drill included the bombing of the north wing of the high school, the blocking of an important road with debris, the breaking of a water main in East Scarsdale, and a serious fire in a Greenacres residence. Even more dramatic was the seizure of the New York Central tracks by a group of pretend saboteurs. All through the southwestern quarter of Scarsdale, the saboteurs fought against members of the state guard, the local police, and the American Legion. Finally, outmaneuvered and outnumbered, they surrendered to the defenders of the community.[58]

Although village residents worked with local, county, state, and federal officials in the matter of home defense, many skirted the recommendations and regulations of the federal government with regard to the purchase of goods in short supply. During the course of the war, the federal government rationed the nation's supply of rubber, sugar, gasoline, coffee, butter, meat, shoes, and other basic commodities. In addition, there were shortages of such other goods as cigarettes, liquor, and chewing gum. How did members of the Scarsdale community respond to the wartime shortages? Time after time the *Inquirer* noted a "disgusting" cycle of behavior on the part of a number of residents. The announcement of impending rationing, despite exhortations from federal officials, would provoke a wave of hoarding. Then, when the rationing went into effect, some residents connived, by lying to the rationing board or by pressuring local merchants, to purchase more than was their due.[59]

The *Inquirer* described such behavior in a tone that grew increasingly shrill. An editorial, written two months after Pearl Harbor, made it clear that the unity of December had vanished. Recognizing that it was "easy" to criticize the administration's handling of the current situation, the newspaper asked, "But is that going to win the war?" The paper went on to attack the widespread hoarding of goods in short supply. "If democracy means nothing but comfort to us," it declared,". . . let's lose the war and have it over with." Somewhat more forcefully the paper stated in May, "It matters not one whit what Scarsdale thinks of Washington. . . . If American citizens are not willing to cooperate in the war effort, . . . our conquerors will teach [us] what sacrifice is." Eight months later the paper was even more indignant. Citing evidence that hoarding was worse in Scarsdale than in other parts of the metropolitan area, the paper said that Scarsdale's "pride" in its "unique[ness]" should turn to "shame." The paper questioned why local families, "just because they have the money, . . . should think it is their right to continue to live as nearly as possible in the way to which they are accustomed, while thousands die of starvation elsewhere." The editorial concluded by quoting the words of Saint Paul, "For many walk . . . whose end is perdition, whose god is the belly and whose glory is their shame, who mind earthly things."[60]

Although not all residents complied fully with federal rationing standards, government regulations had a profound impact on the community. This was particularly true of regulations affecting the use of automobiles. As a result of its restrictive zoning, Scarsdale contained two small business districts inside a large expanse of land that was limited to residential uses. With the community so spread out, residents were accustomed to driving their cars to reach the train, the stores, and the country clubs. When the federal government restricted the sale of tires and gasoline in 1942, and when it banned all nonessential driving in 1943, residents were forced to change their habits. Commuters, who a decade earlier had blocked petitions for bus routes, now rode in buses en route to their trains. Housewives, who used to drive to the store for a single item, now had to plan their shopping with care. Children could no longer count on rides to school or on days at the country club during the summer. For everyone there were fewer social functions and recreational activities. But there were other things to occupy one's time: war work (in victory gardens and Red Cross canteens), housework (now that the servants were working in industry), and community drives.[61]

During 1941 and 1942, residents of Scarsdale seemed to lack enthusiasm for the war-oriented collection drives. Although the village held many drives, including collections of rubber, paper, metal, books, blood, and numerous collections of money, Scarsdale's only record was a humiliating one. Of all the villages in Westchester County, it had the lowest per capita contribution of scrap aluminum, 1.18 ounces compared to 5.26 ounces for Bronxville and 7.10 ounces for North Salem. Scarsdale also failed to reach its quota of $30,500 in the Red Cross Drive of 1942, and belatedly reached a $68,800 target in a combined Community Fund/War Chest Drive that provided funds to twenty-four social welfare agencies close to home, in the nation, and abroad.[62]

In 1943, however, the community's performance in such drives changed. Apparently other residents agreed with the editors of the *Inquirer* who, writing on January 1 of that year, said, "It is about time that Scarsdale took stock of itself. It is about time that . . . [we] woke up to the fact that to talk patriotism is one thing, to practice it another."[63]

The citizens of Scarsdale began practicing a competitive style of patriotism in the Red Cross Drive of 1943. The head of the campaign, Robert S. Gordon, aimed to make Scarsdale "the first community in the nation to go over the top." Gordon lined up 400 volunteers, arranged for heavy publicity, and sent someone to each house in the community on Red Cross Sunday, February 28. By the end of that day, 93 percent of the $52,000 goal was in hand. By the end of the fourth day of the drive, the contributions totaled $53,100. Gordon's "whirlwind campaign" had succeeded. Scarsdale had set a national record and had found its special wartime role. The following year the residents met an $87,500 quota, and in 1945 they raised nearly $90,000 for the Red Cross in one day. During the same three-year period contributions to the Community Fund/War Chest also increased.[64]

Yet Scarsdale's reputation for fund-raising rested more on the sale of war bonds than it did on donations to charities. Although the distinction was important—war bonds were investments after all—Scarsdale's achievement was still striking. The 13,000 residents of the community purchased more than $17,500,000 in government bonds from 1942 through 1945, an average investment of more than $1,345 for every man, woman, and child.[65]

The local war bond drive began conventionally in 1942 with area banks and merchants advertising the value of bonds and squads of so-called Minutemen soliciting pledges. According to the County Trust Company, $18.75 invested in a government bond would enable the country to buy seventy-two dozen bandages, three steel helmets, one field telephone, or one-tenth of a submachine gun. An ad paid for by the Scarsdale National Bank was more dramatic. It depicted an American eagle carrying a bomb with a gift tag attached to it. The tag was inscribed, "With *Your* Compliments." Underneath the picture was the message, "You send Hitler or Hirohito a bomb with your compliments when you buy a Defense Bond." Spurred by such ads, residents cooperated with the government campaign. The Minutemen reported that their household calls were yielding a high percentage of participation. In six months local bond purchases had topped $1,000,000.[66]

Although local support for the first bond drive was undeniable, the second drive of early 1943 generated greater enthusiasm. This drive set as its goal not a monetary figure but something more tangible. Scarsdale would try to become the first community in the country to invest in an entire patrol of planes, specifically nine Thunderbolt fighters. The Thunderbolts, according to drive chairman Gardiner H. Rome, had more speed and firepower than any other fighter plane in the world. With their eight fifty-caliber machine guns, the Thunderbolts delivered "a stream of bullets . . . equal in impact to the force of a five-ton Mack truck hitting an object while going sixty miles an hour." In addition to helping the war effort, the purchase of planes would increase the community's renown. For every $83,000 residents invested in bonds, the name Scarsdale would be painted on the side of a Thunderbolt, along with another name selected by the people of the community.[67]

The Thunderbolt drive tapped the pride of village residents. Within two days they had pledged the money for two planes. Within a week they had purchased a patrol. In a month they had raised enough money to send fifteen Thunderbolts to the United States Air Corps. They named their planes the Scarsdale Scrapper, Rattler, Racer, Blaster, Wasp, Hornet, Tiger, Scorpion, Skylark, Thunderbird, Crusader, Avenger, Challenger, Legionnaire, and the Spirit of Scarsdale. On Memorial Day, 1943, in the course of community ceremonies, the fifteen planes flew over the village. They provided a demonstration not only of formation flying at its most inspiring but also of what the purchase of bonds meant to the country's war effort. In an editorial the *Inquirer* described the planes as "living war bonds."[68]

Up to the end of the war, residents continued to invest in bonds for the purchase of Thunderbolt fighters. They acquired twenty planes in the third bond drive, twenty more in the fourth, twenty-three in the fifth, twenty-two in the sixth, and twenty-five in the seventh, for a total of 125 planes. There was also an increase in the number of individuals who purchased bonds. Back in the first bond drive in 1942, 1,450 residents had participated.

In the seventh bond drive, in June 1945, 4,800 residents bought bonds totaling $4,300,000.[69]

Not surprisingly, that achievement particularly impressed officials at the company that manufactured Thunderbolts. At Memorial Day ceremonies in 1944, after the community had purchased fifty-five planes, the Republic Aviation Corporation, represented by Gordon C. Sleeper, presented a bronze tablet to the people of Scarsdale. Sleeper, a local citizen and high-ranking executive at the company, told the thousands of residents assembled on Butler Field, "No town in America has made greater contributions to the war effort than has Scarsdale. The 22,000 men and women of Republic Aviation . . . are proud of you." From that time on through the end of the war, a sign emblazoned "Thunderbolt Town" hung beneath the name of Scarsdale at the local railroad station.[70]

The war bond drive provided a national outlet for the community's desire to excel. While the return on the money invested was small in interest, it was great in esteem for the community's patriotism and in the recognition of its wealth. In the 1930s, the wealth of many residents had insulated the community from the worst effects of the depression. At that time local attitudes were out of step with national interests. In the 1940s, however, residents strove to place their wealth behind the national effort. As prosperity returned to the country as a whole, the community regained its place as a symbol of what America stood for.

To a degree, it was ironic that a community, reluctant to issue municipal bonds, so heartily supported the national bond issues of 1942 through 1945. Whereas the federal deficits of the depression had brought outcries from village residents, they did not comment on the far larger war-time deficits. That fact reflected local perceptions of the two crises, as well as a shift in federal policy that occurred during the war. Residents of the village viewed the war as a more serious disaster than the depression and thus were willing to suspend their conservative fiscal views. In addition, during the war the national government funneled more of its spending into private corporations. With businesses like Republic Aviation making a large profit, the businessmen of Scarsdale were not likely to complain.[71]

On a more basic level, however, Scarsdale's support for the bond drives of World War II needed no explanation. Surely it was little enough to invest one's money in a cause that required the investment of lives as well.

150

In the course of World War II, 2,025 men and 75 women from the Scarsdale area served in the United States armed forces. Although it is impossible to determine whether, as local residents argued, those figures represented a comparatively large proportion of the population, certain demographic and socioeconomic factors lend credence to the claim. For one, Scarsdale had a larger proportion of men and women in their late teens and early twenties than existed in the general population, because so many young families had moved there during the 1920s. Also, given the upper-middle-class nature of the community, few young men in Scarsdale would have qualified for agricultural or industrial deferments from the draft. Personal drive and community expectations would have affected the number who served as well. World War II was a time of intense patriotism, and many of the young people of Scarsdale would have wanted to prove their devotion to the nation's cause.[72]

Of those who served, seventy-eight died. The number actually seemed far greater. By the second year of the war, the *Inquirer* carried notices almost weekly of one or more young men killed or missing in action. Those notices included people who were not strictly speaking village residents—men who had moved away a few years earlier, men whose wives came from Scarsdale, and men whose families lived in neighboring suburbs that fell within the Scarsdale postal district. All their deaths touched the community. Sadly, as the news of the war grew better, as the Allies mounted their final offensive, the number of young men who died rose higher. Some died in action, like James M. Palmer, a bazooka man killed in the fighting in Germany. Others died in accidents, like Joseph L. Schroeder, whose jeep was struck by a bus in Hawaii. Some were the sons of famous men, like machine-gunner Stephen Hopkins, killed in the island-hopping in the Pacific. His father, Harry L. Hopkins, was President Roosevelt's closest adviser. Others came from modest backgrounds, like pilot Frank A. Pezzella, whose plane was shot down near Sardinia. His father was an Italian immigrant. At least one local woman lost her life in the course of military service. Alice E. Lovejoy, a member of the Women Airforce Service Pilots, died in a plane crash off the coast of Texas.[73]

As those on the home front followed the progress of the war, the exploits of two young pilots captured their attention in a special way. The first was John van Kueren Newkirk, more commonly known as "Scarsdale Jack." A squadron leader in the

Flying Tigers and the first American flier decorated by the British government, Newkirk was credited with downing twenty-three Japanese planes before his death in the fighting in Burma.[74] The other was Edward "Jonesy" Szaniawski. Denied admission to the Army Air Corps in 1940, Szaniawski underwent four eye operations in order to become a pilot. Eventually he commanded three squadrons in more than thirty missions, before he was shot down over Germany in 1944. Szaniawski was captured, sent to a prisoner of war camp, escaped, was recaptured, and escaped again, this time to safety behind Allied lines. Before the end of the war, he had earned the Air Medal with three oak leaf clusters, the Distinguished Flying Cross with two clusters, the Silver Star, and the Purple Heart.[75]

The people at home tried to demonstrate their caring to the men and women in the military. From November 1943, to May 1946, several local organizations provided funds for the publication of the *Home News*, a brief monthly newspaper highlighting what was happening in Scarsdale that was sent free of charge to residents in the armed forces. In addition, some villagers regularly saw off groups of new recruits with hot drinks, sandwiches, and cigarettes, while others entertained the servicemen from New York military bases with an affection appropriate to substitute sons. As the war came to a close, the mayor established a veterans' service committee to ease the young people's adjustment to civilian life.[76]

Yet Scarsdale was slow to recognize its servicemen in a way common to many communities. When a committee of citizens recommended erecting a temporary honor roll listing the names of those in the armed forces, the supervisory boards of the Town Club and the Woman's Club objected on the grounds of utility and aesthetics. They preferred to see the money spent on something useful to the war effort and opposed the construction of "any bill-board type of honor roll" as "undesirable." The American Legion, on the other hand, favored the building of a temporary honor roll, which it described as one of the few feasible ways by which the community could express its gratitude. According to one resident, the younger soldiers, in particular, viewed the "absence of a temporary honor roll" as indicative of a "lack of appreciation" in Scarsdale for the job that they were doing.[77]

Faced with such a division of counsel, the village trustees placed a ballot in the *Scarsdale Inquirer* and called on residents to register their approval or disapproval of the honor-roll plan. Two hundred fifty-five people responded to that request, 174 of whom voiced their approval. Despite the small return, the village board voted on April 27, 1943, to erect a temporary honor roll at Boniface Circle in the Scarsdale business district. At last Scarsdale had a symbol of its concern for the young people in the service, similar to the honor rolls that already existed in towns throughout Westchester County.[78]

The decision to build an honor roll left one matter unsettled, precisely who deserved to be listed. The trustees argued that the list be confined to men and women in military service whose families were currently living within village boundaries, and men and women who had grown up in the village whose parents had moved away no more than two years before they began their military duty. The *Inquirer* considered those standards too narrow. In an editorial, "The Real Scarsdale," it said that every member of the armed forces with a Scarsdale home address, regardless of whether the family residence actually stood inside the village, should be eligible for inclusion, if he or she desired. Eventually the village board yielded to that line of reasoning. In order to pay for the inclusion of 350 names from the larger Scarsdale community, it relied on the proceeds from private donations.[79]

In 1947 the village board approved the recommendations of a committee of citizens for a permanent World War II honor roll: a simple but dignified masonry structure with bronze plaques bearing the names of those who served. The money for the memorial would be raised in the next Community Fund Drive, and as before, the plaques would include the names of servicemen from the larger Scarsdale community. In addition, the board agreed to establish a memorial room in the long-planned-for public library and to set up an endowment for the purchase of books in memory of Scarsdale's wartime dead. This, they believed, would reflect the community's "deep and abiding debt of gratitude" in a way that was useful yet profound.[80]

In the community ceremonies observed during World War II, much was said about "our fellow townsfolk who have entered the service of our country," about "all who have died and will die in a cause dearer than life," and about the sense of national purpose—"no nation is wholly free till all nations are free."[81] Yet local speakers rarely referred to the man who in many

153

communities symbolized the war, President Franklin Delano Roosevelt.

While, after Pearl Harbor, residents of Scarsdale expressed their opposition to Roosevelt less often than they had in the late 1930s, and while they no longer attacked the government's deficit spending, they still resented some of Roosevelt's other policies. His administration's steep taxes on high incomes and the $25,000 wartime ceiling on salaries came in for special criticism. The *Inquirer* claimed that such measures amounted to "a social revolution, and the middle of a war, as Russia and Germany learned in the last war, is not the time for a social revolution." The paper also accused the president of acting on the basis of a "dangerous [fallacy], that riches and democracy do not go together." Thus, even though some of the president's wartime policies benefited big business, such as the guarantee of costs plus a fixed fee for defense contracts, many of the old arguments continued to flare.[82]

In November 1944, village residents again gave a lopsided percentage of their votes to the Republican candidate. Thomas E. Dewey received 76.3 percent of the votes in Scarsdale compared to 23.3 percent for Roosevelt. Nationally, however, Roosevelt succeeded in winning a fourth term as president, although his margin of victory in the popular vote, 7.5 percent, was not as large as it had been in the three previous elections.[83]

Five months later the newly re-elected president died. Bells tolled in Scarsdale as elsewhere, flags on public buildings flew at half mast, ministers eulogized the leader whom so many members of their congregations had opposed. The *Inquirer* went to the heart of the matter:

> All great men have bitter enemies and Mr. Roosevelt had his share of them, but that he was great, no person who had watched him pilot the American nation through the tragedies of the past years would or could deny.

But some observers noted behavior they viewed as inappropriate to the occasion: school children cheering on announcement of the president's death and an absence of flags at private homes during the days of national mourning. One Republican said he was "ashamed" of his fellow citizens of Scarsdale. "Party feeling or no party feeling," he said, "a dead President is worthy of salute."[84]

Victory in Europe came in May 1945, shortly after Roosevelt's death. Victory in Japan occurred in August. The *Inquirer* responded to the news with a sense of renewed consecration: "The victory is only the beginning of the peace and must now be justified. All the best there is in us is still required of us. We have done nothing unless we do all."[85]

Those words echoed the theme of continual striving for excellence that was basic to America's self-understanding and basic to Scarsdale's self-image as well. In 1945, the country had just survived over fifteen years of depression and war. During part of that time, many Americans had questioned whether the United States still merited the title, land of opportunity. They looked at the packed employment gates where thousands vied for a single job and at the abandoned Dust Bowl farms where cotton would no longer grow. They began to question what America stood for and welcomed the efforts of Roosevelt to change the nation's economic system to make it work. But from the perspective of Scarsdale, the American system did work, and the nation's problems were only exacerbated by what they saw as Roosevelt's misconceived efforts to enlarge the government at business's expense. The war helped to bring Scarsdale and the nation together again. Although Scarsdale's experience of the war was a rarefied one—no defense plants, no race riots, no internment camps there—the community's contribution was great in men and money. As the war came to an end and prominent leaders like Henry Luce were speaking of "the American Century" to follow, residents of Scarsdale were certain that their own efforts and values would shape the world as well.

CHAPTER 7

Conservatism and Crisis

The richest town in the world's richest nation—that phrase summed up Scarsdale's claim to distinctiveness in the fifteen years following World War II. As the nation prospered and suburbia boomed, residents took care to preserve Scarsdale's status by tightening local ordinances affecting new housing and by pressuring the village board to dedicate additional properties for open space. At times they pursued opposite policies with equal persistence, adhering to the tenet of pay-as-you-go in village matters while approving large bond issues to support local schools. Basically the postwar era was for Scarsdale a time of conservative consolidation and moderate growth, yet surprisingly it brought to the village a crisis that sorely tested the residents' faith in one another. This crisis manifested on a local level the anticommunist hysteria that swept the United States in the late forties and early fifties. Scarsdale, materially at the height of its glory, was accused of harboring a communist cell.

In 1950, Scarsdale had a total of 13,156 residents, 190 more people than it had had a decade earlier. In the fifties its population climbed over 36 percent to 17,968. The number of inhabitants increased 7 percent in the sixties to 19,229; then, with a decline in family size, the population decreased 8 percent during the seventies.[1]

Although by postwar standards Scarsdale set no records in population growth, it topped the nation in income. The 1960 census revealed that, for 1959, the median family income in Scarsdale was $22,177, while in New York State the median was $6,371 and in the United States $5,660.[2] Of communities in other parts of the United States, Winnetka, Illinois, ranked closest to Scarsdale with a median family income of $20,166. In San

Marino, California, the figure was $16,728; in Millburn, New Jersey, $14,145; in Shaker Heights, Ohio, $13,933; and in Grosse Point Farms, Michigan, $13,119.[3]

Needless to say, Scarsdale's residents were still predominantly upper-middle class. Of the employed males in Scarsdale who were over fourteen years of age, 73.1 percent held professional, technical, managerial, proprietary, or similar jobs compared to 25.4 percent of the employed men in the state and 25.6 percent of the employed men in the New York metropolitan area. Meanwhile, only 7.7 percent of the employed men in Scarsdale worked as skilled or unskilled laborers compared to a state-wide percentage of 42.7 and a metropolitan percentage of 48.4.[4]

Village residents not only held jobs with high socioeconomic status, many had risen to the top of their professions. The 1948 edition of *Who's Who in America* included the names of 170 Scarsdale residents. That figure placed Scarsdale thirty-second among the more than 3,600 communities with residents listed. Moreover, with the exception of Chevy Chase, Maryland, the only communities that ranked ahead of Scarsdale were such large cities as New York, Denver, Chicago, and Dallas, and such university towns as Cambridge, Ann Arbor, Princeton, and Madison. Indeed, the 1948 *Who's Who* listed more residents of the village of Scarsdale than of the entire states of Arizona, Nevada, North Dakota, and Wyoming.[5]

Among the best known residents of the village in the years after World War II were several who moved freely from industry to government. Charles E. Wilson, of Hampton Road, served as president of the General Electric Company, vice-chairman of the War Production Board under Franklin Roosevelt, chairman of the Civil Rights Committee appointed by President Harry S. Truman, director of U.S. mobilization during the Korean War, chairman of the board of W. R. Grace and Company, and president of the People to People Foundation.[6] Malcolm A. MacIntyre, of Mamaroneck Road, served as under secretary of the air force under Dwight D. Eisenhower, president of Eastern Airlines, president of the chemical division of the Martin-Marietta Corporation, a trustee of the Carnegie Foundation, and a director of several companies.[7] Dean Rusk, of Fenimore Road, was president of the Rockefeller Foundation before his appointment by John F. Kennedy as secretary of state. John W. Gardner, of Brite Avenue, headed the Carnegie Corporation before accepting the position of secretary of the Department of Health, Education and Welfare under Lyndon B. Johnson.[8] Other village notables included Arthur S. Meyer, a leading labor mediator; Howard Rusk, a pioneer in the field of rehabilitation medicine; and Kenneth C. Hogate, chairman of the board of Dow Jones and Company, Inc., president of the Barrons Publishing Company, and president of the Financial Press Companies of America.[9]

Although its leading citizens represented both political parties, Scarsdale remained solidly in the Republican camp for the fifteen years following World War II. In 1948, 81.6 percent of Scarsdale's voters cast their ballots for the Republican presidential candidate, Thomas E. Dewey. After that the GOP's proportion of the suburb's presidential ballots declined—to 78.6 percent in 1952, 72.1 percent in 1956, and 64.9 percent in 1960. The drop in the Republican vote probably resulted, at least in part, from the increasing presence in the community of Jews and Catholics, groups that traditionally voted Democratic. Still, it would require the divisive national politics of the 1960s to swing Scarsdale, at least temporarily, into the Democratic column.[10]

With its wealth, stature, and Republicanism, Scarsdale naturally attracted attention. A character in the musical "Guys and Dolls," which opened in 1950, contrasted the sleazy denizens of Broadway to her ideal of a husband. The kind of man she wanted was "a Scarsdale Galahad, the breakfast-eating, Brooks Brothers type" with "strong moral fibre, . . . wisdom in his head, . . . [and a] homey aroma in his pipe." Other allusions to Scarsdale during this period were less poetic and more hyperbolic. In 1949, the *Greensboro* (N.C.) *Daily News* described the community as a place "where Harvard and Columbia degrees are a dime a dozen and where the streets . . . are lined with millionaires." According to the *Richwood* (W.V.) *New Leader*, Scarsdale had "more money per square foot than any other town in the United States." And in 1954, the *American Mercury* referred to Scarsdale as "the gold-plated core of New York's smartest suburb, . . . where Cadillacs run hub-to-hub and the swimming pools are long and deep."[11]

Although even in the postwar years the real Scarsdale did not live up to its image, most residents took satisfaction in the community's reputation for wealth and tried to maintain its high standards. Those standards seemed most vulnerable in the area of housing, especially in view of the intense demand for housing that existed at the end of World War II, the large supply of land that was available for development within the village, and the mass production techniques that developers had begun to apply to residential construction. Under those circumstances villagers recognized that they could no longer depend on ordinances passed a generation earlier to protect their community from the pressures of the housing market. Instead they passed new ordinances to secure the sense of spaciousness, variety, and beauty that had generally marked development in Scarsdale and to require a level of expenditure on new construction that would help keep the community an enclave of the upper-middle class.

Even a desire to aid the veterans could not compete with the goal of maintaining local standards in the area of housing. At the end of World War II, a series of letters in the *Inquirer* pointed to the predicament of former soldiers, men who were now "homeless in their own hometowns." According to an editorial, the residents of Scarsdale had as much responsibility to open their doors to those in need as they would "if enemy bombs had fallen on the countryside."[12] In spite of such rhetoric, only one veteran benefited from the community's postwar compassion. In November 1945, the zoning board of appeals granted a temporary variance that allowed Luke Beckerman and his family to live in the unused doctor's suite of a house in a single-family residence zone. Apart from that incident, local government officials did nothing to alleviate the veterans' housing problems. Instead they rejected further petitions for the establishment of two-family houses and turned down a proposal for the construction of garden apartments on a site near the local business district.[13]

While the village zoning ordinance, as passed in 1922 and amended in the years since then, offered the community protection from the construction of garden apartments and two-family houses, residents feared that builders could still erect one-family dwellings that failed to meet customary Scarsdale standards. In October 1944, fifty-eight homeowners in a largely undeveloped part of the village petitioned the board of trustees to find "some means . . . to protect our section against the erection of low-cost homes." They warned that "such a type of construction" would have "a detrimental effect upon the values of our properties," and added, "That would mean a financial loss to all of us, with no compensating benefit to the village."[14]

Receipt of the petition confirmed the trustees' view that the time had come for a thorough re-evaluation of zoning in Scarsdale. As the first step in the long process of weighing community goals, neighborhood practices, and judicial decisions, the board had already hired a planning expert, Harold M. Lewis. Over the course of the next two years, the board would repeatedly consult with the village manager, the village attorney, the planning commission, and even with Edward M. Bassett, the so-called father of American zoning. Finally, in November 1946, the completely revised ordinance was ready for public discussion.[15]

The ordinance proposed to set policy in a number of areas that the original law had neglected. It would prohibit outdoor displays of food and other merchandise. It would limit the number of gasoline pumps at each filling station. It would require apartment houses, hotels, churches, and other places of assembly to provide appropriate off-street parking.[16]

Most important, in view of the concerns of local residents, the ordinance would incorporate the concept of density zoning. By the end of 1946, the communities of Bronxville, Harrison, White Plains, Garden City, and Greenwich already had density zoning provisions in their ordinances. Under such provisions the one-family residence zone was divided into subsections, each requiring a minimum lot size. In Scarsdale's proposed new ordinance, the Residence A zone, comprising over 97 percent of the town's total area, would become five different density zones, Residence A1 through A5, each with a different minimum lot size. The minimum lot sizes ranged from one acre in A1 to 5,000 square feet in A5. In addition, the ordinance would require minimum frontages of 150 feet, front setbacks of 50 feet, and sideline setbacks of 20 feet for houses built in the A1 zone as compared to frontages of 50 feet, front setbacks of 30 feet, and sideline setbacks of 10 feet for houses built in the A5 zone. Since the purpose of density zoning was to protect the character of a given neighborhood, the board of trustees recommended A1 zoning for the most luxurious sections of Scarsdale (Heathcote, Murray Hill, and the Grange) and A5 zoning for the most modest (Arthur Manor, North End, and Scarsdale Park). It also recommended placing much of the community's undeveloped land in the A2 zone, where the minimum lot size was 20,000 square feet.[17]

Although the trustees anticipated a lively discussion of the proposed revisions, most residents were content to accept the judgment of a special committee of the Town Club appointed to study the law. After the committee endorsed the ordinance as "a plan to protect the future," only a few residents appeared at a public hearing on the subject. The board of trustees formally adopted the revised ordinance on March 11, 1947. In the years that followed, it made only one significant change in the density zoning provisions, the addition of a AA1 zone with two-acre minimum lots, for the properties bordering Heathcote and Sherbrooke Roads and those located in or near the Fenway and Quaker Ridge golf courses.[18]

Perhaps village residents should have viewed the revised ordinance more critically, for they soon came to realize that density zoning would not, in itself, prevent the construction of low-cost houses. Since at least the spring of 1946, plans had been under way for the building of a subdivision, Colonial Acres, in the Quaker Ridge section of the community. At that time the development company, King Ranch Homes, had filed with the village planning commission a map of the subdivision showing the proposed roads and building lots. Not until fall of 1949 did it become clear, however, that the company planned to build the forty-six ranch-style houses all on the same basic plan. With six rooms, one bath, and less than 2,000 square feet of livable floor area, the houses would be small by local standards, although they would be built on the nearly half-acre lots that the zoning law required.[19]

Quaker Ridge residents, perceiving the subdivision as a threat to their property values, pleaded with members of the village board to halt its construction. They decried Colonial Acres as the work of "a speculative builder [who] cares nothing for the community . . . save . . . to reap where he has not sown." Scarsdale, they warned, was peculiarly suited to operations of this kind because it offered large amounts of undeveloped land close to settled areas with "high class" houses. Residents of the district believed that another change in zoning could bring them adequate protection. "The zoning law is not static," said Everett E. Elting, acting chairman of the group. "It must embrace new situations that arise."[20]

Initially, members of the village board seemed indifferent to the pleas of Elting and the others. Saying that "fast action may lead to wrong steps," they watched as the developers of Colonial Acres applied for building permits and began construction on eleven new dwellings. But privately, local officials were hoping to find a loophole in the ordinances that affected construction. In late October, they found what they were looking for. Section 256 of the building code required wood floors with circulating air heat rather than the concrete slabs with radiant heating that the company was planning to use. Armed with section 256 and supported by the members of the village board, building inspector Peter Ferrero revoked the permits he had issued.[21]

The revocation of the permits brought a storm of protest, not only from the representatives of King Ranch Homes, but also from the individuals who had purchased houses, from a number of local residents, and from the New York City press. At a public meeting that lasted for nearly five hours, a lawyer for the company used excerpts from the building code to underscore his point. He stressed the broad discretionary powers the code gave the building inspector, especially in cases of new construction techniques, such as the use of concrete slabs, that the building code had not envisioned. The company president added, "It won't cost a penny more to build with wood floors and air spaces, but it . . . won't give anyone a better house." A prospective homeowner in the development was less temperate in his remarks. He called official explanations of the revocation "a farce" and accused village authorities of attempting to stop the subdivision through tactics of "delay" and "discouragement." Some village residents agreed. Glen V. Dorflinger described himself as "disgusted" by the "dictatorial" actions of the board, and Walter Pleuthner and R. E. L. Howe called on its members to let the construction of the subdivision proceed. Even the *New York Herald Tribune* commented on the case. While sympathetic to the long-run aspirations of Scarsdale homeowners, it criticized the community for "rigging the building code," instead of establishing "broader and more democratic planning measures."[22]

The controversy over the subdivision soon subsided, largely because of the builder's willingness to yield to the community's demands. The company filed new plans with the village, providing for wood floors and circulating air heat. The building inspector promptly reissued the permits, and the construction recommenced.[23]

But although the fight was not a long one, it had a lasting effect on some of the participants. The buyers of homes in Colonial Acres, recalling the bitterness with which established property owners had objected to the building of "rows of houses, one like the other," resolved to free their neighborhood from the onus of "monotony." Through the use of varied building materials, roof lines, and styles of windows, they succeeded in achieving the appearance of custom-built houses. In addition, they agreed to spend thousands of dollars on a comprehensive program of neighborhood landscaping. According to Alfred L. Golden, president of the Colonial Acres Association, they aimed to make their subdivision "a constructive force in the community."[24]

While the residents of Colonial Acres sought to upgrade their properties, the residents of other neighborhoods sought to protect theirs. In mid-December 1949, representatives of the Quaker Ridge section urged the village board to prevent a repetition of the Colonial Acres episode by acting then to adopt stricter laws affecting housing. Six weeks later state senator Pliny Williamson seconded that idea. In a speech to the Town Club, he called for the passage of measures designed to control "the hit-and-run builders of look-alike houses."[25]

The village board responded to such requests in April 1950 by establishing a new and highly original ordinance that aimed "to regulate similarity of appearance in any neighborhood." In order to achieve this purpose, the law established six categories: the height of the roof, the length of the roof, the width of the house, and the location of the windows, doors, and porch. It then forbade any house in a neighborhood from being similar to another in more than three of the six groups, it required a minimum difference of dimensions of two feet in the three dissimilar categories, and it defined the neighborhood of a particular house as the two lots in both directions on the same side of the street and the five houses across the street from these five.[26]

The so-called look-alike law had its supporters, people who said it would protect the village from "blighting, deadly uniformity," as well as its detractors, people who questioned if aesthetics could be "defined by dimensions." Residents also disagreed with regard to its effect on the cost of housing in the community. But although some individuals claimed that the law had "nothing to do with the size or price of a house," it certainly did have an impact on the latter, especially when viewed in conjunction with the operation of density zoning. By 1950, Scarsdale offered no tracts large enough to allow a developer to satisfy the requirements of both density zoning and the look-alike law and still apply mass production techniques. A company such as Levitt and Sons, which developed whole communities on Long Island, in New Jersey, and in Pennsylvania, and which provided "the best house for the money" to a predominantly lower-middle-class market, would have had to change its building methods, its marketing approach, and its prices to succeed in wealthy Scarsdale.[27] Thus, much as the zoning law and building code had made Scarsdale an expensive place in which to build by the standards of the 1920s, so density zoning and the look-alike law achieved the same purpose for the fifties and early sixties. At last, the community had effectively prevented the construction of low-cost houses.

But although the village maintained its standards in the area of housing, the building boom of the 1950s had other repercussions. Between 1950 and 1960 the village added 1,178 single-family dwellings, along with one multifamily residence, and six business buildings. As the number of vacant lots in Scarsdale declined and the number of people living there increased, residents again began to fear the urbanization of their village. In concert with their counterparts a generation earlier, they expressed a desire to keep Scarsdale "as it is."[28] In Scarsdale that phrase proved no empty slogan, as it did in many towns, but a goal for which villagers endured great inconvenience and some expense. They also endured a number of squabbles. In no area was this more true than in the long-term debate between the champions of more open spaces and the advocates of more parking spaces. As long as the population of south-central Westchester continued to grow, this dispute would continue to flare.

In 1937 the Town Club reported that the village, school, and county boards had allocated for public use in Scarsdale "an exceptionally large provision of open spaces," 709 acres out of the community's total area of 4,050 acres. Two decades later that provision seemed less generous. Now there were more people in Scarsdale and more public buildings using formerly unoccupied public land. In 1958 a bequest to the village of 7½ acres from the estate of Wilhelm Weinberg seemed to stimulate the community's interest in preserving its "semi-rural character." To achieve that purpose, the trustees established a series of policies in the 1960s. They required developers to set aside a part of each subdivision as open space. They established a $100,000 land reserve fund in order to obtain strategically located properties and urged the owners of large tracts to notify the village before selling their land on the open market. They offered tax incentives to property owners who "deeded away" the development rights on their extra building lots. Through such policies the village obtained in the sixties and seventies an additional 54 acres, many in prime locations. The trustees also secured agreements from four property owners preventing the subdivision of their land.[29]

The goal of preserving open space entered the realm of controversy only when it came into conflict with a demonstrable village need. From shortly after the end of World War II through the end of the Vietnam era, few village problems received more discussion than the lack of parking in the local business district. Senator Pliny Williamson spoke on the subject; the *Inquirer* wrote editorials on it. The Scarsdale Rotary Club, Town Club, Safety Council, and Realty Board all called for a vigorous program to improve parking conditions. Understandably, members of the Chamber of Commerce were particularly concerned about what they called Scarsdale's "number-one headache." In 1954 they conducted a survey which indicated that an average of 3,614 cars competed for 983 spaces daily. Such a situation hurt local business. "I would prefer to shop in Scarsdale," said one resident, "but I go where there is parking space."[30]

The village board took several steps in an effort to alleviate the problem. In 1948 and 1949 it tried to discourage long-term parking by installing parking meters. In 1953 it converted a landscaped island in a section of a street in the business district to parking. In 1954 it passed an ordinance requiring new business buildings to provide off-street parking facilities.[31]

When none of these decisions brought the village enduring relief, the trustees considered taking bolder action. On the recommendation of three separate studies—one by the firm of Parsons, Brinckerhoff, Hall, and Macdonald in 1951, the second by city planner Matthew Platt in 1956, the third by Tippetts, Abbett, McCarthy, and Stratton Engineers in 1958—they proposed to convert village-owned property on Chase Road across from the post office from a park into a parking lot.[32]

Local merchants united behind the proposal. Lester R. Stewart of the Scarsdale Supply Company, stressing "the tremendous need for additional parking," called the construction of a lot on Chase Road "the only sensible solution." Donald Metz of the Scarsdale Insurance Agency emphasized that planning experts had selected the site, and attorney Benjamin Burstein, speaking for the Chamber of Commerce, blamed a decline in local retail sales on the lack of adequate parking.[33]

But although merchants applauded the proposal, a number of residents found it appalling. They looked at the plan, not in terms of practicality or profit, but in terms of the community's "moral responsibility" to preserve its parks. As one woman put it, "We have no right at all to touch that land." She and others who shared that conviction organized the Friends of the Scarsdale Parks to "see that land acquired by gift or purchase, dedicated and designated as park land, shall not be used for any other purpose." This new group was joined by two older organizations, the League of Women Voters and the Woman's Club, in the crusade to stop the construction of a parking lot on "the last open green spot in the business district."[34]

In 1963, after seven years of contention, the village board held a formal public hearing on the proposal. In the course of that hearing, the community's merchants found themselves subjected to a barrage of insults. According to one man, parking in the business district did not matter since the stores were so poor they could be dispensed with. Another, following through on that point, noted that if the entire business district were eliminated Scarsdale's "financially 'comfortable'" citizens could absorb the tax increase. A third speaker demanded, "Are we [the residents] here to serve them or are they [the merchants] here to serve us?"[35]

Faced with such a sharp expression of public disapproval, the trustees gradually abandoned the project. But, along with the author of a letter in the *Scarsdale Inquirer*, they probably wondered what the commotion was about. After all, their proposal had not called for a grotesque display of twisted concrete or flat expanse of asphalt, but an extensively landscaped parking area which, in the view of at least one resident, combined the beauty of a park with the utility of a parking lot. Yet others emphasized the importance of having a park visible from the business district. In the words of Mrs. David Rumsey, the Chase Road park stood "as reassuring evidence of Scarsdale's zoning pattern, Scarsdale's residential character, and Scarsdale's responsibility to its future recreational needs."[36]

In 1971, after another unsuccessful effort to convert a park— the one by the train station—into a parking area, the trustees settled on a different approach to the problem. They voted to build a five-story garage that would accommodate 500 automobiles in what the *Inquirer* called an "already blighted" part of the village. The site, known as the Freightway, was next to the commuter railroad tracks and behind the apartment buildings that lined Garth Road. But if the location was inconspicuous from the stores and offices of the village, it was also inconvenient to the vast majority of them. Nevertheless, local merchants, desperate for relief of the parking situation, agreed to bear one-third of the project's $1,800,000 cost.[37]

The improvement afforded the village by the construction of the Freightway parking garage proved to be short-lived. Only two years after the facility's completion, the newspaper was again calling attention to the community's inadequate parking. Yet, as villagers searched for parking spaces to the din of honking horns, they could take comfort in the sight of the swatches of green that ringed the business district—the Chase Road park, saved from destruction in 1963; the station area park, similarly protected in 1964; and De Lima park, purchased by neighboring property owners as a gift to the village in 1972.[38]

Although, in their desire to exclude cheap housing and preserve open space, village residents followed through on a pattern that dated back to the 1920s, another aspect of village policy in the postwar era was of more recent vintage. The unstable economy of the 1930s, together with an aversion to the programs of the New Deal, had prompted the village to adopt a more conservative fiscal policy. During the 1940s that policy acquired a name, some local champions, and a loyal following, but its end result proved disappointing, for pay-as-you-go did not deliver the low taxes that its proponents had promised. Only slowly would residents come to recognize that the fault lay, not with the doctrine, but with the incompatibility of their various goals. Nothing, not even the most prudent fiscal measures, would allow the citizens of Scarsdale to maintain their community's residential character, to enjoy superior municipal services, and at the same time to retain low taxes.

"A village without a bonded indebtedness and the lowest tax rate in America"—that was the vision of Kenneth C. Hogate as he took over the office of mayor in the spring of 1941. "We have reached the point in Scarsdale," he said, "where we can run the village on a pay-as-you-go basis . . . without the loss of any worthwhile funding. It is within the power of Scarsdale if its citizens want it." A few months later a federal ban on nonessential construction rendered Hogate's challenge irrelevant, and more pressing wartime issues came to dominate the public mind, but by 1946 the idea of pay-as-you-go had gained a new champion, Mayor H. Beach Carpenter and the entire community were discussing a report the village board had circulated. "Scarsdale's $1,066,000 Question," *American City* magazine called it.

The figure represented the cost of improvements that the village would soon need to build. The question concerned the method of financing. Should the village government rely on long-term, low-interest bonds; should it accumulate the savings to pay in cash; or should it use a combination of short-term bonds and accumulated savings?[39]

The mayor and trustees made it clear that they favored the second option. Pay-as-you-go would, in their words, "induce caution in planning and undertaking projects" and enable the village to avoid the problem of "inflexible debt service . . . in lean years." Specifically, such a financial program would cost more than bonds in the short run—at least $13.20 more a year for ten years on a $10,000 assessment, but it would save residents money in the long run—the lack of interest payments would keep future taxes low.[40]

Most residents responded enthusiastically to the pay-as-you-go idea. In the two weeks after the trustees issued their report, they received more than 100 letters on the subject. Three-fourths of these approved full pay-as-you-go financing. A manufacturing executive put the matter succinctly. "This is the proper policy for an individual," he said, "and it appears to me it is also proper for our village." A former mayor expanded, "It would be easy to borrow at low rates a sum which we would be cussing about every tax-paying date for years." "Things are pretty good now," he added, "but that could easily change. There is no surer way of making them change than for Scarsdale to load itself with debt and the charges of debt."[41]

Assured of public support, the trustees began to set aside anywhere from $25,000 to more than $300,000 from current taxes for future construction. From this reserve came the funds for a number of village improvements—a library in 1951, a police headquarters in 1954, an incinerator in 1959, a storm drainage project in 1961, and a highway improvement program in 1963. All totaled, the village succeeded in paying for more than $4.1 million of major capital expenditures between 1946 and 1965, while accumulating an additional reserve of $1.14 million. At the same time, it managed to reduce its bonded indebtedness from $1.01 million to $385,000 without incurring any new debts to the general fund.[42]

But, although by 1965 the village had greatly reduced its bonded indebtedness, it had not succeeded in achieving Mayor Hogate's other goal. Indeed, far from enjoying "the lowest tax rate in America," local residents paid three times more in village taxes than they had twenty years earlier. In fiscal 1944–45, village taxes, not including school taxes, had been $6.878 per $1,000 of assessed property and the average assessment was $20,750. By 1965 the tax rate was $22.253 per $1,000, and the average assessment had risen to $21,697.[43] To some extent the increase resulted from inflation, for a 1965 dollar bought less than three-fifths the goods and services a 1945 dollar had purchased. But the increase also reflected the community's interest in securing new services (such as village-run day camps for the children in the summer), in continuing other quality services (such as backyard garbage collection three times a week), and in providing village employees with benefits deemed unnecessry two decades earlier. In 1964 the state comptroller reported that Scarsdale spent $108 per capita on village operations compared to a state-wide expenditure per capita for villages of $48.52.[44] Since Scarsdale had no industry, few apartment houses, and only a small number of businesses of any sort, most of the burden for those expenses fell on the homeowners of the community.

Increasingly, those homeowners voiced their concern. In 1954 a committee of the Town Club said there was "a real hazard" that "inordinately high taxes" would drive people out of Scarsdale. It urged the village to take "corrective measures before it is too late." In 1958 one man noted the discrepancy between the desire to keep Scarsdale "the way it is" and the drive for lower taxes, warning, "It is by no means unjustified to predict that Scarsdale will ultimately destroy itself by becoming over-burdened and over-taxed to maintain [village services and a school system] beyond its capacity." In 1965 a village leader asked, "How can Scarsdale possibly solve this problem of tax escalation beyond reason, holding to its present position about the physical character of the community?"[45]

In the latter half of the sixties, village residents tacitly answered this question much as they had in the twenties. Forced to choose between maintaining the community's distinctiveness, in both its residential character and its quality services, and receiving a degree of tax relief, they generally accepted the need for extremely high taxes. At the same time they decided to abandon the once almost religious commitment to pay-as-you-go financing. In 1967 the village board held its first referendum in twenty-nine years. The referendum involved a $690,000 swimming pool complex, an item to which successive village boards had given a low priority but which local voters approved by a margin of 1,623 to 339. That same year the trustees voted to build a village hall with the last of the funds they had reserved under the pay-as-you-go system.[46] The expectations of village residents and village employees, the imbalance in the local tax base, and the impact of national inflation had combined by the late 1960s to make one point perfectly clear. Gone was the time when the operation of the richest village in America could be among the country's least expensive.

If pay-as-you-go was the watchword in village policy in the postwar era, spending for excellence was the theme in the schools. Between 1945 and 1965, the voters approved large bond issues to construct new buildings and large budgets to support the educational program. But although the residents were willing to spend for new and even exciting buildings, they were generally unwilling to experiment with exciting, new educational ideas. In 1958 the former principal of Scarsdale High School, Lester W. Nelson, tried to explain why "communities with the greatest opportunities and resources seem to be [those] most opposed to experiments." He concluded that their conservatism resulted from the apparent success of their schools. People who had moved to the community "because they liked the schools . . . think they can maintain quality by maintaining the status quo."[47]

Nelson's analysis held a portion of truth, but it glossed over the tensions that had marked education in Scarsdale, and in the nation, since the end of World War II. While progressive ideas had begun to have an impact on the physical structure of school buildings, progressive teaching methods had become the subject of intense public criticism.[48] Tangentially related to that criticism was another, sharper attack. Between 1949 and 1954, a small group of residents repeatedly charged that communists had infiltrated the Scarsdale schools. Although the school board's handling of the controversy ultimately enhanced the community's reputation for fair play, for a time the barrage of charges created doubts about the suburb and serious dissension within it. Only slowly would the community recover its zest for experiment, its eagerness to lead. The conformity that affected many circles of American society in the wake of the McCarthy era affected the people of Scarsdale as well.

Ever since the community's educational experiments of the 1920s, Scarsdale's name had been prominent in the field of education. Educational journals featured numerous articles on a wide range of local policies, from the role of the guidance counselor, to the benefits of heterogeneous grouping, to the scheduling of school facilities for maximum use.[49] Local administrators enjoyed reputations well beyond the community's borders. As principal of Scarsdale High School from 1933 to 1953, Lester Nelson served on the board of trustees of the Educational Testing Service, presided over the Middle States Association of Colleges and Secondary Schools, and received honorary doctorates from Colgate University, Colby College, and the University of Pennsylvania. Archibald B. Shaw, Scarsdale's superintendent of schools from 1949 to 1959, eventually headed the department of educational administration and higher education at Michigan State University. His successor, Harold Howe II, later served as U.S. commissioner of education and vice-president of the Ford Foundation for education and research.[50]

Most residents took pride in the schools' reputation. In the opinion of the *Scarsdale Inquirer*, the schools constituted "the village's greatest single asset." The newspaper continued, "Neither expense nor effort is spared in maintaining them at high level, and the result is a system probably unsurpassed in the nation."[51]

Although the *Inquirer*'s last claim was difficult to prove, it was clear that during the postwar era residents spent large sums of money to support their schools. From 1945 to 1965, as the number of children in the schools in district one increased from 2,339 to 4,346, the voters approved bond issues totaling $10,207,000. The money went for the construction of a new elementary school, a junior high school, two additions to the senior high school, and improvements at the old elementary schools. In educational matters residents easily justified their departure from the pay-as-you-go policy. In the words of a former school board member, "There is no reason why present homeowners should be forced to pay in full for . . . large school structures that will be enjoyed by Scarsdale children ten, twenty and thirty years hence."[52]

The school board intended the facilities to last not only in terms of size, but in terms of concept. While all the new facilities contained interesting features, the most original was the Heathcote Elementary School, which opened in September 1954. Designed by the architectural firm of Perkins and Will, the school had separate wings and separate play areas for children of similar age levels; hexagonal, almost circular, classrooms with portable furniture and large windows; coordinated facilities for science, shop, and home economics; and a library with a fireplace fueled by wood the children gathered. Although the school board did not emphasize the point, such features reflected a number of progressive ideas. Clearly Heathcote was a child-centered school where learning was a part of doing, and science a part of life.[53]

While a few residents, including Donald H. Ogilvy, questioned the value of "building a super-duper school," they were decidely in the minority. The $1.4 million bond issue for Heathcote passed by a margin of 551 to 47. Within a few years *Life* magazine, describing Heathcote as "a forerunner of the schools of the future," had devoted four pages of pictures and print to the structure, and *Architectural Forum* had featured the school as its cover story. Back in Scarsdale, a school board spokesman declared, "Heathcote has without question increased Scarsdale's prestige—and enhanced the value of all homes in the village."[54]

In the postwar era, residents not only committed themselves to long-run expenditures for new school facilities, they also accepted the burden of large annual budgets. Although school spending increased from $909,930 in 1944–45 to $5,932,570 in 1964–65 and school taxes from $12.85 per $1,000 of assessed valuation to $48.91 per $1,000, most residents emphasized their desire to continue the schools' tradition of excellence and to avoid false economies. In 1958, when the voters for the first time in the district's history rejected a budget recommended by the board, they actually added money to it. One man's statement expressed the attitude of many residents: "If the time comes that I cannot afford to pay the cost, I would prefer to move rather than to hope that the standards would be lowered to meet my budget."[55]

But although the community's residents enjoyed the renown of their school district and paid high taxes to maintain the district's quality, they did not hesitate to criticize its operation. In 1947 the education committee of the Town Club published a thirty-eight page report that aimed to raise the scholastic achievement of Scarsdale pupils, particularly in reading, spelling, grammar, geography, and history. Committee chairman William H. Conant, a New York business consultant, placed the blame for "a bliss of ignorance in pivotal studies" on "too much progressive education" in the community's elementary schools. He added, "Our pupils have been high in arithmetic only because progressive education could find no way to fiddle with the multiplication table." The committee recommended a return to more traditional approaches, an emphasis on the use of maps in geography, a return to "undiluted" history instead of current events, more drill work in spelling and grammar, and larger quantities of homework in the earlier grades. "The carefree school days of ultraprogressive education," said Conant, "are fading into the realities of survival of the fittest."[56]

Twelve years later the Town Club's education committee issued another report. While more restrained in tone and more thorough than the 1947 report, the 1959 document reiterated the call for a return to fundamentals. Central to its analysis was a set of statistics the *Inquirer* termed "frightening." Although the Scarsdale schools spent nearly three times the national annual average to educate each student, local children of "'A' ability" tended to be "only C+ students in college." The committee offered no simple solutions to this problem. But while it recognized that "it is not the function of a citizens' committee to prescribe educational improvements for the Scarsdale schools," it urged the schools to devote more hours per day to academic subjects and questioned the inclusion of such subjects as driver education, instrumental music, and shop in a college preparatory curriculm.[57]

Both Town Club reports provoked wide discussion in the community. Both led to some changes within the schools. Indeed, the 1959 report may have precipitated the resignation of Superintendent Archibald B. Shaw. But although the first report attracted national attention as the portent of a conservative reaction against progressive education, the second report received little notice outside Scarsdale. It was a small part of the re-evaluation of educational standards that occurred throughout the United States after the Soviet launching of the first earth satellite.[58]

While the two Town Club reports questioned the quality of the academic training provided by the schools, another group of critics attacked the values the schools were inculcating. At first, this second attack seemed to be a part of the reaction against progressive education. In speeches and letters to the editor, men like Otto E. Dohrenwend, a Wall Street broker and papal Knight of Malta, and William C. Kernan, the assistant minister at St. James the Less Episcopal Church, criticized the schools' emphasis on experience, social adjustment, and growth without reference to God's moral law. But soon these men were questioning not only the secular orientation of the Scarsdale schools but their political orientation as well. As one of Kernan and Dohrenwend's supporters phrased it, "Secularism [is] the ally of communism." "We must wake up!" said another. "We are fast walking our youth right behind the 'iron curtain,' where there are no such characters as Washington, Jefferson, Lincoln— and God Almighty."[59]

These statements appeared in the *Scarsdale Inquirer* in January 1949, after the House Un-American Activities Committee had begun its probe of communist influence in the national government, but before Senator Joseph R. McCarthy had moved to the forefront of the anticommunist crusade.[60] From about that time through 1954, the charge that communists were infiltrating the Scarsdale schools absorbed a large part of the energy of the community. In pressing their claims, Dohrenwend, Kernan and the others used language and tactics similar to those employed by McCarthy. Yet, unlike McCarthy, the local anticommunists never succeeded in gaining significant vocal support for their charges. Their failure, at a time when many communities were joining the spy hunt, pointed up the unusual nature of the local population. Scarsdale residents, with their wealth, education, and social status, or at least their aspirations to wealth and status, did not usually make good converts to what historian Richard Hofstadter has called "the paranoid style in American politics."[61]

Throughout the controversy the anticommunists in Scarsdale made the following basic charges. They said that "communist apologists" had written some of the books on the shelves in the high school library, recommended on class reading lists, and used in courses. In addition, "communist apologists" had spoken or performed at assemblies held in the schools, meetings sponsored by the Parent-Teacher Association, classes of the Scarsdale Adult School, and courses for the local teaching staff. According to Otto Dohrenwend, such a "pattern of communist influence" could not have occurred in Scarsdale "by coincidence." "You cannot have a conspiracy without conspirators," he said.[62]

The school board had a consistent response to these charges. Affirming its belief in the "freedom of inquiry" and the "competition of ideas," it refused to exclude books from the library "solely on the ground of alleged un-American convictions or associations of their authors." It asserted that "vigorous teaching" would protect against subversion better than "repressive censorship" and denied there was cause to question the loyalty of any members of the schools' professional staff. It concluded, "The Scarsdale schools are not infiltrated with communism and never have been."[63]

The lines of argument in the controversy hardened quickly. Early on the majority of village residents sided with the school board and tried to demonstrate their support of its policies. Yet the anticommunist clique, propelled by American setbacks abroad and the growing power of McCarthy at home, managed to agitate the question for five full years. Their activities showed how an unscrupulous minority could abuse the democratic process, frustrate majority sentiment, and create bitterness and dissension in a relatively tranquil community.

Repeated direct clashes between the anticommunists and the school board marked the first year of the controversy. Beginning at the public meeting of the board in September 1949, and at almost every meeting thereafter through the following April, one or more members of the so-called Committee of Ten raised questions concerning the selection of books for the Scarsdale High School library. In particular, their charges focused on the historical fiction of Howard Fast, who was then a Communist Party member and who would eventually be imprisoned for contempt of Congress. At the meeting of the school board in February 1950, Cyril S. Treacy detailed the committee's objections to one of Fast's books. According to Treacy, *Citizen Tom Paine* contained numerous "infractions of good taste," "continued cursing," and "not . . . complimentary" descriptions of the country's first leaders. In addition, the book followed "the Communist Party line" by portraying the Revolution not only as a war against Britain but as a class struggle as well. Attacking "the type of deluded liberalism which regards an undefined right to teach anything as more important than the souls of the young," the members of the committee called on the school board to remove *Citizen Tom Paine* and the other "subversive" books from the shelves of the high school library.[64]

Meanwhile, other citizens voiced their opposition to the views of the Committee of Ten. The Scarsdale chapter of the American Veterans Committee passed a resolution opposing the effort at censorship and a group of eighty-one prominent citizens publicly expressed its confidence in the board. Other citizens spoke out in public meetings. Rudolf P. Berle said, "You can't beat bad ideas by burying them. You beat them with good ideas. I challenge anyone to say that the Scarsdale schools are not teaching children to be first-class citizens." Harry J. Liese asked, "Are we to blink at facts in history and try to make our children think every American is a saint?" Charles A. Perera added, "All of us here despise communism, . . . but all of us know of the class struggle in this country, the slavery, the sweat shops. I am not afraid to tell my children what has been wrong in the past. I know what I believe and what I think is right."[65]

Members of the school board tried to respond to the committee's charges in a restrained and thoughtful manner. First, they drew up a report explaining how the high school staff selected the books used in courses and those made available in the library. Concluding that the school district already employed "proper methods" of book selection by "qualified persons . . . fully devoted to the American way of life," the board decided to continue the process of book selection and to withdraw no books selected under that process. Later, as the Committee of Ten focused its attack on *Citizen Tom Paine*, the board asked three members of the school's professional staff, the head librarian and the chairmen of the English and social studies departments, to evaluate the book. The three concluded that the book provided suitable reading for high school students. Indeed, they found that in a few instances where the author "could have followed the communist line," he "had opposed it."[66]

Unhappy with the board's responses, members of the Committee of Ten became more combative and even insulting. They accused the board of "indifference" to their charges, demanded to know which teachers had ordered the books, and vowed to take the issue outside Scarsdale. Repeatedly members of the committee insisted that their goal was to help the community by "keep[ing] communism out of the Scarsdale school system." "It's already there," said William Kernan at the April meeting, "and you don't know communism when you see it."[67]

Apparently the school board could only satisfy the anticommunists by acceding to their wishes. Agreed that to do so would be in "the worst possible interest of our schools and our children," eager to turn to other matters, and encouraged by a show of support at the annual school district meeting, its members decided to end oral presentations on the subject of book selection. Any further questions in that regard would have to be submitted to the board in writing.[68]

Intended to quell the controversy, the board's decision served to intensify it. When school board President A. Chauncey Newlin announced the decision at the beginning of the May meeting, the members of the Committee of Ten opened a new line of attack. This time they focused on the left-wing connections of Bert James Loewenberg, a professor at Sarah Lawrence College who had organized a course for teachers that was held at Scarsdale High School. Members of the school board pointed out that the course was held at the high school simply for the convenience of area teachers, that it was actually under the aegis of New York University and Sarah Lawrence, that Loewenberg was a qualified scholar at an accredited college, and that the board did not investigate the teachers of courses its staff members took. In the words of one member of the board, Robert G. Fuller, the Loewenberg issue amounted to "the same subject from a different angle." Accordingly, President Newlin ruled further attempts to discuss the issue out of order. To cries of "dictatorship" from the Committee of Ten and its supporters, he adjourned the meeting slightly more than an hour after it had begun.[69]

The "mad house" atmosphere of the May 8 meeting left the members of the Committee of Ten feeling aggrieved and some members of the community perplexed. They wondered why the school board had "taken a line of stubborn resistance to the dangers of communism that a minority group of citizens ha[d] tracked down." One woman said, "It is because they are good Americans that they . . . will not let the subject drop."[70]

Desirous of airing the issue to the satisfaction of the community, the school board agreed to make a concession to the Committee of Ten. On June 19, 1950, the board held a special meeting to determine whether the evidence warranted something the committee demanded: a full-scale investigation of communist influence in the schools. Nearly 1,400 citizens listened intently as the members of the committee—Dowrenwend, Kernan, Edward O. McConahay, F. Lawrence Chandler, Andrew P. McLaughlin, I. Herbert Schaumber, Edward A. Wetzel, Mr. and Mrs. Robert J. Fitzpatrick, and Dr. August W. Brustat, pastor of the Trinity Lutheran Church—presented their testimony. Much of the ground they covered was familiar, a bit of it was new. But as the *Inquirer* pointed out, "There was no evidence given by any of the speakers reflecting on individual Scarsdale teachers or members of the board of education."[71]

After the members of the committee spoke, Superintendent Archibald B. Shaw took the lectern. Seeking especially to reassure the hundreds of families who had recently moved to Scarsdale, he devoted his remarks, not to alleged communist influences in the selection of library books and program speakers, but to the individuals who had a daily influence on the community's children, the 133 teachers who taught in the Scarsdale schools. Shaw began by emphasizing the fact that "[133] is a very small number, a very 'knowable' number, especially when we change it from a statistic to people working in four schools." He then went on to describe the process of selecting the teachers, their duties, differences, and common concern for the children of Scarsdale. He concluded, "We have competent teachers, loyal teachers, decent, wholesome teachers. In their hands our children, our American way, both are safe." As the superintendent ended his remarks, a deep silence fell over the audience for a moment, then nearly everyone joined in a long, standing ovation. Shaw at least for the moment had succeeded in transforming the issue from one that played on the element of fear in the community to one that emphasized the element of trust.[72]

At its July meeting, officially the first of the 1950–51 academic year but psychologically the last of 1949–50, the board of education heard Superintendent Shaw rebut the specific charges raised by the committee in June. Its members then agreed that the use of "carefully gleaned passages often quoted out of context" did not constitute evidence of communist infiltration. Stressing that further discussion of the matter would "impair seriously the morale of our teachers with inevitable harm to our school children," they refused to hold the investigation that the committee demanded.[73]

Most members of the audience greeted the board's decision with applause. They had long since come to the conclusion that, in the words of Sylvia R. Failes, "The members of the board have been badgered and beleaguered by an insignificant but persistent little clique." Paul S. Smith agreed. In his view the "battle of the books" had become the "battle of the bloc." He added, "Individual and minority rights are to be respected but not to the extent of thwarting the will of the majority." Oscar S. Blinn expanded on that idea. Charging that the members of the Committee of Ten were "violating some of the fundamental principles of our representative system," he said,

[Since they] have had a fair opportunity to be heard by a governing body of public servants, at reasonable length, and their arguments have been weighed and considered, and the body has taken action on the merits, the issue must be regarded as settled.[74]

As the controversy moved into its second and third years, the board of education succeeded in preventing the issue from dominating its public meetings. Yet far from regarding the question as settled, the local anticommunists, now calling themselves the Citizens' Committee, continued to press their charges. As the ongoing crisis attracted increasing attention outside the community, tempers grew more taut within. Repeated demonstrations of support for the school board from a very large number of Scarsdale residents drew only renewed accusations of conspiracy from its critics.

On September 14, 1950, a member of the Citizens' Committee gave an extended presentation at a meeting of the school board for the last time during the controversy. At eleven o'clock, after attending to new business, the board recognized Edward O. McConahay, a graduate of the United States Military Academy, a life insurance executive, and a major in the Army Reserves who was about to report for active duty. McConahay then delivered a nine-page speech based on the premise that "the battle we have been fighting in Scarsdale in the educational field is part of the same battle that is being waged by our country and its allies in Korea." According to McConahay, Superintendent Shaw, either through gullibility or guile, was a key figure in the communist conspiracy's local successes. He termed the superintendent's statements "preposterous," accused him of resorting to "old trick[s]" in trying to evade the committee's charges, and claimed he had violated laws aimed at inculcating patriotism and morality in the public school children. When McConahay asked, "How can an educator stoop so low?" many of his listeners probably wondered the same thing of the major. At the end of the speech, Lillian C. Brown, a member of the school board, commented, "I do not feel that this meeting should close on the level to which it has sunk. Tonight we have seen freedom of speech become license." In giving McConahay the opportunity to speak, the board had recognized its debt to a soldier-patriot. In abusing that opportunity, McConahay had violated the community's sense of fair play. The following month the board announced an end to further discussion of the issue of communist influence in the schools. This time community sentiment allowed the board to adhere to its decision.[75]

Having exhausted their grace at the school board, members of the Citizens' Committee had to rely on other methods of keeping the issue before the public. They regularly sent letters to the *Scarsdale Inquirer* and occasionally paid for advertisements in the paper as well. They mailed "advisory circulars" containing new charges to every household in Scarsdale and spoke to groups both in and outside the community. Eventually their cause received a sympathetic hearing in such periodicals as the *American Mercury* and the *Catholic World*. In April 1951, Rabbi Benjamin Schultz, the coordinator of the Joint Committee Against Communism in New York, called on Governor Thomas E. Dewey to conduct an investigation into the matter. Schultz said, "What we want to know is: who is pulling these strings? What person (or persons) . . . has arranged [for] . . . the evil and successful infiltration of pro-communists into the entire school set-up in Scarsdale?"[76]

As the accusations continued, letters to the editor in the *Scarsdale Inquirer* often referred to the existence of "rancor" and "dissension" in the village. Virginia Sandberg wrote, "One's heart becomes heavy to hear so much bitterness in Scarsdale, the place one was once proud to call home." Most writers blamed the school board's critics for the problem. Alfred P. Slaner suggested that the Citizens' Committee had "borrowed the big smear technique of Hitler and Stalin" for it had "not revealed the presence of a single communist after two years of haranguing." Kenneth M. Gould added that, if the present "atmosphere of thought control" were long continued, freedom would "perish as surely as if this nation were conquered by Red armies or our government were overthrown by internal treason."[77]

Gould's remarks came in the wake of the committee's charges that Otto Klineberg, Edward C. Lindeman, and Ernest O. Malby had communist connections. Klineberg was a village resident with three children in the public schools, and all three men were respected academics who had lectured under the auspices of either the Scarsdale Adult School or the P.T.A. In defending his friends and fellow scholars, Gould, the editor of *Senior Scholastic* magazine, said, "We are living under a system of punishment by extra-legal publicity for the most trivial of deviations from a dead level of orthodoxy." He called on village residents to reject the efforts of "self-appointed censors" to sow suspicion among them and concluded by paraphrasing a statement Norman Cousins had made while speaking in Scarsdale, "We need to restore to our human relations the practice of trust in the fundamental decency of the great majority of our neighbors."[78]

The groundwork for a restoration of community trust was laid in the spring of 1952 when the school board and its supporters survived a direct challenge from its critics. On March 27, the Citizens' Committee held a large public meeting in the auditorium of the Edgewood School, which it had rented for the occasion. Reiterating the charges it had made for nearly three years, the committee accused the members of the school board of "irresponsibility and indifference to the major issue confronting the American people—the survival of our country in the face of the attack on it by the communist conspiracy." Otto Dohrenwend gave the key address. "Who brought the influence of individuals like [Howard] Fast . . . into the Scarsdale schools?" he asked. "Up to now the school board has refused to say. As parents and taxpayers you have the right to know." He concluded by challenging to a public debate the members of the school board who faced re-election.[79]

After years of dealing with the committee's distortions and in accordance with Scarsdale's tradition of uncontested elections, the two candidates, Malcolm C. Spence and Amelie Rothschild, declined to debate. Nevertheless, the weeks from March 27 to May 6, the day of the election, proved to be a time of intense activity as numerous individuals and groups rallied to the support of the regular candidates. The superintendent, the principals of the local schools, and the Scarsdale Teachers Association issued statements defending the actions the school board had taken. The Town Club announced its decision to study the activities of the Citizens' Committee and paid for the mailing of several proschool board statements to every household in the community. A group of residents drafted a petition that approved the job the schools were doing, endorsed the decisions of the board of education, deplored the methods of the Citizens' Committee, and called on the members of the community to attend the annual election meeting. Nearly 3,000 people signed the petition, which appeared as a two-page advertisement in the *Scarsdale Inquirer*.[80]

On May 6, 1952, 1,392 eligible voters attended the annual school district meeting. In their bids for re-election, Rothschild and Spence received 1,352 votes each. In addition, there were

26 write-in votes, only 15 of them for members of the Citizens' Committee. Even more stunningly than in previous years, the community had demonstrated its support for the school board. The liberal magazine, *The Nation*, praised "Scarsdale's Victory." "The impressive vote, . . . " it said, "demonstrates that even the zeal of demagogues is no match for an aroused public. What happened to McCarthyism in Scarsdale can be made to happen elsewhere."[81]

Although people in Scarsdale were less certain than the editors of *The Nation* that they had "lifted the seige against the schools," the 1952 school election represented a turning point in the controversy. Over the course of the next two years, the schools' critics would write more articles and letters, mail more circulars, and hold another public meeting, but while their behavior was often exasperating (as when August W. Brustat labeled the Town Club's report on the subject as "the best proof" that communists had infiltrated Scarsdale), they would never again pose a serious threat to the community.[82]

In the late spring and early summer of 1954, as the Army-McCarthy hearings galvanized the nation, the school board and its critics clashed once more. This time the committee questioned why the sixth-grade teachers at Edgewood School had chosen a play for their pupils to perform that was written by communist sympathizers and allegedly fostered class tensions. The play was "The Lonesome Train," a song-filled story of Lincoln's funeral train and the thoughts of various people whom it passed.[83]

The members of the school board stuck to their usual position. They refused to condemn the play simply on the basis of its authors' associations, and they generally defended the play's interpretation of the past. But they went further. In a brilliant move they told the members of the Citizens' Committee to hand over the evidence they had accumulated to the proper authorities at the Federal Bureau of Investigation. The board promised to cooperate fully with any investigation the federal government might make, but refused to discuss the matter any further with a group of private vigilantes.[84]

Gradually the controversy sputtered to a halt. Although the *Inquirer* announced in mid-July its intention to print no more letters on the subject, it continued to do so for over a month. Finally its editors gathered the nerve to act on their warning. After August 1954, the columns of the *Inquirer* no longer reeled with insinuations and invective. Three months before the Senate voted to condemn Joseph R. McCarthy, Scarsdale had disarmed his local counterparts.[85]

In the prize-winning book, *The Politics of Fear*, historian Robert Griffith closely analyzed the rise and fall of Joseph McCarthy. According to Griffith, McCarthy succeeded in part because of his gall: his willingness to violate the patterns of deference and courtesy that prevailed in the Senate, his tendency to attack most fiercely when the evidence was slim, and his ability to dramatize events in a way that captured the headlines. But, Griffith said, the encouragement of fellow Republicans and the mistakes of leading Democrats, especially in the years 1950 through 1952, played a large part in McCarthy's rise as well. Indeed, the Senator from Wisconsin fell from power not so much because Americans experienced a change of heart about the pervasiveness of the communist threat as because his Republican colleagues came to agree that, in attacking the Eisenhower administration, McCarthy was undermining the party's seat of power.[86]

The members of the Scarsdale Citizens' Committee showed a willingness to transgress the boundaries of accepted group behavior similar to McCarthy's. Drawing large conclusions on the basis of little evidence, they launched repeated attacks against respected members of the Scarsdale community. Yet the local anticommunists could not benefit from decades of partisan rivalry as McCarthy had done. Scarsdale residents were overwhelmingly Republican in national and state matters and just as devoutly nonpartisan in local matters. The existence of this political concensus thwarted the committee's efforts to gain a stronghold in the community.

What then kept the anticommunists going? They were sustained by what they interpreted as evidence of America's vulnerability— the so-called loss of China, the end of the nation's atomic monopoly, and the discouraging course of the war in Korea. They were also impressed by evidence of McCarthy's growing power as, one by one, his political enemies experienced defeat and as crusades similar to their own blossomed throughout the country. In addition, they drew strength from local sources. As overwhelming as the opposition to the Citizens' Committee appeared to be, the group did have a small band of supporters. Though not confined to a single church or neighborhood, support seemed to be strongest among Catholics living in the more modest sections of the community.[87]

Ironically, those who condemned the public schools for propagating the Marxist doctrine of class struggle themselves played on status differences within the community as well as resentment toward the establishment in the nation as a whole. An appeal for funds in the American Legion publication, *The Firing Line*, read:

> The long battle between the Americans and the phonies is still raging in Scarsdale, New York. Plenty of money and mud buckets on the side of the stuffed shirt anti-antis. Plenty of fighting heart and perseverance on the side of the embattled Scarsdale Citizens' Committee.[88]

In this regard it was significant that approximately half the adults in Scarsdale never committed themselves publicly to one side or the other. No doubt, the continual barrage of charges and countercharges was confusing to many residents, especially those new to the community and unfamiliar with its mores. Moreover, many residents probably felt torn between a desire to identify themselves with the community's image of stature and wealth, as represented by support for the school board, and a sense of not belonging in Scarsdale, as represented by support for the Citizens' Committee. Complicating matters further was the fact that Scarsdale was beginning to attract large numbers of Jewish residents. Since for decades nativists had tended to equate Jews with radical activities, there may have been an element of anti-Semitism in the charges of communist infiltration of the community, although the Citizens' Committee did not limit its specific attacks to Jews or make any explicitly anti-Semitic statements.[89]

The richest town in the world's richest nation seemed at first an odd place for charges of communist subversion to arise. With their long history of devotion to the Republican Party and their efforts to keep Scarsdale an upper-middle-class town, village residents seemed liable to criticism more from the left wing of American politics than from the right. Yet, from the perspective of the local anticommunists, Scarsdale's very prominence made it "perfect meat for propaganda." To quote a supporter of the Citizens' Committee, "This is the richest community in the nation, and if [the communists] can succeed here, among the 'upper crust,' their task is much nearer completion."[90] By the same logic, victory for the anticommunists in a town as prominent as Scarsdale would have brought their cause even more serious attention in the nation as a whole. But the anticommunists did not succeed in the New York suburb, and that fact underscored an important point about the residents of the community. For all their concern about restricting low-cost housing, avoiding village bond issues, and teaching fundamentals, Scarsdale's citizens were not consistently conservative by the standards of the late 1940s and 1950s. Instead, they clung to the liberal faith in the primacy of reason and the free exchange of ideas. That faith sustained the community during the years of the attack upon its schools. In the times that lay ahead, the limited liberalism of village residents in the postwar era would evolve into a force for change in Scarsdale and the nation.

CHAPTER 8

The Embarrassment of Riches

The affluence that had been a source of pride to residents of Scarsdale in the immediate postwar era became in the 1960s and early seventies a point of embarrassment to some of them, to other newer residents, and to many of the children of both groups. As Americans in general became aware of the short-comings of their democracy, some residents of Scarsdale did what they could to effect reform. They espoused a variety of causes, including revision of the nonpartisan system, racial integration of local housing and schools, and withdrawal from the war in Vietnam. In calling for basic changes in community attitudes and institutions, the reformers appealed to Scarsdale's tradition of national leadership. Yet many residents of the village perceived the reformers' demands as threatening the very aspects of civic life that had attracted them to Scarsdale. The debate that resulted divided the community, its neighborhoods, and often its families. At times it even alienated individuals from a sense of satisfaction in what they had accomplished. Yet, despite all the tension the discussion engendered, now more than ever before the community's practice of placing itself on the barricades seemed appropriate. For what was central to the spirit of the sixties was a questioning of the meaning of success, a questioning of the meaning of America, and, in the symbolic usage of a number of contemporary commentators, a questioning of the meaning of Scarsdale.

The sixties were, in one sense at least, a relatively stable decade for Scarsdale. The population growth of the fifties subsided, and with little land left for development, the issues that had preoc-cupied the village in the past underwent a transformation.[1]

But the small increase in the total population from 1960 to 1970, as well as the small decline of the following decade, masked a significant change in the ethnoreligious composition of that population. While urban families continued to move into Scarsdale when their children entered school and move out of Scarsdale when their children were grown, the families that left the community were disproportionately WASP, the families that entered disproportionately Jewish. In 1940 approximately 69 percent of Scarsdale's families could be categorized as white, Anglo-Saxon Protestants; 16 percent were Roman Catholic in affiliation or background, and 15 percent were ethnically Jewish. Twenty years later, the percentage of WASPs had declined to 42, the percentage of Jews had risen to 35, and the percentage of people from Catholic ethnic groups had increased to 23. In 1980 Jews comprised the largest ethnic group in the community, constituting roughly 50 percent of the total number of families. Protestants counted for 24 percent of the total, Catholics 21 percent. Asians, blacks, and others comprised the remaining 5 percent.[2]

Although the change in the ethnic composition of the population provided a source of strain in the community, neither the change nor the strain was often the topic of recorded discussion. Only on a few occasions did the newspaper refer to the existence in Scarsdale of "a definite deep-seated prejudice here" or "a deep cleavage along religious lines" or "an undercurrent of anti-Semitism."[3] Nevertheless, such a problem existed, as an incident that served as a prelude to the soul-searching of the sixties made clear.

The incident concerned what the *Inquirer* called "the biggest social event of the season," the annual debutante party at the Scarsdale Golf Club, better known as the Holly Ball. In 1960 one of the debutantes chose as her escort a convert to Episcopalianism whose father was Jewish. When the ball committee rejected her choice, the girl cancelled her debut.[4]

The incident came to public attention nearly two weeks after the ball in a sermon delivered by George F. Kempsell, the rector of the Church of St. James the Less. Kempsell recognized the issue as "a very complex religious and social one" but said he felt compelled to act because the boy, the girl, and instrumental figures at the golf club were all members of his parish. The rector's sermon did not mince words. He described the decision to exclude the young man "as morally reprehensible, . . . a sin against God and against a member of this congregation." He continued, "What we are saying is that if Our Lord Jesus Christ had come to earth in Scarsdale in time for the Holly Ball, he would not have been allowed to escort a young lady of this parish to that dance." He concluded,

> Therefore, I feel it is my responsibility as your pastor to say that anyone who has in any way, by word or in thought or deed, acquiesced with this position of the Scarsdale Golf Club [or who in his . . . mind agrees with that decision] is no longer welcome to receive Holy Communion at this Altar . . . until such time as he had worked out his own peace with God in his way.[5]

The sermon electrified the congregation and the community. The *New York Times* reported that one of Kempsell's parishioners resigned from the church and several other parishioners expressed their sorrow regarding their involvement in the affair. Meanwhile, a local rabbi praised Kempsell's "uncompromising courage and clarity," and a number of Protestant ministers voiced their "Amen[s]." Several residents made similar statements, a few using the occasion to call for "an all-out attack against bigotry." One woman stated confidently that anti-Semitic actions were "as doomed as segregation in the South." The *Scarsdale Inquirer* was less optimistic. In a front-page editorial it spoke of "The Wall of Fear"—fear of "encroachment by an alien group" that separated Christians and Jews in Scarsdale. The incident, it felt, had caused a worsening, not an improvement, in relations between the two groups. It believed, "the barrier, clearly, will not be overthrown," but hoped that "those who dislike walls . . . might find ways" of scaling this one.[6]

In the years after the incident, there were some indications that the wall was crumbling. In September 1961 thirty residents met to organize a local chapter of the National Conference of Christians and Jews. In January 1964 the village board, hoping to foster "mutual esteem, justice, and equity among the diverse groups of the community," agreed to establish an advisory committee on human relations. Within fourteen months of its formation, that committee was acting to end discrimination in housing sales against Jews and non-Caucasians. In a different vein in the 1970s, such community organizations as the Scarsdale Bowl Committee stopped holding social functions at restrictive private clubs. Perhaps most significantly the Scarsdale Golf Club, the site of the old Holly Ball, quietly began to admit Jewish members. The *Inquirer*'s observation of 1961, that relations between Christians and Jews were confined to "a plane of polite non-intercourse," no longer held true. Although differences still existed—most notably on the use of public land for the display of a Christmas crèche—economics, demography, and history had conspired to bring the two groups somewhat closer.[7]

In addition to the change in the ethnic composition of the local population, there was also a change in its political orientation. These two shifts were to some extent related. The increase in the percentage of Jews and Catholics in Scarsdale, traditionally Democratic voting groups, probably contributed to the declining size of the Republican majorities in the presidential elections from 1948 to 1960. Between that year and 1964, however, a dramatic reversal of voting patterns occurred that marked a new era of independence on the part of the Scarsdale electorate. In 1964 the Democratic candidate, Lyndon B. Johnson, won 64.8 percent of the presidential ballots in Scarsdale, almost exactly the proportion the Republican candidate, Richard M. Nixon, had received in 1960. Four years later 5,280 villagers cast their ballots for the Democrat, Hubert H. Humphrey, while 4,292 voted for Nixon and 92 for the American Independent candidate, George Wallace. In the next presidential election the Republicans won a slim majority of the local ballots. Although 5,117 voters preferred the Democratic candidate, George McGovern, 5,299 supported the incumbent, Richard M. Nixon.[8]

The revival of two-party politics in Scarsdale, for county and state as well as national elections, along with a rekindling of interest in abstract political questions, spurred opposition to the nonpartisan system. For decades the overwhelming majority of residents had acquiesced in the Town Club's view that Scarsdale's nonpartisan government was "*the* source of local strength." As late as 1957, Harry J. Liese argued that his preference for the Democratic Party in national matters had "nothing to do with municipal government." "The village is a corporate enterprise," he said, "that has to be run efficiently and nonpartisanly for the resident stockholders."[9] Within a few years, however, the nonpartisan system had begun to come under sustained attack from Liese's fellow Democrats, who, convinced of the correctness of their political principles and made bold by signs of their growing strength, began demanding reforms in the system. To illustrate the urgency of these demands, the Democrats' official party caucus withheld its support from the nominees of the nonpartisan committee from 1963 to 1970. In two of those years individual Democrats, without party endorsement, opposed the nonpartisan candidates, and in 1970 the party formally sponsored a slate that ran against the nonpartisan choices. Although these contested elections, the first in nearly forty years, nevertheless resulted in victories for the nonpartisan candidates, they did not produce a renewal of faith in Scarsdale's political traditions. Scarsdale's method of political operation had too many kudos to its credit to be defeated, but it was too remote and too decorous to inspire a deep sense of attachment.

In the early 1960s, when the Democrats began withholding their support from the nonpartisan process, they said that they were acting "as a matter of principle and without reference to the individual candidates." In their opinion, the process, as currently constituted, was "not nonpartisan, nor democratic, nor representative, nor responsive." To correct these failings, they demanded several changes in its structure and operation: the direct election of the citizens' nominating committee; the replacement of the so-called nucleus committee (which then consisted of the presidents of the Town Club and Woman's Club, one representative selected by the presidents of the neighborhood associations, and two at-large members selected by the outgoing nominating committee) with officers of the committee's own choosing; the abolition of artificial ratios for representatives of the two parties and sexes; and the institution of public forums for candidates to express their views.[10]

As the party set forth its ideas, individual Democrats made incisive remarks. In a speech to the League of Women Voters, J. Robert Moskin stressed the elitist aspects of Scarsdale's government. Pondering a phrase often favorably associated with the nonpartisan system, "the job seeks the man," he reminded his audience that "a job is an inanimate thing which cannot seek anything." In his opinion, the phrase actually implied that "those who hold power seek the man of whom they approve." Here, he said, "power does not come up from the people but down from those who possess it." He concluded that such a situation was lamentable in Scarsdale "because I cannot think of another community better fit to govern itself."[11]

More caustic than Moskin was Robert J. Koblitz. He compared the lack of choice among candidates in Scarsdale's elections and the lack of open discussion at village board meetings to the operation of the Prussian monarchy and the Soviet state. When a former mayor described Scarsdale's government as "a special brand of democracy," Koblitz retorted, "Distrust of the people and dislike of contested elections" were *not* unusual or special. "The point is," he said, "they are seldom called 'democratic.'"[12]

By 1965 the Town Club, after making a few minor changes in the nonpartisan nominating procedure, seemed willing to undertake its thorough reform. Stating that the nonpartisan system should not be viewed as "sacrosanct," the club called for continuing efforts "to simplify the system and to strengthen its representative characteristics." Two years later the club approved "controlled direct elections" of the nonpartisan nominating committee "with built-in safeguards for the majority [Republican] party." After another two years it had dismantled the nucleus committee and abolished the sex and political ratios. It was also considering methods of holding candidate forums.[13]

Yet those changes did not come rapidly enough to satisfy the system's strongest critics. In 1967 Koblitz, a political science professor at Bard College, and Emily F. Korzenik, a teacher of social studies, opposed the election of the nonpartisan citizens' slate. The two criticized the "ceremonial" and "perfunctory" nature of the political process in Scarsdale and accused the village board of failing to provide "leadership in discussion" and "opportunity for dissent."[14]

While Koblitz and Korzenik lambasted the system, the nonpartisan nominees, in accordance with tradition, tried to avoid any campaigning. The candidates selected in 1967 were representative of the type of executive talent that the nonpartisan committee had always prized. The candidate for mayor was Malcolm A. MacIntyre, a vice-president of the Martin-Marietta Corportion. Nominated for seats on the village board were Richard Darrow, the president of Hill and Knowlton, a leading public relations firm; Saul Horowitz, the president of the HRH Construction Corporation; and Hartselle Kinsey, a recently retired vice-president of Union Carbide.[15]

While MacIntyre and his colleagues refrained from campaigning, those who supported their candidacy did not. In the weeks before the election, they wrote letters to the newspaper, circulated petitions, and purchased ads. Such efforts helped to secure a relatively large turnout for the election and a four-to-one margin for the citizens' slate. But the nonpartisan victory did not settle the issue. If the 600 residents who voted for Koblitz and Korzenik wanted contested elections and more open government, then the nonpartisan system was in for more trouble.[16]

That trouble was not long in coming. In 1968 Korzenik again ran for office, and despite no official Democratic endorsement, she narrowed the margin between her opponents and herself.[17] Two years later, in 1970, the Democrats formally opposed the nonpartisan slate. They reached this decision late in the weeks before the election, after the nonpartisan committee, whose members had been elected by the voters in neighborhood district meetings, nominated candidates the Democrats deemed too conservative. The party, which had based its earlier withdrawal from the nonpartisan process on "principles, not persons," now opposed candidates selected through a process that the Democrats had forced to reform. This exceedingly contradictory behavior seemed more comprehensible in the context of the times. The Democrats had moved further to the left in the course of the decade. Because they wanted trustees who favored the building of low-income housing and the racial integration of the community, they nominated Herbert Beenhouwer, Lloyd Meeker, and Olivia Sachs to oppose Albert Foreman, Burnham Finney, and especially Jane Hackett, whose husband was Scarsdale's most outspoken conservative. Yet once again a majority of the active citizens rallied to the support of the nonpartisan system. In the Foreman-Beenhouwer race the vote was 2,466 to 828; in the Finney-Meeker election it was 2,285 to 894; and in the choice between Hackett and Sachs, it was 2,174 to 1,066.[18]

The defeat quieted the Democrats for a while, but it did not reconcile them to the revised nonpartisan system. Throughout the 1970s and into the 1980s, the Democrats, insisting on more direct voter-candidate exchanges, continued to withhold their support from the nonpartisan candidates, and in 1971 the Republican caucus began to take similar action. Within a decade this disaffection had spawned a new movement that called for the holding of contested, nonpartisan elections, but in its first test at the polls, the Open Government Coalition lost by a nearly three-to-one margin, as had earlier insurgents.[19]

Still, the agitation of the past twenty years had not been in vain. Indeed, it had helped to cause some important changes. Now that the voters, gathering in neighborhood district meetings, elected the members of the nominating committee, and now that the committee could select candidates without regard to party or sex, the nominees for village office included more Jews and more women. In addition, the candidates of the nonpartisan nominating committee, so long berated for their remoteness, were beginning to engage in some low-key campaigning. Though they still avoided open forums when there was a rival slate, they expressed their opinions in newspaper interviews and tried to meet the members of the electorate by attending local meetings.[20] The time had passed when the candidates nominated by the committee were known to the voters almost entirely through the achievements listed on their résumés. The comparison that earlier residents had delighted in making between the governance of Scarsdale and that of a major corporation no longer appeared quite so appropriate.

The liberalism, by local standards radicalism, of a significant group of Scarsdale's citizens affected not only the process of sifting candidates for local office but also the process of winnowing potential buyers and renters of property. As the southern-based civil rights movement exploded into the national black power movement, village residents began to feel that Scarsdale was not immune from either the blame for, or the ramifications of, the racial and economic stratification that marked the metropolitan area and the country. Declaring that "Scarsdale is not an island," many called for an end to racial discrimination in residential sales and rentals, while some wanted a change in the zoning ordinance to permit the erection of low-income housing.[21] These appeals for a sharp break from past community goals irritated some other residents who felt they were being both pressured and patronized. As the gulf between the two groups grew, village leaders did not lose sight of compromise. The Scarsdale of 1980 would be neither as different as the reformers had called for, nor as different as their opponents had feared.

"Scarsdale has become a symbol," said soon-to-be trustee Carol Stix in the mid-1960s. "Just as every American boy can grow up to be president, every family who wants to should be able to live here if they can afford it."[22] That ideal underlay a lot of effort on the part of village reformers, particularly from 1961 to 1967. The movement began with the organization of the Scarsdale Fair Housing Group. Like twenty-five already-existing organizations in the New York metropolitan area, the SFHG aimed to eradicate racial discrimination in housing. To achieve that end, members offered to accompany blacks who were looking for houses and tried to solicit the names of homeowners who were willing to sell to black families. But the SFHG soon encountered a problem. Most village homeowners and real estate brokers seemed reluctant to sell to blacks, not because they opposed open housing "in principle," but because they feared "offending their neighbors" or "displeasing potential customers."[23]

With this in mind, the leaders of the SFHG decided to launch a campaign that would show the pervasiveness of prointegration feeling in Scarsdale. In 1965 they drew up a "Good Neighbor Pledge" that publicly committed those who signed it "to welcome new neighbors . . . without regard to race, religion, color, or national origin and . . . to promote brotherhood in our community." Within a short time the pledge had received the support of nearly 1,000 individuals, as well as several church, neighborhood, and community organizations.[24] In the meantime, the village board had begun working, through its advisory committee on human relations, to inform residents of the terms of a state law that forbade discrimination in housing. Although the members of the board argued for a time that further action on their part was unnecessary, they passed a resolution urging "all citizens to support the principle of open housing," in November 1966, and two years later they approved an ordinance that provided for the use of court injunctions and the levying of fines in cases of discrimination.[25]

Such actions made the editor of the *Inquirer* ecstatic. In his opinion, they "give the lie to those who misjudge our village . . . [as] wealthy, smug, [and] self-satisfied." By supporting open housing, he said, "we tell the world that Scarsdale is far from smug, that Scarsdale believes in human dignity and decency and fairness, and that the people of Scarsdale are prepared to support their beliefs with their acts."[26]

As enthusiasm for the idea of open housing swept through the community, one section of Scarsdale turned the other way. At a meeting of the Arthur Manor Association, residents voted fifty-nine to forty-two against group adoption of the good neighbor pledge. Instead, they voted to leave decisions on transactions regarding housing to the "individual consciences of residents of the area." Although an editorial in the *Inquirer* labeled the association's decision "disturbing," it could not have been entirely surprising.[27] With its comparatively small lots and modest houses, Arthur Manor was one of the only sections of Scarsdale where there was reason to believe that many blacks could afford to purchase property. Whether the residents of other areas were actually more enlightened or simply less directly threatened was a question that defied a clear-cut answer. In any case, in 1968, when the focus of reformist zeal turned from the goal of providing equal access to the housing that existed to the notion of providing new units for low- and moderate-income families, opposition developed on a community-wide basis.

The equation of expensive single-family houses with peace, beauty, and the good life had long been a central tenet of the orthodox suburban faith. To that end, the village board had passed both a restrictive zoning ordinance in 1922 and a demanding building code in 1923. In 1947 the board had added minimum acreage requirements, and in 1950 it had adopted the so-called look-alike law to prevent the construction of mass-produced houses. More recently, in 1962, the zoning board of appeals had confirmed the community's commitment to single-family residences by denying the use for a nonprofit music school of a twenty-three-room mansion on a nine and a half-acre estate, and in 1965 the village trustees voted to replace the awkward look-alike law with a more flexible, more powerful board of architectural review.[28]

This latest addition to the series of local ordinances that regulated construction came only three years before the Scarsdale Fair Housing Group began demanding changes in those ordinances that would permit the construction of multifamily dwellings for those with low and moderate incomes. The SFHG recommended a number of sites scattered throughout Scarsdale. Of these the land, owned by the village, known as the Freightway received the most serious attention. Located near the business district and next to the railroad tracks, the site had already been mentioned for use as a parking garage. Proponents of the housing project proposed to build a large structure combining several stories of parking with several of apartments.[29]

In arguing for the plan, reformers like Herbert Beenhouwer, Emily Korzenik, Robert Ostrow, and Ethel Robinson, underscored the shortage of "decent housing at reasonable cost" in the metropolitan area, and Westchester in particular. They appealed to the sympathies of local residents, reminding them that many of the people employed in Scarsdale could not afford to live there. They appealed to the residents' sense of urgency, stressing the seriousness of the urban crisis and its potential for disaster. Most of all, they appealed to the villagers' pride. They asked, "If Scarsdale, one of the nation's richest communities,

[can] not put up one low-to-middle income apartment house, what community [can]?" All Scarsdale needed was the will to do it, they insisted. "We can do anything we want to," Korzenik said, "and we should have done it yesterday."[30]

Other residents disputed the wisdom of the proposed housing project. On the most fundamental level they objected to the suggested location. There were too many drawbacks to the site: the danger of proximity to the tracks, the lack of play space, the seriousness of traffic congestion, and the isolation of Freightway from the residential districts of the community. A citizens' committee, advising against the project, said, "Housing any minority group, white or black, at a site inferior to other areas in Scarsdale could accentuate the very real differences we wish to reconcile."[31]

Residents also objected to the proposal's probable impact on local spending and taxes. They stressed the strain that an increased population would place on local schools and services and questioned the equity of providing subsidized housing to people with incomes little lower than those of 30 percent of the families already living in Scarsdale. While asserting that they were "not unaware of the problems that are tearing our nation apart," they argued, "you do not have to hurt white people . . . to help break caste barriers."[32]

Finally, residents made it clear that they objected to any basic change in the physical layout of the community or in its class structure. One man said the plan would lead to "the Queensification of Scarsdale, . . . the proliferation of the ugly." Another asked, "Is there anything immoral about a better neighborhood—provided we let all aspire to it and share it when they can afford it?" A woman stated, "I cannot see any point in trying to destroy this community. . . . If people are concerned about the problem, they should go where the problems are."[33]

These considerations formed the basis for a statement issued by the village board in October 1968. In rejecting the proposal for the construction of a low- to moderate-income apartment house in the Freightway area, the trustees spoke of the problems of creating "an isolated ghetto unsupported by recreational facilities," of placing an "extra financial burden . . . on many of our neighbors least fitted economically to bear these costs," and of undermining "the present environment for living in Scarsdale." The trustees stressed their commitment to the racial integration of the community but not to its economic integration. They concluded their statement with the following promise:

> We intend to formulate a program that will give clear credibility to our welcome for those black citizens who in increasing numbers are attaining the ability to purchase homes here. We will seek, directly or indirectly, to encourage, accelerate, and augment this movement so that these citizens will take their places freely interspersed among us.[34]

The program the trustees alluded to was formally established two months later as the Scarsdale Open Society Association. Endorsed by the village board but not under its direct supervision, SOSA consisted of a nonprofit organization empowered to lend funds originally set at $80,000, later increased to $175,000. The fund would be used to overcome one of the chief obstacles to the purchase of houses in Scarsdale by members of racial minorities—lack of capital for a sufficient down payment to complete the financial arrangements. By applying to SOSA, a minority group member with a good credit rating could acquire a second mortgage for the amount he or she needed. Consequently, the program would help to achieve the goal the trustees had set for Scarsdale, racial integration of the community without a change in its class structure.[35]

Although most village residents approved of the plan, a few felt differently. One man termed it "unlawful and undemocratic" on the ground that it would discriminate in favor of certain racial groups. Another called attention to its implicit elitism by parodying the inscription on the Statue of Liberty:

> Give us your educated, your affluent, your intellectuals,
> Your upper class, . . . inconspicuous, uniformed in white collars
>   and gray flannel Brooks Brothers suits.
> And Scarsdale will open its golden gate to the promised land.[36]

In spite of such criticism, SOSA persisted and made a small difference. Although the number of blacks living in Scarsdale declined from 833 in 1960 to 314 in 1980, the decline resulted from a sharp drop in the number of black servants living in the community. Meanwhile, the number of heads of primary families who were black increased from fewer than 20, most of whom resided on isolated Saxon Woods Road, to about 50 scattered throughout the community. Although SOSA was not directly responsible for all this increase (by 1981 only 15 black families had accepted loans from the association and half of those had moved away), the association's existence probably helped to attract some black families who required no assistance to purchase houses.[37]

For whatever reason blacks were attracted to Scarsdale, it was clear they did not come as a result of concessions in zoning. Despite continued agitation for the building of low- and middle-income housing, the village board stuck by its policy statement of 1968. Rejecting as unsound the building of housing projects "solely for 'showcase' purposes," it at first called for efforts to solve the housing crisis on a county-wide or regional basis. Then, in 1974, when the New York Urban Development Corporation wanted to construct a forty-unit complex on land donated by the Westchester Ethical Humanist Society, the village board refused to grant permission for the project. Although the proposal had the support of former mayors Malcolm MacIntyre and Saul Horowitz, Jr., the board considered it "inconsistent" with Scarsdale's "fundamental philosophy that the village is a residential community essentially of single-family houses."[38]

For better or worse, the board applied that principle not only to proposals for the construction of low-income housing, which would have required tax abatement from the village, but also to proposals for the construction of luxury apartments, which would have enlarged the tax base. In 1970 the trustees tabled a suggestion from Eggers and Higgins Architects to use village-owned land near the Scarsdale station for two apartment buildings of sixteen and twenty-four stories each. Six years later they rejected a request from the heirs of George G. Allen to erect cluster-housing condominiums on a part of the family's twenty-five acre estate. Additional proposals for the construction of multifamily residences seemed certain to be rejected if the trustees heeded neighborhood sentiment.[39] Thus, sixty years after the passage of its zoning ordinance, Scarsdale was still "a village of homes," though now an occasional black family might be able to purchase one of them.

Whereas concerning housing most Scarsdale residents came to accept a compromise position—favoring the racial integration of the community without its economic integration—concerning education they appeared to be more deeply divided. While no one quarreled with the principle of allowing residents of all races to send their children to the schools, and while no one opposed permitting a few southern blacks the chance to finish high school in Scarsdale, they disagreed sharply over plans to bus minority children from a neighboring district into the Scarsdale schools. The depth of feeling on the issue resulted in part from the importance the community placed on education, but other factors—from worsening racial tensions, to the widening generation gap, to a diminishing faith in authority—played a part as well. Though the sources of division were national in scope, many residents blamed the school board for its local manifestation. The board misread a large part of the public on the issue of busing, and these residents let the board feel their displeasure.

In 1965 Kenneth W. Thompson, the new president of the board of education, a scholar in the field of international relations, and a vice-president of the Rockefeller Foundation, told the readers of the *Inquirer*, "The cutting edge of educational advance is in the hands of pacesetters like Scarsdale. . . ." He made it clear that, during his tenure as president, the school board and staff would engage in "discussion of new techniques," but, he assured his readers, "the overarching end remains in 1965, as in 1915, the best education for the largest possible number of students."[40]

Three years later Thompson, retiring from the board, was still in a pioneering mood, though now that his interests had gained a focus his words had greater urgency. "School boards," he said, "should be concerned with the 'great burning issues of our times.'" The country and the world were undergoing a social revolution, and he believed that that revolution should be "encouraged, fostered, helped." The citizens of Scarsdale, he implied, could best foster change by cooperating with the proposals their board of education had placed before them.[41]

During the preceding three years, Thompson and his various colleagues on the school board—two lawyers, an accountant, a builder, an architect, an investment counselor, and four housewives, along with school superintendent Donald G. Emery—had initiated two programs and were pondering a third, all of which were intended "to broaden channels for mutual understanding and cooperation between whites and blacks." The first was the Student Transfer Education Program. Established in 1966, it enabled black students from segregated schools in the South to spend their last two years of high school in Scarsdale while living with local families. This program was small-sized but long-lived.

In 1968 there were six STEP students attending Scarsdale High; in 1971 there were twelve; in 1981, one.[42]

The second program, the Summer Cooperative Project, was more ambitious, more controversial, and less enduring. The project's goal was to bring together 100 junior high school students from predominantly white Scarsdale and largely black Mount Vernon. These "high potential but low achievement" students would receive six weeks of special classes and intensive tutoring in mathematics, science, and the language arts. Scarsdale would provide the facilities and the direction. A racially balanced teaching staff would be recruited from both school districts. The federal government, under Title III of the Elementary and Secondary Education Act, would pay the $55,000 bill.[43]

More than a year of planning had gone into the project when, in January 1968, one man began to express disapproval. In a letter to the *Inquirer*, Robert S. Hackett questioned the propriety of "one of the wealthiest communities in the nation" applying for federal aid. He charged that the board had sought outside funding because its members knew that, if it meant a small rise in taxes, busing pupils from "less opulent districts" would not win voter approval. He reminded the school board it did not have "a mandate to tamper with the principle of our neighborhood schools" and said that such "tampering . . . [was] more apt to destroy a superlative standard than to elevate general educational performance."[44]

A few weeks later, at a school board meeting, Hackett proved that his position had broad support. Presenting a petition bearing 533 signatures, which he said he had collected in three days, Hackett called on the board to withdraw its application for federal funds. If such a program were to be undertaken, he said, it should be financed entirely by local taxes and only if a majority of residents voted to do so in a referendum on that question.[45]

But the board did not withdraw its application for the grant or hold a referendum on the Summer Cooperative Project. In a formal statement it reminded the public that, "generally speaking, [the American system of governance] operates not on the basis of plebiscites but through representative government." The board explained that its members constituted "a duly elected body . . . [whose] long hours and excessive homework give it a basis for decisions . . . seldom matched in the community." While it promised to be "attentive to public opinion," it recalled the tradition of earlier boards, "unwilling to yield their sacred trust on fundamental educational matters to pressure groups, however worthy their cause or mission."[46]

In May 1968, the board of education received the funding it had requested. The program was held that summer, and according to a team of evaluators from Sarah Lawrence College, it achieved its "major objectives . . . with good to excellent measure of success." Plans to repeat the project proceeded, but in the spring of 1969 funding for educational summer programs was eliminated by Congressional cutbacks.[47] These developments received little attention from village residents, however, because the Summer Cooperative Project had been eclipsed by another more far-reaching proposal.

The new proposal was the logical outgrowth of the kind of thinking then current in educational circles. In such works as the Coleman Report and *Racial Isolation in the Public Schools*, experts pointed to the racial unrest in American cities as evidence that the time had come for changes in the relationship between black inner-city school districts and white suburban districts. Underscoring the growing disparities between the underfinanced, academically weak city schools and the tax-rich, academically sound schools of the suburbs, they implied that whole metropolitan areas would be engulfed in turmoil if no steps were taken to ease the inequities.[48]

In the mid-1960s several educators brought these points home to the people of Scarsdale. In 1966 Robert Dentler, the deputy director of the Center for Urban Education and a professor at Columbia Teachers College, said, "Scarsdale is on the inner ring of suburbs and is gradually being absorbed into the urban core. The challenge is to provide the kind of leadership and stimulation needed to bring quality education to a vast area." "Certainly some problems hit the inner city first," he continued, "but sooner or later they are everywhere." In 1967 Kenneth Clark, the president of the Metropolitan Applied Research Center and a professor of psychology at the City University of New York, urged a Scarsdale audience "to take the initiative in organizing school districts that transcend political boundaries . . . to include ghetto areas." He warned, "The problems of the inner city area are and will be your problems, tomorrow if not yesterday." A few months later Scarsdale's own superintendent, Donald G. Emery, published an article in *Look* magazine. Predicting the almost total segregation of Northern schools "if the nation holds to its present course," he called on the North's suburban school districts to bear the burden of integration with the cooperation of city districts and vast amounts of state and federal aid.[49]

By the time Emery wrote those words, some metropolitan areas had already heeded the call for urban-suburban cooperation, albeit in pilot programs. In the Hartford area, there was Project Concern, in Rochester, Project Unique. In Boston, the Metropolitan Council for Educational Opportunity (METCO) oversaw the busing of 917 inner-city children to schools in twenty-eight suburban towns.[50] How could Scarsdale fail to meet what Emery had once called "the challenge of a new excellence for a new era?" "Our only danger is that we may think too modestly, be overly cautious, or fail to aspire to the stature which is possible for us," he said.[51]

In view of the idealism, urgency, and ambition expressed by Emery and school board president Thompson, the plan they placed before the public seemed to be quite moderate. The plan grew out of the work of two groups: a high school faculty committee on civil rights and, in particular, a parent-teacher committee on Scarsdale's urban responsibility. In its first year of implementation, targeted for 1969–70, the plan would involve the busing of six randomly selected first-grade children and six kindergarten children, probably from black neighborhoods in Mount Vernon, to each of Scarsdale's five elementary schools. In subsequent years the thirty children already enrolled in each grade would move up through the system while thirty new pupils would enter on the kindergarten level. Eventually the program would involve a maximum of 390 black pupils from outside Scarsdale. The sender community would contribute the amount of money it normally spent per child and the state would make up the difference between that amount and Scarsdale's costs. To ease the loneliness of the bused-in pupils, Scarsdale parents would agree to serve as host families, providing lunchtime meals and after-school entertainment.[52]

From March 1968, when the proposal was first aired, to March 1970, when the Mount Vernon board of education voted to reject it, the issue of busing, more than any other, convulsed the community. On the one side, many people agreed with the *Inquirer*'s endorsement of the program as "a moral imperative" and "a social necessity." With "our country hurtling down a collision course," said Mrs. Marvin S. Traub, "we each of us have little enough opportunity to directly shape our world. Here is one way to reach out, to embrace a sense of humanity."

Proponents of the program also emphasized its potential benefits for Scarsdale students. According to a letter signed by 229 high school seniors, the plan would help "to end the isolation that we [students] experience in Scarsdale" and better "prepare us for a diversified world environment." Finally, the plan seemed to express the community's sense of striving. "If we are half as good as we think we are," said high school principal Aaron Fink, "we can accommodate these children."[53]

On the other side of the issue, a large number of people doubted whether the program would ease racial tensions or prove advantageous to either the students in Scarsdale or those who were bused. One man dismissed the program as "pure tokenism," another called it "a futile gesture." A third wondered if "exposing our children to a few new and darker faces for a few hours daily [would] truly benefit either group." Harry B. Gilbert, a psychologist for thirty-two years in the New York City schools, said he opposed the integration plan because "it obfuscates the real problem of how to teach slum children." He termed the program "psychologically and educationally unsound for the bused students," of dubious advantage to Scarsdale students, and "fraught with possible negative attitudes." He concluded, "I am hardly against what is needed to break down barriers, but I am sensitive for the Negro students."[54]

Some residents who opposed the plan voiced concern over the issue of cost. Although representatives of the board of education repeatedly stated that outside sources would cover any expenses the program entailed, a few taxpayers remained unconvinced. They reminded the board that outside funding was usually granted as "seed money" with the implication that the local district would eventually absorb the costs. They added, even if the state and federal governments continued to pay the expenses, that still affected the size of their total tax payments.[55]

A few proponents of the program were impatient with those who raised objections to it. A teen-ager said she was "disturbed about the mercenary attitude [being] expressed." A woman agreed, "The preoccupation with finances in one of the wealthiest communities in the United States fill[s] me with shame." A couple implied that racism underlay the objections of many opponents: "This group does not want black kids going to school with their children . . . or other Scarsdale children." A college student was more direct, "Those of you who want to subvert the program and believe Negroes should stay in their place should say so and not hide behind [other arguments]."[56]

While one side accused its opponents of racism, the other said those who favored the program were acting out of guilt. A student critic of the program charged that, because residents had "a guilty conscience for putting the black man where he is today," they wanted to try to "save their souls" by letting blacks make up a small fraction of the schools' population. In a similar vein, a couple asked whether "showing off a number of poor Negroes" would help assuage the residents' guilt.[57]

As residents clashed, not only over the program's probable costs and benefits but over each other's motivations as well, the question of a referendum again came to the fore. As he had argued in the case of the Summer Cooperative Project, so again Robert S. Hackett accused the school board of seeking "OUTSIDE financing . . . [in order] to evade any necessity for obtaining a favorable vote on the proposal BEFORE its implementation." He continued,

> It would seem crystal clear that ANY program of the class currently under discussion would have a better chance of success and a better chance for doing all the good expected of it if it could be launched with the knowledge that it had won well-deserved approval before introduction.

Still, the members of the school board resisted Hackett's demand. According to its president, Kenneth W. Thompson, the board was required by its mandate to exercise a certain "arrogance of conscience." "The board must act as it believes the great mass of people would act if they had the same available facts, [and] had given the subject the same amount of time and study."[58]

Theoretically the board was on solid ground, politically it was not. What Thompson called the board's "arrogance of conscience," some citizens interpreted as sheer conceit. In the spring of 1968, they made the board's unwillingness to hold a referendum the central issue in a contest for its two vacant seats. While the regular candidates, Jackson B. Browning and Joseph B. Ullman, supported the board's tradition of "independent, impartial decisions," the challengers, John P. Laware and Ward L. Reed, Jr., tried to make the election "a referendum on a referendum." They were not antibusing or against the nonpartisan system; they were simply proreferendum, they said. The results showed that a large number of citizens supported their position. In the Browning-Laware race the vote was 1,836 to 1,767; in the Ullman-Reed race it was 1,795 to 1,788.[59]

With fewer than seventy ballots separating the candidates in one election and only seven in the other, the Committee for a Referendum (CFR) petitioned the state commission of education for a new election. Since some irregularities had occurred in the election process, the commission agreed. This time, with 50 percent more citizens voting, the regular candidates won by a somewhat safer margin. Browning defeated Reed by a vote of 2,810 to 2,611, and Ullman defeated Hamilton V. Howry, Jr. (who had replaced Laware), 2,858 to 2,655.[60]

In the months after the special election, the members of the board of education tried to steer a middle course. While reaffirming their interest in providing an educational program suited to "the realities of a multi-racial society," they postponed the date for implementing such a program to 1970–71. In addition, they decided to decrease the number of bused children in each grade to twenty-five; to preselect them for maturity, self-motivation, and academic potential; to distribute them to the schools where crowding was least severe, and to evaluate the program after two years to see if it should be continued. These modifications, along with the board's promise to allow a full airing of citizens' views before the program's formal adoption, helped to explain the unspectacular showing of the CFR candidate in the June 1969 election.[61]

Nevertheless, in the fall of that year, it became clear that the community remained deeply divided. At a series of six public hearings on the integration plan, the board heard from critics who considered the proposal too risky, as well as from critics who considered it too tame. Proponents appeared to dominate one of the hearings, opponents dominated two, the audience split evenly in three. Competing advertisements, each with more than 1,000 sponsors, appeared in the *Inquirer* in early December. The PTA Council and the League of Women Voters supported the plan; the members of the Town Club voted against it.[62]

Presumably the hearings, the ads, and the organizations' resolutions were supposed to inform the board of the people's wishes. But as the day approached when its members were to cast their votes on the proposed experiment, many citizens were becoming convinced that they were "powerless to affect" the board's thinking. According to Raymond Davies, who had attended one of the hearings, "The whole tone of the board's utterances, despite their protestations to the contrary, seems to indicate a mind already made up to proceed with their plan." Davies urged the board to reconsider its position on the holding of an advisory vote and warned that failure to do so would intensify "the strong current of resentment" that already existed.[63]

The board of education did not hold a referendum, however. On December 8, 1969, its members voted six to one to adopt the modified integration plan. The president of the board, Leonard Howard, explaining his "yes" vote, described the program as "wholesome . . . not fearsome. . . . The good concerned citizens of Scarsdale of generations past built such bridges toward better education and I feel we are following in that tradition." Trustee Joseph B. Ullman agreed: "If the result helps one iota to ameliorate the disastrous race relations situation facing this country, that should be another reason to accept the plan, not a reason to condemn it." But, to the man who cast the dissenting vote, the issue looked more complicated. In a prepared statement, Jackson B. Browning said that, while he saw "no fatal defects in the proposed experiment itself," he voted against its adoption because he perceived such action "to be in defiance of the public will." In this time of reductions in state aid and increase in school taxes, he thought, the board should be "more, not less, responsive" to popular opinion. Moreover, the program's adoption in an atmosphere of deep division undermined its potential for a positive impact. Since the program was basically "a gesture of good will," it "should be made by the community if it is to be effective," not by the school board "in a spirit of uncertainty as to the willingness of the community to participate."[64]

The people of Scarsdale never learned how the experiment in integration would have worked. On March 5, 1970, the members of the Mount Vernon board of education voted not to participate in the plan. The decision came after two public hearings at which a small group of people expressed disparate views. While several residents of the city cautiously endorsed the program, others raised objections to it. One black parent worried about the criteria used in selecting the children. "The cream of the crop will be taken out of [Mount Vernon] and sent to Scarsdale," he said. A rabbi questioned the propriety of using hundreds of thousands of dollars of state funds to bus black children to a wealthy white community when money was desperately needed to upgrade the schools in black neighborhoods. But the argument that seemed to have the greatest influence on the eight white board members who voted against the plan came from a representative of Scarsdale's CFR. With the Mount Vernon school board already attempting to fight court-ordered busing within its city limits and with white residents of the city threatening to sue the board if it established a program open exclusively to blacks, Harold J. Reynolds pointed out that the board would find itself in an untenable position. On the one hand, it would be trying to oppose busing to achieve an interracial balance within its own area of jurisdiction, and on the other hand, it would be trying to support busing to achieve integration in another community. In vain did representatives of the National Association for the Advancement of Colored People argue against Reynolds's position. In the end, only Mary Ellen Cooper, the board's sole black member, voted for the plan.[65]

The proposal for interdistrict busing was dead, but the ramifications of the Scarsdale board of education's effort to "ram . . . the proposal . . . down the community's throats" were just beginning to be felt. In two trips to the polls, on May 12 and June 4, the voters rejected the more than $11 million budget the board of education had approved. The first defeat seemed partly the result of a low voter turnout. Only 1,437 citizens had voted—815 against the proposal—compared to a turnout of more than 4,000 the preceding year. But the second defeat, by a vote of 2,105 to 2,225, could not be blamed on voter apathy. Though a 3.5 percent increase in the property tax on top of new assessments no doubt played a part in the considerations of the people who voted against the budget, many used this opportunity to express dissatisfaction with the board's "inept" and "misguided" actions and "obdurate," "contemptuous," and "cavalier" attitude. Six months after the board's yes vote on busing, a large number of citizens said no to the board.[66]

With a state-mandated austerity program looming over the schools, the budget passed in its third try, but the school board recognized its constituents were not pleased. In July 1970, the board elected as its president Jackson B. Browning, the man who had voted against the adoption of busing. Under his direction its members committed themselves to "do better in understanding and harmonizing community aspirations and requirements." In September the board took an important step in that direction by setting up a series of citizen-staff committees to assess the job the schools were doing. In January 1971, it hired a consultant to improve communication between the board and the community, and in May it appointed a new superintendent. With the departure of Donald Emery to head the National Reading Institute, the board selected a candidate who, citizens hoped, would not "use Scarsdale as a stepping stone to greener pastures." That summer thirty-nine-year-old Thomas Sobol, a graduate of Harvard and Columbia Teachers College, inaugurated an era of quiet leadership. During the rest of the 1970s, the Scarsdale schools paid more attention to the needs of local residents and less attention to the problems of the metropolitan area.[67]

A recalcitrant school board and rising taxes were the most important causes of the budget defeats in 1970, but the belief that the schools were inculcating radicalism was high on the list. As day-time teach-ins on the war in Vietnam gave way to off-campus protests, the members of the school board and staff found themselves caught between the students' increasing sense of urgency and the taxpayers' increasing doubts.[68] To seal those doubts, a story appeared on the front page of the *New York Times*: "Guerilla War Tactics Taught at Scarsdale High." Although many people disputed the *Times*'s depiction of the course, the article sufficed to make Scarsdale look ridiculous, thus adding a pang of embarrassment to the pain of deep division.

The article concerned a class taught in the high school summer session of 1969 by thirty-four-year-old Stephen Kling. Toy rifle and grenade in hand, he was pictured there on page one, pointing the way to a few of the thirteen students who had taken "to the woods . . . to put into practice the revolutionary theories they [had] learned." The article detailed the rules of the war game and the course of the action as the "guerillas" overpowered the "government forces" with water pistols, water balloons, and cans of shaving cream. The article also told how, in an earlier version of the course, Kling had had the students map a strategy for taking over Scarsdale. The teacher explained that they had made "a dry run" by staking out the police, fire, and power stations and in the process learned how "very easy" it would be to sabotage the village.[69]

Picked up by the wire services, the story appeared in the press all over the world and was broadcast nationally on radio and television. "The ultimate in academic nonsense" was the pronouncement of outside commentators, but several people living inside the village interpreted the story in a more paranoid fashion. "Put in its simplest form," said Godfrey Hammond, "Scarsdale High School is teaching a group of youngsters how to take over, by violent means, the village of Scarsdale."[70]

The board of education scrambled in an effort to undo the damage. It investigated the course, sent out press releases, and mailed a newsletter to every family in the school district. These explained that the *Times* article had described only the last day's assignment in the course on the two occasions it was taught. These half-humorous exercises came after seven weeks of lectures, readings, discussions, and written examinations concerning six revolutions of the twentieth century. But the board could not settle the doubts of all of its constituents. Said one disgruntled resident, "You, gentlemen, believe that anything the yippie type wants goes, and so you use my tax dollar to teach guerilla warfare tactics to a bunch of kids who, for all I know, will turn around this fall and start putting into practice some of what they learned."[71]

The outrage expressed by a large number of residents regarding the so-called guerilla warfare course reflected, not only a waning faith in the school board and a widening gulf between young and old, but also the existence of sharp differences over American involvement in the Vietnam War. Ever since 1965, when President Johnson had increased the American commitment to South Vietnam, Scarsdale had served, according to the *New York Times*, as "the center of the anti-war movement in Westchester." In an editorial in April 1965, at the beginning of U.S. escalation, the *Scarsdale Inquirer* had opposed the war. In a telegram to the White House, in January 1966, fifteen local clergymen, representing all the major faiths, had called on the president to negotiate a peace. Scarsdale had a draft counseling service by December 1967, a "dump Johnson" movement by January 1968, and a strong surge of pro-Eugene McCarthy sentiment in the spring and summer of that year. Perhaps most significantly, on May 26, 1970, in the wake of the Cambodian invasion and the deaths at Kent State, 450 business and professional men and women from Scarsdale went to Washington to "lobby for peace" by meeting with members of Congress and officials of the executive branch.[72] Yet, despite the existence of widespread opposition to the war, the opinions expressed in the letters column in the *Inquirer* showed that many Scarsdale residents supported the government's war effort.[73] No incident better displayed the division of feeling on this issue than the debate surrounding the visit of Dean Rusk to the community, in May 1967.

Rusk came to Scarsdale to receive the first public service award ever presented by the Town Club. He certainly fulfilled the criteria the club had set. While a resident of the village from 1952 through 1961, he had actively participated in a variety of civic organizations; and both as president of the Rockefeller Foundation in the fifties and as secretary of state in the sixties, his influence had been felt far and wide.[74] Yet many residents questioned the wisdom of granting an award to "one of the architects . . . and chief government apologists of our position in Vietnam." Some took a cautious tone. As five couples wrote, "At the risk of having our objections misinterpreted as disrespect for an esteemed Scarsdalian, . . . we must still dissent [from the decision to honor the secretary of state]." Others were more strident. In the opinion of Gloria S. Karp, Rusk was "a living symbol of an American war which has been characterized as brutal, costly, unspeakable, and a blunder." "Because our Town Club is quasi-governmental," she observed, "the nation-at-large can only infer that the village of Scarsdale condones and supports the war in Vietnam."[75]

While a few individuals dismissed such criticism as "immature and irrelevant [sniping]," the members of the Town Club's convocation committee tried to defend the choice in a reasonable manner. They stated that "nothing in this award represents an endorsement of any view whatsoever . . . on Vietnam [or any other issue]." They argued, further,

> To suggest that we could honor only someone who has avoided all problems which might be controversial or someone whose every position we agree with would, we believe, represent a narrowness of vision, a demand for conformity, and a requirement for disengagement from the world which is antithetical to the very best for which Scarsdale stands.[76]

That argument satisfied some residents and failed to satisfy others. To C. M. Ferguson, Rusk was "a decent, able, and honest man trying to do a difficult job well." In a similar vein, the *Inquirer*, despite its opposition to the war, called on the people of Scarsdale to honor Rusk "not for what he symbolizes in one specific matter but for his many years of contribution to our village and to the nation." However, in the opinion of others, that "one specific matter" of Rusk's involvement in the war happened to be "the critical controversy of our time." According to Louise Feldman, the village ought to be telling Rusk, "Your shame today exceeds your contributions yesterday."[77]

The Rusk convocation was held as scheduled. On a stormy Sunday afternoon, 1,000 sympathizers filled the seats of the high school auditorium where they heard the secretary of state promise "to do everything possible to bring the struggle in Vietnam to a successful conclusion." As a token of the community's esteem, Mayor Malcolm MacIntyre presented Rusk with a crystal glass eagle and a parchment citation. Meanwhile, outside the building, 500 protesters held a silent vigil in heavy rains and gale force winds. Ten representatives of the group met with Rusk after the ceremony and presented him with a petition signed by approximately 1,000 residents, calling for an end to the bombing and the serious pursuit of a negotiated peace. Although they hoped that an appeal signed by Rusk's former neighbors would have a "special influence" with him, the ten emerged from the meeting "unconvinced and troubled."[78]

The protest surrounding the Rusk convocation inspired a column by James Wechsler in the *New York Post* a few days later. Speaking of "the quiet turmoil in sedate places," Wechsler said that the protest portrayed "in miniature . . . an unprecedented rebellion of respectability steadily spreading through the middle-class sectors of society. Many who stood outside in Scarsdale's rain are unaccustomed to carrying placards on Sunday—or any other day of the week." Wechsler noted that, while there was certainly pro-war sentiment in Scarsdale, what was becoming "increasingly clear" was "the deepening intensity of the division" between hawks and doves and "the advent of a new breed of insurgent who no longer heads from Ivy League to ivory tower and disdains dissent as a malaise of the lower classes."[79]

The final word on the significance of the Rusk convocation belonged to a man whose views had nothing to do with the war in Vietnam. In a letter to the *Inquirer*, Thomas B. Graham said he was puzzled over the motivation behind the granting of the award. Although it was normal, he said, for a man's boyhood community, or college, or graduate school, to take pride in his accomplishments, Rusk was in no way "formed" by his years in Scarsdale. He had moved to the village only after achieving "considerable public stature," and even then his work was in

New York—he merely slept in the suburb. Graham concluded by raising a pair of rhetorical questions: "Does Scarsdale honor Dean Rusk with this citation? Or does Scarsdale project its own little wonderland image for the outlanders to admire by the creation and sponsorship of this award?"[80]

Throughout the sixties and early seventies, as the Rusk convocation showed, the course of events in Scarsdale took on added meaning because of the interplay between the community's self-consciousness and its national reputation. The convocation was probably motivated in part, as Graham suggested, by a desire to publicize the fact that people as successful as Rusk lived in Scarsdale, and precisely because they lived there, the protest against the secretary of state was particularly newsworthy. In event after event, the same dynamic was at work. The residents of the community and its outside observers shared a common assumption about it. Here was an entire community of the "best and the brightest," hence it must reflect national hopes and frustrations in a special way.

Certainly this was true in the early to mid-1960s, when the predominant mood in Scarsdale, as in the United States, was one of aspiration. In rhetoric that reverberated with the idealism of the New Frontier and the Great Society, local leaders challenged village residents to fulfill the mission of the community. In the words of village trustee Carol Stix, Scarsdale "has always been a leadership community and once again [it] is thinking in these terms." According to Rita Satz, the president of the League of Women Voters, "Scarsdale is a symbol, whether we like it or not. We must be a leader in today's modern world." And John S. Snyder, the former president of the board of education, said, "Scarsdale's role in the past has been that of innovator and pacesetter in community affairs. . . . It should not now abrogate its responsibility in the face of drastic change."[81]

But at some point in the late 1960s, the rate of change became too drastic. The unending news of racial unrest, student demonstrations, political assassinations, and mounting deaths in Vietnam, coupled with local demands for contested elections, low-income housing, and school integration, gave rise to "a feeling of desperation." In 1970, village resident Janet Wells told *Time* magazine that a sense existed in Scarsdale "that somehow things are getting out of hand but no one can do anything about it."[82] By this time, instead of a symbol of American achievement, Scarsdale had become a symbol of America's faults.

The most famous statement identifying Scarsdale with what was wrong in the nation originated with a radical student but gained notoriety as the title of an article in the *New York Times Magazine*, in April 1969. "You Have to Grow Up in Scarsdale to Know How Bad Things Really Are" discussed the causes and goals of the student protest movement. After quoting that young man, Yale psychologist Kenneth Keniston wrote that, while

> the comment might sound heartless to a poor black, much less to a citizen of the Third World . . . [the student] meant something important by it. He meant that *even* in the Scarsdales of America, with their affluence, their upper-middle class security and abundance, their well-fed, well-heeled children, and their excellent schools, something is wrong. Economic affluence does not guarantee a feeling of personal fulfillment, political freedom does not always yield an inner sense of liberation and cultural freedom; social justice and equality may leave one with a feeling that something else is missing in life.[83]

Almost immediately, the phrase "you have to grow up in Scarsdale" was taken up by six Cornell students from Scarsdale, who were "grasping for words to express [their] convictions" about the causes of disturbances at their university. "[The radical] student spoke for us," they said. "The American ideals and priorities, the holding up of affluence and 'success' as goals have not been satisfying." Calling for a reordering of American values, they continued, "We in Scarsdale have material security, yet the goal of personal dignity for all men—students, workers, blacks— has not been realized."[84]

In Broadway plays and popular magazines, the late sixties and early seventies yielded other examples of the symbolic use of Scarsdale, but the statement that seemed best to reflect the disillusionment and disorientation of many in the community was written by a young man for local readers. "I am a resident of Scarsdale, New York—one of the most affluent villages in the world," he began. "Somewhere in Southeast Asia is another village which is burned out and destroyed—the village of My Lai." The two villages, the writer went on, had once been "similar in many ways," but, whereas Scarsdale still had its "comfortable homes," "rich green trees," and "healthy children," My Lai contained only "ashes," "ruins," and "memories of her young." He concluded, "My Lai is a village (which was five hundred years old) that America has destroyed, and Scarsdale is a village that a consumption-oriented America has created."[85]

From hope to desperation, from self-righteousness to shame, the years of the sixties and early seventies were a time of stark contrasts. In the effort to bring about equality, Scarsdale and the nation learned about diversity. In the effort to bring about peace, they learned about strife. In the effort to make over the world in their own images, they learned how tarnished those images were. Some goals were achieved, but others, at times attempted in a fumbling fashion, were set aside as unattainable. The proponents of change had been chastened. Yet one man had lost neither his interest in reform nor his faith in Scarsdale's capacity for leadership. Speaking in 1972, Kenneth W. Thompson, the former president of the board of education, attempted to tap the community's idealism:

The one mandate I put before you is that we try—in this favored community with all its strengths and resources. Having tried, we shall rest easier with ourselves and with those who went before and come after us. More important still, if we should take even modest steps, we might give the nation hope that a community known for its wealth was more deservedly known for its courage, wisdom, and justice. And if enough Scarsdales were renewed, who can say whether a divided nation with an uncertain view of itself and its domestic and international relations might have a rebirth.[86]

In 1972 not even Scarsdale rose to the challenge. Like the nation, the community was turning inward.

Epilogue

During the course of the last ten years, events have conspired to make the name of Scarsdale more familiar to Americans than ever. A best-selling diet book and two sensational murders, the more famous of which did not even occur in the village, brought Scarsdale to the attention of people who would otherwise not have known of the suburb. Yet, while millions pondered the ramifications of the so-called Scarsdale Letter in the Jean Harris murder trial, Scarsdale's mayor told reporters, "Most people here couldn't care less."[1] Instead, village residents were preoccupied with the size of their tax bills, the strength of their zoning code, the quality of their schools, the effectiveness of their nonpartisan system, and relations between Christians and Jews and men and women.

By 1980–81 the village tax rate had risen to $56.8627, the school tax rate to $130.6630, and the average assessment to $23,879. This meant that the average property owner was paying more than $4,500 to support one year's operation of the village government and schools. Yet, despite these high taxes, residents of the village did not join the national trend toward tax revolt. Instead, they seemed willing to accept the explanations of officials that they were doing what they could to control costs without sacrificing quality.[2]

In other ways village residents showed that they were eager to maintain Scarsdale's traditional standards. In 1976, and again in 1982, they defeated proposals for the construction of luxury multifamily housing units, despite arguments that such units would bring them needed tax relief. In 1979 they accepted a further increase in taxes by approving a $1.5 million bond issue

217

for the renovation of the auditorium at the Scarsdale High School.[3]

But while village residents remained committed to keeping Scarsdale "a village of homes" with "education . . . the only industry," developments that occurred outside the village threatened to force a modification of local standards. One change in village standards resulted from a new judicial definition of what constituted a family for the purposes of zoning. Although the village ordinance restricted the use of single-family residences to either biological families or no more than five unrelated persons living as a family, and although it explicitly prohibited the establishment of any "institution for the feeble-minded," the board of trustees did not intervene when the Westchester Association for Retarded Citizens purchased a house in the village for eight retarded adults and their two supervisors. The trustees based their decision not to act on recent court rulings that had set aside local ordinances by approving the establishment of group houses in single-family residence zones. When a private citizen went to court to get a new ruling in this instance, the judge declared,

> The community residence conforms to the zoning requirements
> of the Scarsdale village code . . . [since it] intends the creation
> of a generic family unit and is not classifiable as an institution.

However laudatory its purpose and however invisible its impact, the opening of the group home, in the summer of 1979, represented an easing of Scarsdale's zoning requirements.[4]

Another judicial decision, one which concerned the method of financing public education in New York State, posed a more serious threat to local standards. In 1978, in the case of Levittown v. Nyquist, a lower court judge ruled that the state's heavy reliance on local property taxes to finance the public schools violated the equal protection clause of the state constitution by discriminating against the children who lived in poor districts. He also found that the existing formula for the distribution of state funds to local districts was inequitable.[5]

While the state's determination to appeal the decision delayed its implementation, representatives of the Scarsdale school district worked to win a new ruling in the case. In 1979–80 they spearheaded a drive, eventually joined by eighty-five school districts, all receiving the minimum amount of state aid per pupil, to present an *amicus curiae* brief. As Scarsdale's superintendent of schools, Thomas Sobol, told the *Inquirer*;

> We advocate equity for pupils and taxpayers in less affluent communities, but not at the expense of whatever quality we have achieved, nor of local control of education. We think there are sound arguments for our position and that they should be made before the court.

In October, 1981, the Appellate Division of the State Supreme Court rejected the arguments of Scarsdale and the other flat grant school districts, but eight months later New York State's highest court, finding merit in those arguments, reversed the rulings of the lower courts by a six-to-one margin. The decision confirmed the right of village residents to tax themselves steeply for educational purposes, averted a massive reallocation of state funds, and seemed likely to have far-reaching consequences. For in defending their own interests, Scarsdale and the other flat grant districts helped to develop legal arguments that could have an impact in states other than New York.[6]

Not all the threats to the traditional standards villagers were working to protect originated from outside the village. Although large numbers of residents no longer agitated for lower class housing and school busing, the spirit of the sixties lived on in Scarsdale, at least in a willingness to confront basic issues.

The clearest legacy of the 1960s was a renewal of the debate over the viability of the nonpartisan system. This time the attack was led by Paul Feiner, a law student at St. John's University who challenged many of the procedures and decisions of the village board of trustees. But Feiner's main complaint centered on the lack of choice in local elections and, consequently, on the candidates' failure to address the issues that faced the community. When the Town Club rejected his proposal to sponsor a village-wide referendum on the holding of contested elections for local office, Feiner organized the Ad Hoc Committee for a Change, later known as the Nonpartisan Coalition for Open Government. In 1981, in its first test at the polls, the coalition's candidates lost by a nearly three-to-one margin, but twelve months later Feiner was carrying through on his promise to "do the same thing next year, [only] we'll work harder." Although Feiner's candidates did not win, it was doubtful that Scarsdale would return to the punctilious politics of an earlier era.[7]

The debate over the use of public land for a Christmas crèche caused even more of a strain than the arguments over contested elections. Every December since 1957 a committee representing eight area churches had, with the approval of the village board, placed a nativity scene on village property in the business district. Up to 1973 the board's decision had been unanimous, but that year trustee George Szabad abstained from the voting and in subsequent years a growing number of the citizens of the community and their trustees came to question the policy. In 1978 the board's vote was five to two; in 1980 it was four to three, and in 1981 the board withheld its approval by a one-vote margin. Though letters criticizing the decision flooded the newspaper and the offices of the village board, the wonder was, not that the trustees had taken the action they did, but that in a community with such a large non-Christian population it had taken them so long to do so. Still, in the months after the decision, the trustees equivocated. Seeking to appease all groups, they proposed to transfer to the ownership of a private foundation a small piece of village park land, to be known as Heritage Plaza and to be used for patriotic and religious displays. Thus, the dispute wore on.[8]

Perhaps the most significant development of the 1970s and early eighties concerned the role women were playing in the community. The 1980 census was certain to reveal that in Scarsdale as elsewhere a dramatic increase had occurred in the percentage of women who worked, but in few communities had women so clearly moved into positions of power. For the first time in Scarsdale's history a woman was elected as the local representative to the county government, another woman was elected mayor, two women served as presidents of the board of education, and two were awarded the Scarsdale Bowl. In keeping with these changes, the Town Club, which a federal judge had ruled could continue its male-only policy, voted to admit women as members. Although they had always played an active role in the civic life of the community, more women were now receiving recognition for their efforts.[9]

While in Scarsdale the developments of the 1970s and early 1980s involved both the continuation of traditional standards and adaptations to broader social change, these contradictory trends carried through on an earlier pattern. As Scarsdale was being opened to fuller participation by all its residents, the maintenance of local standards in zoning and government expenditures assured that the level of one's income would continue to be the primary determinant of a sense of belonging. As writer J. Anthony Lukas once remarked, "The flip side of community is exclusiveness." What he meant was that, whenever there is a strong sense of community identity, the members of that community must have some means of determining who belongs and who does not. In Boston, Massachusetts, according to Lukas, the key factor is race;[10] in Logan, Utah, it is religion, and in Scarsdale, New York, it is social class. By the early 1980s, Scarsdale conformed more nearly to its ideal of community than ever. It could indeed lay claim to being a capitalistic utopia, open to all of society's economic achievers with little regard to race, religion, or sex.

APPENDIX A. Economic and Social Affiliations of the Members of the Village Board of Trustees, 1915–1933

Name, Date and Place of Birth	Education	Subdivision or Street Address	Church	Public Service	Executive Positions	Professional Organizations	Benevolent, Patriotic, and Cultural Assoc.	Clubs
Jacob Aronson, b. 1887, Brooklyn	St. Lawrence University; Brooklyn Law School	Westover, later Fox Meadow	Jewish Community Center	Village Trustee, 1931–33; Bd. of Appeals, 1935–51	Vice-Pres., NY Central Railroad; Dir., Central Federal Savings and Loan Assoc. and Scarsdale Nat. Bank	Vice-Pres., Chamber of Commerce of N.Y. State; Assoc. of American Railroad; ABA, N.Y. Bar	Trustee, Brooklyn Law School; Chrm., Union of American Hebrew Congregation, Railroad Y.M.C.A.	Traffic Club; Masons; Fairview Country Club; Quaker Ridge Golf Club; Town Club.
Frank O. Ayres, b. 1862, Oldham, Mass.		Murray Hill	St. James the Less (Epis.)	Pres., Town Club, 1916–17; Village Trustee, 1922–24; Village Pres., 1924–26.	Vice-Pres., Metropolitan Life Ins. Co.; Dir., Caleb Heathcote Trust Co.			Scarsdale Golf Club; Town Club
James Baird, b. 1873, Vanceburg, KY.	U. of Mich. (captain, quarterback—football team)	Greenacres		Village Trustee, 1926–27.	Pres., James Baird Construction Co.; former Pres., George A. Fuller Construction Co.		Donated N.Y. State park; endowed U. of Ariz. scholarship fund.	U. of Mich. (NY & Tucson); El Rio Club (Tucson); American Guernsey Cattle Club; Cosmos Club of Wash.; Pres., Scarsdale Golf Club; Town Club.
Wm. A. Bassett		Greenacres		Village Trustee, 1922–26; Town Super., 1924–27.				Town Club
Frank H. Bethell, b. 1870, Newburgh, Ind.	Evansville (Ind.) Business School; Bklyn. Inst.	Murray Hill	St. James the Less (Epis.)	Village Pres., 1915–17; Village Trustee, 1917–18; Planning Com., 1917–19; Pres., Town Club, 1920 Member, Bronx Pkwy. Com.	Pres., Bell Telephone Co.; Dir., Hudson Ins. Co. and Scarsdale Nat. Bank	Telephone Pioneers of America Merchants Assn. (NY)		Racquet & Tennis; Railroad; Town Club Manursing Island; Pres., Scarsdale Golf.
Chas. E. Birge, b. 1871, Algona, IA	U. of Wisc.; MIT, Ecole des Beaux Arts in Paris	The Grange	St. James the Less (Epis.)	Planning Com., 1921–24; Village Trustee, 1927–32	Architect			Westchester-Biltmore Country Club; Town Club

Name, Date and Place of Birth	Education	Subdivision or Street Address	Church	Public Service	Executive Positions	Professional Organizations	Benevolent, Patriotic, and Cultural Assoc.	Clubs
Arthur Boniface, b. 1879 Hastings, Eng.	British Naval School	Sherbrooke Park	St. James the Less (Epis.)	Village Trustee, 1918–21; Village Pres., 1921–22; Planning Com., 1919–21; Village Eng., 1922–43	Civil Engineer; employed by village as "manager" in 1922	ASCE; A. P. Works Assn; Nat. Municipal League; NE Water Works Assn; Nat. Soc. Pro. Eng.; NY State Soc. of Eng.	University Glee Club	Scarsdale Golf; Rotary; Masons; Royal Standard Lodge of Nova Scotia; Engineers Club; Town Club
Gail Borden, b. 1871 Brewster, N.Y.		Weaver Street		Village Trustee, 1923–29	Gentleman farmer and sportsman (grandson founder Borden Co.)			Larchmont Shore Club; Town Club
Wm. T. Brewster, b. 1870 Lawrence, Mass.	Harvard, BA, MA; Hon. D. Litt., Columbia	Greenacres		Village Trustee, 1930–32	Prof. of English, Provost at Barnard College; author, editor			Phi Beta Kappa; Century; Harvard Town Club
Laura C. Burgess, b. Scarsdale, New York		Burgess Road	St. James the Less (Epis.)	Village Trustee, 1921–24	Organizer of Scarsdale's Community Farm; Husband, Vice-Pres., Nat. Sulphur Co.			Scarsdale Golf; Fox Meadow Tennis; Woman's Club
Josephine Castle		Overhill	Imac. Heart of Mary (Cath.)	Village Trustee, 1921–24	Husband a movie producer			Woman's Club
Robert E. Christie Jr. b. 1893	Princeton	Greenacres	Hitchcock (Pres.)	Village Trustee, 1925–27; Mayor, 1929–31; Aide to Under-Sec. of War, WWI; helped draw up Fed. Sec. Act	Partner, Dillon, Read & Co.; Dir., A. G. Spaulding; Dir., Goodyear Tire & Rubber; Dir., Hartsdale Nat. Bank	Pres., Bond Club of NY; Pres., Investment Bankers of Amer.	Children's Welfare Assn. of Westchester County; Scarsdale Foundation	Town Club
George B. Clifton, b. 1880 Baltimore, MD	Baltimore City College (Name of a high school)	Arthur Manor	Scarsdale Congregational	Village Trustee, 1924–30; Pres., Town Club, 1930–32	Local banker-officer, Scarsdale Nat., then Caleb Heathcote Trust Co.; then Vice-Pres., County Trust Co.		Scarsdale Foundation; Scarsdale USO committee; family welfare community service.	Town Club; Rotary Club
Walter J. Collet		Old Orchard Lane & Carstensan Road	reportedly a former Catholic	Village Trustee, 1928–31	Pres., Collet Constr. Corp.			Pres., Scarsdale Golf; Town Club

Name, Date and Place of Birth	Education	Subdivision or Street Address	Church	Public Service	Executive Positions	Professional Organizations	Benevolent, Patriotic, and Cultural Assoc.	Clubs
Warren W. Cunningham, b. 1885, Elizabeth, NJ	Princeton; NY Law School	Popham Park	Scarsdale Congregational (earlier St. James the Less)	Pres., Town Club, 1925–26; Village Trustee, 1926–27; Mayor, 1927–29; Bd. of Appeals, 1925–26, 1929–30	Partner in law firm—Hall, Cunningham & Howard; Dir., Trojan Powder Co.; Amer. Maize Products Corp.; Homelight Corp.; County Trust Co.	ABA; State & NYC Bar		Union League; Princeton; Univ.; St. Andrew's Golf; Amer. Yacht; Town Club; Scarsdale Golf
Edwin L. Dillingham	Yale	Weaver Street	St. James the Less (Epis.)	Village Trustee, 1930–32	Gen. Mgr. of Charles Scribner's Sons			Phi Upsilon; EnglewoodCountry; University; Yale; Graduates (New Haven); Scarsdale Golf; Town Club
Gardiner S. Dresser b. 1878, Brooklyn, NY	Cornell	Heathcote		Village Trustee, 1931–32	Dresser & Escher Bond Brokers			Scarsdale Golf; Orienta Beach; Cornell of NY; Delta Upsilon; Lawyers; Town Club
Arthur F. Driscoll, b. 1885, No. Brookfield, Mass.	Brown; Harvard Law	Heathcote	Immaculate Heart of Mary (Cath.)	Bd. of Appeals, 1926–28, 1930–32; Village Trustee, 1929–30; Pres., Town Club, 1937; Mayor, 1939–41	Partner, O'Brien, Driscoll & Rafferty law firm; Dir., Caleb Heathcote Trust Co.	ABA; State, West County & NYC Bar; NY County Lawyers Assn.	Scarsdale Foundation; Society of Friendly Sons of St. Patrick; Knights of Columbus; Trustee, White Plains Hospital	Pres., Scarsdale Golf; Pres., Fox Meadow Tennis; Harvard of NY; Brown of NY; Town Club
Lawrence Dunham, b. 1856	MIT	The Post Road	St. James the Less (Epis.)	Village Trustee, 1917–18	Banker with Corn Exchange Bank			Scarsdale Golf; NY Yacht Club; Commander, New Rochelle Yacht Club; Town Club
Emery L. Ferris, b. 1876, Hillsboro, OH	Miami Univ.; Harvard Law	Murray Hill	St. James the Less (Epis.)	Village Trustee, 1931–36	Partner law firm, Gasser, Ferris, Hayes & Anderson			Town Club
George W. Field, b. 1875, Worcester, Mass.	Yale; NY Law School	Popham Park	Scarsdale Congregational	Planning Com., 1918–19; Village Trustee, 1919; Village Pres., 1919–21; Pres., Town Club, 1921–23; Town Sup., 1927–28	Law partner Platt, Field & Taylor; Dir., Scarsdale Improvement Corp.; Scarsdale Nat. Bank; & Scarsdale Supply Co.			Town Club; Yale in NY.; Leewood Golf; Nantucket Yacht (Mass.)

Name, Date and Place of Birth	Education	Subdivision or Street Address	Church	Public Service	Executive Positions	Professional Organizations	Benevolent, Patriotic, and Cultural Assoc.	Clubs
Guy Forbes, b. 1872, Perth Amboy, NY	Holderness School in NH	The Grange	St. James the Less (Epis.)	Village Trustee, 1918–23; Village Pres., 1923–24; Jus. of Peace, 1920–31	Associated with silk firm of Schwarzenbach, Hubert & Co.		Pres., Central Westchester Humane Soc.	Orienta Beach; Town Club
Charles A. Furthman, b. 1872, NYC	NYU Law		Scarsdale Congregational	Village Trustee, 1915–18; Town Sup., 1918–23	Law partner Furthman & Riesick	Founder, Bronx Bar Assn.; North Side Bd. of Trade		Town Club; Masons; Schnorer Club (Bronx)
Louise Glover		Rochambeau Road	Scarsdale Congregational	Village Trustee, 1928–30; Planning Com.	Chrm. Bd. *Scarsdale Inquirer*, (husband, sr. partner accounting firm)		Girl Scouts	Woman's Club; Scarsdale Golf
Charles C. D. Gott, b. 1872, Brooklyn		Fox Meadow	Hitchcock (Pres.)	Village Trustee, 1929–31	Vice-Pres., Self-Winding Clock Co.			Railroad Club; Town Club; Scarsdale Golf
John M. Hancock, b. 1883, Emerado, ND	U. of ND (4 varsity sports)	Murray Hill	Hitchcock (Pres.)	Village Trustee, 1932–35; Mayor, 1935–37; WWI, naval rep. to War Industries Bd.; WWII, mem. War Resources Bd.; alternate UN Atomic Energy Com.	Partner in Lehman Bros.; Dir. of 21 corps., including Sears, Roebuck & Co., Int'l. Silver Co., Lever Bros.		Trustee of Hamilton College, of MIT, of U. of ND, of Wesley College in ND and of Inst. for Advanced Study at Princeton	
Charles E. Herrman, b. 1882, NYC	City College	Heathcote	Scarsdale Congregational	Village Trustee, 1919–22	Exec. Vice-Pres., of Texas Oil Co.; Pres., Caribbean Corp.; Pres., Moose Mt. Ltd.; Vice-Pres., Midland Securities Co.; Dir., US Realty and Improvement Co.; Dir., Scarsdale Improvement Corp.		Trustee of Wells College; Metropolitan Museum of Natural History; Theater Guild	Scarsdale Golf; Whitehall; Sleepy Hollow; Westchester-Biltmore; NY Ath. Club
Kenneth Hogg		Overhill	Scarsdale Congregational	Village Trustee, 1921–24	Insurance exec.			Scarsdale Golf; Town Club

Name, Date and Place of Birth	Education	Subdivision or Street Address	Church	Public Service	Executive Positions	Professional Organizations	Benevolent, Patriotic, and Cultural Assoc.	Clubs
Richard R. Hunter, b. 1877, Jackson Co., IA	Brown U.	Murray Hill	Hitchcock (Pres.)	Village Trustee, 1918–22; Village Pres., 1922–23; Pres., Town Club, 1923–24; Chrm. Bd. Appeals, 1925–31; WWII, mem. Price Adjustment Bd.	Sr. Vice-Pres., Chase Nat. Bank; Exec. of other banks, incl. Equitable Trust Co., Caleb Heathcote Trust		New England Society	Scarsdale Golf; Boulder Brook; Amer. Yacht; Broad St; NYC Club; Brown U. in NY
Margaret H. Johnson		Church Lane		Village Trustee, 1924–28				Woman's Club
Fred Lavis, b. 1871, Torquay, Eng.	St. Luke's College (left school at 14)	Greenacres		Village Trustee, 1915–17; Pres., Town Club, 1924–25; Mayor, 1931–33	Consulting eng.; Pres., Int'l. Railways of Central America	ASCE; Inst. CE of GB; Amer. Railways Eng. Assn; Amer. Inst., Consulting Eng.; Assn. Amer. & Chinese Eng.	Council of Pan Amer. Soc. of NY; St. George's Soc.	Union League; Railroad Club; Scarsdale Golf; Town Club
Herbert Mc-Kennis, b. 1881, Albany, NY	Dartmouth; Columbia Law	Greenacres	Immaculate Heart of Mary (Cath.)	Planning Com., 1922–25; Village Trustee, 1932–35; Leader in home rule & taxpayer's assn. in Westchester Co.	Attorney		Bedford Reformatory Bd. of Visitors	Scarsdale Golf; Town Club; Lawyers Club of NY; Phi Beta Kappa; U. Club of White Plains; Dartmouth Club of NY
Wm. Walker Orr, b. 1872, Worcester, Mass.	Harvard	Heathcote	St. James the Less (Epis.)	Village Trustee, 1915–17; Planning Com.; 1917–19; Jus. of Peace, 1920–23	Sec., Johns-Manville Co.	Asst. Sec., Nat. Assn. Credit Men; Exec. Sec. NY Credit Men's Assn.	NY Bd. of St. Luke's Hospital in Tokyo; Sec. Church Army in Amer.; active on Epis. diocesan com.; Bd. Amer. Church Bldg. Assn.	Town Club; Harvard Club of NY
Malcolm Pirnie, b. 1889, NYC	Harvard, BS, MCE	Popham Park	Scarsdale Congregational	Village Trustee, 1931–33; Mayor, 1933–35	Malcolm Pirnie Engineers, Won Hoover Medal for excellence & leadership in eng. Devised plans to divest Ger. & Japan of potential for war (after WWII)	Pres., ASCE; Amer. Water Works Assn; Amer. Inst. Consult. Eng.; NE Water Works Assn; FL Eng. Soc.	Trustee, White Plains Hospital; Trustee, Com. of Econ. Develop Robert College, Istanbul, Turkey	Town Club

Name, Date and Place of Birth	Education	Subdivision or Street Address	Church	Public Service	Executive Positions	Professional Organizations	Benevolent, Patriotic, and Cultural Assoc.	Clubs
Allan H. Richardson, b. 1880 Montville, Mass.	Yale	Fox Meadow	Baptist	Village Trustee, 1927–29; Treas. Puerto Rico, 1912–16	Pres., McCall Corp.; Vice-Pres., Atlantic Fruit & Sugar Co.; Controller, Vassar College	Pres., Periodical Publishers Assn.	Dir., Westchester Co. Children's Assn.	Yale & U. of NY; Skull & Bones; Boule Delta Kappa Epsilon; St. Andrew's Golf; St. Mary's Country; Whitehall; Town Club
Harrison M. Robertson, b. 1893, Albermarle Co., VA	U. of VA, BA, LLB	Mamaroneck Road		Village Trustee, 1930–31	Gen. council of British Amer. Tobacco, Ltd. & Brown & Williamson Tobacco Corp.			Phi Beta Kappa
Jesse E. Waid, b. 1888, Denver, CO	Harvard, BA, LLB	Kelwynne Road	Hitchcock (Pres.)	Jus. of Peace, 1924–31; Village Trustee, 1927–30	Attorney			Kappa Sigma; Town Club; Harvard Club
Hugh White, b. 1877, Lapern, Mich.	U. of Mich, BA, LLB (football captain)	Old Orchard Lane	St. James the Less (Epis.)	Village Trustee, 1924–26; Village Pres., 1926–27	Pres., Chrm. Bd., Geo. A. Fuller Co.; Pres., Scarsdale Improvement Corp.; Vice-Pres., Scarsdale Nat. Bank; Pres., Fort Hill Estates			U. Mich.; Town Club; Whitehall; Scarsdale Golf (Pres.); University; Lawyers; Blind Brook; Boulder Brook; Manursing Is.; St. Maurice Fish & Game Club of LaTique, Can.
Rush Wilson, b. 1870, Bethesda, OH	Mount Union College; Ohio State Univ. Law School	Fox Meadow		Pres., Town Club, 1913–15; Village Trustee, 1915–17; Village Pres., 1917–19; Jus. of Peace, 1920–21	Asst. Gen. Land and Tax Agent for NY Central (retired, 1915); Pres., Scarsdale Nat. Bank; Pres., Scarsdale Improvement Corp; Pres., Heathcote Land Corp.			Sigma Alpha Epsilon; Town Club

Name, Date and Place of Birth	Education	Subdivision or Street Address	Church	Public Service	Executive Positions	Professional Organizations	Benevolent, Patriotic, and Cultural Assoc.	Clubs
Charles W. Young, b. 1876 Yaphank, NY	NY Law School		Hitchcock (Pres.)	Village Trustee, 1917–18	Member, banking firm of Emerson, McMillan and Co.; Pres., Kelly Springfield Motor Truck Co.; Vice-Pres., Amer. Light and Traction Co.; Pres., White Star Coal Co.; Dir., Bolton Barnsley Mills Corp., James C. Enskine Corp., Southern Light and Traction Co.		Sec., World Court League	Town Club; Phi Delta Phi; Waccabue Country; Gedney Farm Golf

Abbreviations Used in the Notes

An. Rep.	Annual Report of the Board of Trustees of the Village of Scarsdale
Bd. of Ed.	Minutes of the Meetings of the Board of Education of Union Free School District No. 1
Dist. Meet.	Minutes of the District Meetings of Union Free School District No. 1
NYT	*New York Times*
Plan. Comm.	Records of the Planning Commission of the Village of Scarsdale
Proceedings	Proceedings of the Board of Supervisors of the County of Westchester
RD	*White Plains Reporter Dispatch*
Records	Records of the Meetings of the Board of Trustees of the Village of Scarsdale
School Report	Annual Report of the Board of Education of Union Free School District No. 1
SI	*Scarsdale Inquirer*
TC Minutes	Minutes of the Meetings of the Town Club
TC Yearbook	Yearbook of the Town Club
Town Board	Records of the Meetings of the Board of the Town of Scarsdale
WC Yearbook	Yearbook of the Woman's Club

Notes

PREFACE *(Pages vii–x)*

1. *Life*, April 1936, p. 32.
2. *New Yorker*, 2 April 1979, p. 29.
3. *SI*, 5 March 1964 (See Appendix B, p. 000, for abbreviations).

CHAPTER ONE *(Pages 1–15)*

1. U.S. Bureau of the Census, Unpublished Population Schedules for Westchester County, New York, 1790 and 1840, Genealogical Library of the Mormon Church, microfilm reels 589,904 and 017,210. For information on Scarsdale's founding and early history, see Dixon Ryan Fox, *Caleb Heathcote: Gentleman Colonist* (New York: C. Scribner's Sons, 1926), pp. 107–16; Harry Hansen, *Scarsdale: From Colonial Manor to Modern Community* (New York: Harper & Brothers, 1954), pp. 9–88; Diana Reische, *Of Colonists and Commuters: A History of Scarsdale* (Scarsdale: Junior League of Scarsdale, 1976), pp. 14–67.
2. Hansen, *Scarsdale*, pp. 89, 92; U.S. Bureau of the Census, Population Schedules, 1860, reel 803,881.
3. A comparison of the population schedules for the 1860 and 1880 census (reel 1,254,947) shows that the occupational structure of society in Scarsdale barely changed during the intervening years. Although similar information is not available for 1890, the fact that the population increased by a total of only fourteen people between 1880 and 1890 suggests that Scarsdale experienced little change during that decade. U.S. Bureau of the Census, Published Census Statistics, *Eleventh Census of the United States, 1890, Pt. 1, Population*, p. 295; N.Y. State, Secretary of State, *Enumeration of Inhabitants*, 1915, p. 295; N.Y. State, Unpublished Population Schedules for Scarsdale, 1905, 1915, and 1925, Westchester County Clerk's Office, White Plains, New York, and the Mormon Genealogical Library, reels 589,664, 589,671, and 589,904. In determining whether a head of household belonged to the upper-middle class, the author relied mainly on the listing of his or, occasionally, her occupation. In cases where this designation seemed vague, she considered whether the household included live-in servants and occasionally, as a

233

last resort, the social status of the people living in the immediate neighborhood.

4. Robert H. Wiebe, *The Search for Order: 1877–1920* (New York: Hill and Wang, 1967), pp. 111–32 and Kenneth T. Jackson, "The Crabgrass Frontier: 150 Years of Suburban Growth in America," in *The Urban Experience: Themes in American History*, ed. Raymond A. Mohl and James F. Richardson (Belmont, Calif.: Wadsworth Publishing Co., 1973), pp. 197–207.

5. U.S. Bureau of the Census, *Seventh Census of the United States, 1850*, p. lxxii and *Eleventh Census, 1890*, p. 288; Jackson, "Crabgrass Frontier," pp. 199–200.

6. Otto Huffeland, "Early Mount Vernon" (Mount Vernon: Mount Vernon Public Library, 1940), pp. 27–29; Victor Mays, *Pathway to a Village: A History of Bronxville* (Bronxville: Nebko Press, 1961), pp. 103–107; Robert Creamer, ed., *The Story of a Town: Eastchester, 1664–1964* (Tuckahoe: n.p., 1964), pp. 20–21.

7. Article on Scarsdale in the 1890s, *SI*, 17 February 1923; Hansen, *Scarsdale*, pp. 141, 228–29, 253–56.

8. *SI*, 17 February 1923; promotional material for Arthur Manor as quoted by Fred Lavis and the Local History Committee of the Town Club, in "The Story of Scarsdale," (unpublished manuscript, 1946), pp. 16–17; Westchester County Deeds, 16 September 1892, Liber 1284, pp. 247–49 (deed of Arthur Suburban Home Company to Edward F. O'Connor); *SI*, 28 January 1904.

9. This information was drawn from the official maps for the various subdivisions filed in the land record offices of Westchester County, White Plains, New York.

10. Philip Colt, "The Making of a Suburban Colony," *Country Life in America*, August 1904, pp. 350–52.

11. N.Y. State, Population Schedules, 1915.

12. U.S. Bureau of the Census, *Eleventh Census, 1890, Pt. 1, Population*, p. 295 and *Thirteenth Census, 1910*, III, p. 206; N.Y. State, Secretary of State, *Enumeration of Inhabitants, 1915*, p. 295. For developments in transportation see *SI*, 13 February 1912; 15 March 1912; 10 August 1912 and 7 September 1912; also Roger Arcara, *Westchester's Forgotten Railway* (New York: n.p., 1962).

13. Sample included every twentieth deed involving a sale of land, filed with the Westchester County clerk and listed in the index for the period 1898 to 1910.

14. *SI*, 23 February 1905 and 19 January 1912.

15. TC Minutes, 7 October 1904, p. 1; George E. Mowry, *The California Progressives* (Chicago: Quadrangle Books, 1963), pp. 45, 86–104; Samuel P. Hays, "The Politics of Reform in Municipal Government," in *Understanding the American Experience*, ed. James M. Banner et al., v. 2 (New York: Harcourt Brace Jovanovich, 1973), pp. 174–77.

16. Of the original sixteen members there were three lawyers, three builders, two realtors, an engineer, a chemist, and six business executives. The next group of members included three lawyers, two bankers, one realtor, a doctor, an editor, an artist, an engineer, a farmer (also the town supervisor), and three business executives. Occupational infor-

mation based on New York State, Population Schedules, 1905. for Scarsdale. The limit on membership set in the original constitution was abolished in 1915, TC Minutes, pp. 2, 72.

17. *SI*, 4 July 1901; 2 January 1902; 28 January 1904; 13 December 1906; 20 November 1902. Angell sold the paper in 1910 to the Bronx Valley Press, which merged the *Inquirer* with the *Bronxville Review* and, in July 1919, suspended its publication completely. The Scarsdale Woman's Club purchased the newspaper a few months later and operated it until 1959. Since that time the newspaper has had four different owners. See Hansen, *Scarsdale*, pp. 271–75 and chapter five of this work.

18. *SI*, 20 November 1902; 28 January 1904; 3 May 1929; 31 May 1913 and 19 July 1913; Hansen, *Scarsdale*, p. 230.

19. Town Tax Assessment Rolls, 1890, pp. 1, 5, 45; 1914, p. 157. See also the slip of paper included in the 1914 roll book for figures on the 1914 budget. An. Rep., 1915, p. 5; 1924–25, p. 5.

20. *SI*, 1 April 1909; 30 July 1909; 20 August 1909; 12 September 1901; 10 October 1901; 24 October 1901; 27 August 1909; 3 September 1909.

21. *SI*, 10 September 1909; 3 September 1909; 17 September 1909; 10 October 1901; 27 August 1909; Hansen, *Scarsdale*, pp. 127, 325; *NYT*, 24 December 1934, p. 13. Secor owned seventy-seven acres in 1909, whereas White owned fewer than six acres. Tax Assessment Rolls, 1909, pp. 50, 55, 65, and 67.

22. *SI*, 1 October 1909, 22 October 1909; 9 November 1909.

23. Cleveland A. Dunn, *SI*, 3 May 1929; *NYT*, 11 July 1936, p. 15.

24. Hansen, *Scarsdale*, p. 117; *SI*, 31 January 1914.

25. TC Minutes, 11 June 1908, p. 19; 11 January 1910, p. 29; 13 December 1912, p. 48; 13 January 1913, p. 50; Town Board, 15 January 1913; *SI*, 30 August 1913.

26. See the comments of Benjamin J. Carpenter and Philip W. Russell, *SI*, 6 September 1913, and of Clarence McMillan, *SI*, 13 January 1914.

27. See the editorial and the comments of A.B. Crane, *SI*, 30 August 1913, and the comments of Cleveland A. Dunn, *SI*, 31 January 1914.

28. See editorial and comments by Dunn and Russell, *SI*, 31 January 1914.

29. *SI*, 7 February 1914; *NYT*, 1 February 1914, sec. 2, p. 12.

30. TC Minutes, 25 September 1913, p. 56; 8 January 1914, p. 61; 14 May 1914, p. 64; *SI*, 27 February 1915; 20 March 1915; 27 March 1915.

31. *SI*, 27 March 1915.

32. *SI*, 5 June 1915; 12 June 1915; *NYT*, 17 June 1915, p. 20.

33. Records, 26 June 1915, pp. 1–2.

34. Letter from "Half Century," *SI*, 22 May 1922.

CHAPTER TWO *(Pages 17–42)*

1. *SI*, 20 November 1902.

2. N. Y. State, Secretary of State, *Enumeration of Inhabitants, 1915,* p. 295; *SI*, 5 December 1925; Records, 10 April 1918, p. 74; *NYT*, 30

May 1920, sec. 8, p. 1; 25 November 1923, sec. 10, p. 2; 4 January 1925, sec. 11, p. 2; An. Rep., 1925–26, p. 5.

3. Records, 6 April 1917, pp. 126–27; 7 April 1917, pp. 128–30; *SI*, 25 April 1917; N. Y. State, Population Schedules, 1915.

4. *SI*, 25 April 1917; 6 June 1918; Records, 7 April 1917, pp. 128–29. The general anti-German hysteria is discussed in John Higham, *Strangers in the Land: Patterns of American Nativism, 1860–1925* (New York: Atheneum, 1963), pp. 194–217, and in David M. Kennedy, *Over Here: The First World War and American Society* (New York: Oxford University Press, 1980), pp. 67–68.

5. *SI*, 19 December 1917; Hansen, *Scarsdale*, p. 186; *SI*, 14 March 1917; 4 April 1917; 11 April 1917; 18 April 1917; 23 October 1918.

6. According to the *Inquirer*, the leaders of the New York State Suffrage Association considered the community farm to be "suffrage propaganda" of the type that would tend to dissolve "many arguments held against universal suffrage" (*SI*, 11 April 1917). In general, the Scarsdale Suffrage Club supported the moderate tactics of Carrie Chapman Catt. Its members said they were "not at all in sympathy with the militant and aggressive suffragists" (*SI*, 22 May 1915).

7. *SI*, 11 April 1917; 23 May 1917.

8. *Ibid.*; article by Burgess, *SI*, 17 February 1928.

9. *SI*, 25 April 1917; "Taking Scarsdale Off the Market," *New Republic*, 2 June 1917, pp. 125–26; *SI*, 20 June 1917; editorial, *SI*, 19 December 1917.

10. Quotation from Benjamin J. Carpenter, *SI*, 6 September 1913. A detailed discussion of the provision of these services appears in chapter two of the author's "Scarsdale, 1891–1933: The Rise of a Wealthy Suburb" (Ph.D. diss., Yale University, 1976).

11. *SI*, 9 December 1922; 27 January 1923; 13 April 1928.

12. *SI*, 17 November 1923; 13 March 1926; 17 April 1926; 13 April 1928.

13. An. Rep., 1924–25, p. 6.

14. *SI*, 13 June 1925.

15. *SI*, 30 July 1926.

16. *SI*, 3 September 1926; 24 June 1927; 9 March 1928; 30 November 1928; 28 December 1928; 29 March 1929.

17. An. Rep., 1930–31, p. 22.

18. Records, 28 February 1923, p. 52; 26 March 1923, p. 77; 26 September 1923, pp. 298–301; 24 October 1923, pp. 316–21; 14 November 1923, p. 324; letter from P. Compton Miller, *SI*, 13 October 1923.

19. *SI*, 12 January 1924.

20. Arthur Boniface, "The Disposal of Organic Waste by the Beccari System at Scarsdale, New York," *Transactions of the American Society of Civil Engineers*, December 1927, p. 820. See also Boniface, "The Problem of Waste Disposal in a Small City," *American City*, October 1927, pp. 466–68 and Records, 28 February 1923, pp. 46–51.

21. *SI*, 10 March 1923; 10 February 1928; Boniface, "Disposal of Organic Waste," p. 820.

22. *SI*, 12 January 1924; 26 April 1924; 27 March 1926; Boniface, "Disposal of Organic Waste," pp. 821–22.

23. An. Rep., 1927–28, pp. 19–20.

24. Records, 26 September 1923, pp. 298–301; *SI*, 12 January 1924; 26 April 1924. References to the collection of "mixed waste" indicate that the village board had capitulated to the people's laziness, An. Rep., 1926–27, p. 19.

25. *SI*, 27 January 1928; An. Rep., 1927–28, pp. 19–20; *SI*, 13 December 1929; 20 December 1929, 17 January 1930; An. Rep., 1934–35, p. 36.

26. An. Rep., 1934–35, p. 31.

27. *SI*, 20 March 1926.

28. An. Rep., 1925–26, p. 42; letter from Heinrich Hirschenthaler, *SI*, 14 October 1922.

29. *SI*, 2 May 1914.

30. Hansen, *Scarsdale*, pp. 141–42; see the advertisements, *SI*, 1919–20, and the editorial, *SI*, 14 December 1912.

31. *SI*, 1 May 1920; 8 May 1920. The bank changed its name to the Scarsdale National Bank and Trust Company on 15 October 1924.

32. *SI*, 1 May 1920; 14 May 1921.

33. *SI*, 22 July 1921; 16 January 1926; J. Pearce in "The Rough Road Column," *SI*, 16 September 1922. The bank described the order of its priorities as follows: "Safety is first. Service is next. Profit comes last." *SI*, 27 May 1922.

34. *SI*, 17 December 1921; 14 May 1921.

35. *NYT*, 23 November 1920, p. 26; *SI*, 27 November 1920.

36. *SI*, 27 November 1920.

37. *SI*, 10 February 1923; 21 June 1924.

38. *SI*, 17 October 1925, 24 April 1926; 10 December 1926; 19 August 1927, 16 December 1927; 3 August 1928; *NYT*, 29 January 1927, p. 26; *SI*, 8 April 1927; 17 June 1927; 15 July 1927; 6 January 1928; 27 July 1928.

39. What the *Inquirer* called the "fresh and forcible arguments in favor of town or city planning" drew the attention of Scarsdale residents as early as 1912. *SI*, 28 December 1912.

40. Charles N. Glaab and A. Theodore Brown, *A History of Urban America*, 2nd ed. (New York: Macmillan Co., 1976), pp. 239–44; Seymour Toll, *The Zoned American* (New York: Grossman Publishers, 1969), pp. 122–29, 193.

41. Toll, *Zoned American*, p. 168; Records, 13 July 1921, p. 157.

42. Records, 9 March 1921, p. 50; 11 January 1922, p. 5; 30 April 1925, pp. 200–205; Mel Scott, *American City Planning Since 1890* (Berkeley and Los Angeles: University of California Press, 1969), pp. 120–22, 228; John L. Hancock, "Planners in the Changing American City, 1900–1940," *American Institute of Planners Journal*, September 1967, p. 296.

43. Records, 29 March 1922, p. 73.

44. Village President Arthur Boniface and George W. Field, the lawyer who represented the realtor, Frederick Fox, *SI*, 8 April 1922.

45. Records, 29 March 1922, pp. 89–93.

46. *SI*, 8 April 1922; Records, 4 April 1922, p. 101.

47. Records, 4 April 1922, p. 101.

48. *SI*, 13 May 1922; 25 October 1924.

49. Records, 29 March 1922, pp. 74–98. In his book on Scarsdale, Harry Hansen quotes Malcolm Pirnie, one of the opponents of the original zoning law, as saying, "The first version of the law showed the business zone extended on both sides of Popham Road from the railroad to the White Plains Post Road and on both sides of the Post Road to the White Plains line and also of Fenimore Road to Hartsdale. The only way the law could be changed was by action of the village board, urged by petition of taxpayers." (Hansen, *Scarsdale*, p. 174.) The law never made such generous provision for business, though what provision it did make aroused deep resentment in the community.

50. Records, 19 April 1922, pp. 140, 121, 123; 10 May 1922, p. 166; 24 May 1922, p. 176. See also the letter from Emily O. Butler, *SI*, 18 April 1925.

51. Records, 19 April 1922, p. 128.

52. S. L. Angell spoke for Mary Lockwood, William P. Platt, and the Popham Estate, Records, 19 April 1922, p. 135; letter from "Prospective Property Owner," *SI*, 27 May 1922.

53. "A Resident of the Popham Tract" and "Woodlands Place," *SI*, 26 April 1922. See also the letter on apartments from Alfred William Anthony, *SI*, 17 February 1923.

54. *SI*, 10 June 1922; 13 May 1922.

55. *SI*, 10 June 1922; letter from "A Former Resident of Woodlands Place," *SI*, 13 May 1922.

56. *SI*, 7 October 1922.

57. John M. Digney represented the Pophams. *SI*, 10 June 1922.

58. *Ibid.*

59. *Ibid.*

60. *SI*, 16 September 1922.

61. Records, 27 September 1922, pp. 295–97; 11 November 1922, p. 348, *SI*, 23 September 1922; 30 September 1922.

62. Records, 11 July 1923, pp. 223–25.

63. Records, 13 June 1923, p. 176; letter from Richard L. Edwards, *SI*, 23 June 1923; An. Rep., 1923–24, pp. 7, 21; Records, 11 July 1923, pp. 223–25.

64. *SI*, 29 December 1923; 12 January 1924; An. Rep., 1923–24, p. 7.

65. *SI*, 24 November 1923.

66. Letter from Walter Pleuthner, *SI*, 24 November 1923.

67. Dixon Ryan Fox, *SI*, 15 March 1924; Pliny Williamson, *SI*, 1 March 1924; Jesse Waid, *SI*, 29 March 1924.

68. *SI*, 15 March 1924.

CHAPTER THREE (*Pages 43–64*)

1. From 1920 to 1930 Scarsdale grew more rapidly than any other "minor civil division" in Westchester except Pelham Manor, which grew 180 percent, U.S. Bureau of the Census, *Fifteenth Census, 1930, Population*, I, pp. 746, 750, 764–5. See also Jackson, "The Crabgrass Frontier," pp. 211–16.

2. An. Rep., 1925–26, p. 5; *NYT*, 25 November 1923, sec. 10, p. 2; L. Ward Prince of Prince and Ripley Realtors, *NYT*, 4 January 1925, sec. 11, p. 2.

3. Letter from Stephen L. Angell, *SI*, 19 December 1925; articles on the Westchester County Bureau of Public Information, *NYT*, 18 October 1925, sec. 12, p. 1; 29 November 1925, Sec. 11, p. 2; 25 April 1926, sec. 11, p. 1; *SI*, 9 July 1926; *NYT*, 5 July 1925, sec. 11, p. 3; 21 March 1926, sec. 11, p. 3; 12 June 1927, sec. 10, p. 2.

4. Records, 27 June 1917, pp. 230–32; Plan. Comm., 23 July 1917, pp. 1–2; 5 February 1918, p. 27; Records, 29 March 1922, pp. 74–98; 11 July 1923, pp. 223–25. The role played by the village government and local citizens in enforcing minimum standards of construction in Scarsdale differed from the process of "regulation without laws" that Sam Bass Warner has described in *Streetcar Suburbs: The Process of Growth in Boston, 1870–1900* (New York: Atheneum, 1969), pp. 117–52. Warner argues that, although no fewer than 9,000 separate builders were engaged in the development of the suburban towns he studied, because of the large financial risks they undertook, they "uniformly clung to traditional and popular methods in order to make their profits more certain."

5. *SI*, 1 October 1926; Plan. Comm., 5 October 1926, p. 374; *SI*, 26 November 1926; Records, 8 May 1928, pp. 185–87; Henry Hellman, pres., Grange Improvement Co., quoted in *SI*, 26 November 1926.

6. For a discussion of the subdivisions opened in the years from 1891 to 1915, see chapter one. The Eastman estate became the focus of community interest in the early 1960s when the Hoff-Barthelson Music School applied to the zoning board of appeals for permission to convert the mansion to a school. When the board denied the request, the land was sold to a developer and subdivided into building lots. The mansion itself was demolished. *SI*, 1 March 1962; 15 March 1962; 22 March 1962; 17 May 1962; 28 June 1962.

7. *SI*, 2 August 1929.

8. *Ibid*. See brochure, "Construction by Collet," (n.p., c. 1931).

9. *NYT*, 21 September 1930, sec. 13, p. 19; 5 October 1930, sec. 12, p. 14; 3 May 1931, sec. 11, p. 5.

10. *NYT*, 22 March 1931, sec. 11, p. 4; 3 May 1931, sec. 11, p. 5.

11. Westchester County Deeds, 18 December 1931, Liber 3202, p. 376 (deed of Crane-Berkley Corp. to Warren P. Shipway).

12. Advertisements for Berkley began to appear in the spring of 1930, poor timing in view of the economic conditions. Ten years later Crane and Collet had made more than sixty sales. See the deeds listed under the heading, Crane-Berkley Corp., grantor, in the index to the Westchester County deeds for the village of Scarsdale.

13. *SI*, 23 January 1926. See brochure, "Construction by Collet."

14. Westchester County Deeds, 28 August 1926, Liber 2700, pp. 29–31 (deed of Sherbrooke Park, Inc. to Arthur Boniface); *SI*, 23 January 1926; 20 March 1926; the author examined each of the thirty-eight deeds listed under the heading, Sherbrooke Park Inc., grantor, in the index to the Westchester County deeds, for the village of Scarsdale.

15. *NYT*, 6 June 1926, sec. 11, p. 5; 13 June 1926, sec. 10, p. 3; Westchester County Deeds, 28 July 1926, Liber 2628, p. 380 (deed of Heathcote Land and Development Corp. to Setrak E. Avdayan); 23 November 1927, Liber 2811, p. 313 (deed between the company and Ida W. Nybum); the author examined each of the fifty-nine deeds listed under the heading, Heathcote Land and Development Corp., grantor, 1926–30, in the index to the Westchester County deeds for the village of Scarsdale.

16. *SI*, 20 December 1924; Records, 10 February 1925, p. 61; *SI*, 14 February 1925; see the letters from Fred Lavis, William T. Brewster, Marie D. Kling, and thirteen prominent citizens, *SI*, 7 March 1925; 21 March 1925; 4 April 1925; 25 April 1925; for speeches and petitions see the account of the village board meeting, *SI*, 28 March 1925; Records, 30 April 1925, pp. 177–243; editorial, *SI*, 18 March 1927.

17. *SI*, 14 March 1925; 28 March 1925.

18. Editorial, *SI*, 18 April 1930.

19. *SI*, 14 March 1925; 25 April 1925.

20. *SI*, 11 April 1925; 18 April 1925; Records, 30 April 1925, p. 225.

21. Petition presented by John W. Dickinson with more than 1,000 signatures, Records, 30 April 1925, p. 243; *SI*, 23 May 1925.

22. Records, 8 March 1927, pp. 102–7; 22 April 1927, pp. 212–14, *NYT*, 24 April 1927, sec. 10, p. 2; *SI*, 29 April 1927.

23. Herbert McKennis spoke on the implications of recent court decisions at the open meeting of the village board on 22 April 1927, *SI*, 29 April 1927; Wulfson v Burden, 241 NY 288 (1925); *SI*, 2 January 1926; Toll, *Zoned American*, pp. 232–33; Euclid v Ambler Realty Co., 272 U.S. 365 (1926), p. 394.

24. Euclid v Ambler Realty Co., 272 U.S. 365 (1926), p. 397; for local response to the Euclid decision, see editorial by Warren W. Cunningham, *SI*, 3 December 1926.

25. *SI*, 8 July 1927; affidavits in support of petition sworn by Everett Jacobs, 8 March 1927 and 29 June 1927, and by Andrew J. Thomas, 8 June 1927, Fox Meadow Estates v William Livingston, County Clerk's File 4660, 1927; arguments of Judge William Cunningham, counsel for the plaintiff, *SI*, 8 November 1929.

26. Testimony of Mrs. I. S. Eshleman, Herbert McKennis, and Rush Wilson, *SI*, 12 April 1929, and 29 March 1929; affidavit of Robert Whitten, sworn 12 May 1925, Exhibit 1 in matter of Fox Meadow Estates v Livingston, County Clerk's File 4660, 1927; see also the editorial, *SI*, 23 August 1929.

27. Herbert McKennis, quoted in *SI*, 2 May 1930; concluding remarks of Gov. Miller, *SI*, 8 November 1929.

28. Ernest P. Goodrich, zoning expert, witness for plaintiff, *SI*, 29 March 1929; Gov. Miller's concluding remarks, *SI*, 8 November 1929, George B. Ford, zoning expert, witness for defendant, *SI*, 29 March 1929. Curiously, Ford, who testified for Scarsdale, and Goodrich, who testified in behalf of Fox Meadow Estates had long worked as partners (Scott, *American City Planning*, pp. 122–23 and 228–31).

29. Governor Miller, *SI*, 8 November 1929; George B. Ford, *SI*, 29 March 1929; Pliny Williamson, *SI*, 10 June 1930.

30. Morschauser's decision, pp. 4–7, Fox Meadow Estates v Livingston, Clerk's File 4660, 1927; *NYT*, 17 April 1930, p. 16.

31. *Ibid.*; Pliny Williamson, quoted in *SI*, 25 April 1930; Herbert McKennis, quoted in *SI*, 2 May 1930.

32. Fox Meadow Estates v Culley, 233 App. Div. (NY) 250 (1931); see also the findings of fact cited in *SI*, 31 July 1931.

33. *Ibid.*

34. See, for example, the following articles in the *Proceedings of the National Conference on City Planning*: George B. Ford, "Regional Planning and Metropolitan Planning," v. 15 (1923), pp. 4–5; Robert Whitten, "Regional Zoning," v. 15 (1923), pp. 85–114; Hugh R. Pomeroy, "Regional Planning in Practice," v. 16 (1934), pp. 122–23.

35. Toll, *Zoned American*, p. 258; Joseph L. Arnold, "City Planning in America," in *Urban Experience*, ed. Mohl and Richardson, pp. 29–31.

36. Fox Meadow Estates v Culley, 261 NY 506 (1933); editorial, *SI*, 13 January 1933.

37. U.S. Bureau of the Census, *Fifteenth Census, 1930, Population*, I, pp. 750, 765; *SI*, 26 November 1926; 24 April 1926; 12 December 1925. A more complete analysis of the topics discussed in this section, as well as an analysis of additional topics, appears in chapter five of the author's dissertation, note 10, notes to chapter 2, above.

38. Plan. Comm., 2 June 1920, p. 130; Records, 23 June 1920, p. 133; 1 November 1922, p. 333; 24 February 1925, pp. 74–78; *SI*, 9 May 1925.

39. Records, 12 October 1926, pp. 381–82; *SI*, 22 October 1926; see also *SI*, 6 March 1926.

40. The purchase of the Fox Meadow School site and the Kelwynne Road school site were approved by votes of 87 to 8 and 72 to 18, respectively: *SI*, 24 December 1926; Bd. of Ed., 27 December 1926, p. 266; the purchase of the Mamaroneck and Kelwynne tract (160 to 59), Post and Fenimore tract (156 to 59) and Davis Park tract (157 to 61) all approved: Records, 4 April 1927, p. 158; tract at Olmsted and Post Roads approved: An. Rep., 1928–29, p. 5; Records, 27 May 1930, p. 191. In all, the voters approved the purchase of 65.459 acres of land by the school and village boards for a total of $873,416: An. Rep., 1937–38, p. 13 and Bd. of Ed., 27 December 1926, p. 266; 2 May 1928, p. 91; 28 May 1928, p. 97.

41. Quotation from An. Rep., 1927–28, p. 45. The social-homogeneity argument for purchasing parks appeared in *SI*, 6 March 1926 and the Town Club Report of the Committee on Public Buildings, Grounds and Highways, 1926.

42. Records, 13 October 1927, p. 458.

43. Letters from County Engineer Charles MacDonald and residents Marguerite F. Luckhardt and Martha Washburn, Records, 13 September 1927, p. 415; 11 September 1928, p. 292; 23 October 1928, p. 333; 27 December 1927, pp. 524–25; 27 December 1928, pp. 389–411.

44. Records, 20 June 1929, pp. 249–51; *SI*, 28 June 1929; Proceedings, 17 June 1927, p. 100; 1 July 1929; pp. 135–38; 5 August 1929, pp. 176–79.

45. Records, 26 March 1929, pp. 126–27; Proceedings, 8 April 1929, pp. 900–901; 4 August 1930, pp. 121, 197–98; *SI*, 15 August 1930; Records, 9 September 1930, p. 325; 11 November 1930, pp. 391, 398; Proceedings, 17 November 1930, pp. 384–86; 24 November 1930, pp. 388–90; *SI*, 21 November 1930; 5 December 1930; 28 November 1930; 12 December 1930.

46. Records, 23 September 1930, pp. 337–38; *SI*, 26 September 1930; resolution of Greenacres Association, *SI*, 24 October 1930.

47. Records, 17 May 1926, pp. 192–96; letter from F.F. Bayer, *SI*, 22 May 1926.

48. Records, 26 April 1932, pp. 172–74; letters from "An Impartial Observer" and "A Twenty-Year Resident," *SI*, 10 June 1932; 3 June 1932.

49. Heathcote Association, Middle-Heathcote Association, Drake Road Neighborhood Association, Fox Meadow Association—all opposed. Arthur Manor Association, divided: 138 opposed of 217 canvassed. Records, 14 June 1932, pp. 210–15; *SI*, 17 June 1932.

50. Records, 28 June 1932, p. 221; letter from William T. Brewster, *SI*, 8 July 1932; Hansen, *Scarsdale*, p. 171.

51. Records, 13 July 1927, p. 371; *SI*, 15 July 1927; 1 November 1924; 13 December 1924; 22 July 1927; interview with Ruth Nash Chalmers, 18 March 1971; *SI*, 5 August 1925. The significance of the hot-dog incident is discussed by Martha W. Lear, *The Child Worshipers* (New York: Crown Publishers, 1963), pp. 120–21.

52. *NYT*, 14 July 1927, p. 13. The *Times* carried seventeen news articles and one editorial on the subject between July and December 1927. "Ruth Chalmers Remembers," *SI*, 20 November 1969; *SI*, 16 December 1927; "Our Newly Won Hot Dog Fame," *SI*, 22 July 1927; see also the lament by Mary S. Hogg, *SI*, 3 February 1928 and the editorial, "Leave Us Lay," *SI*, 7 August 1931. The latter piece included the statement: "Apparently Scarsdale is only news if it can be treated as a precocious child."

53. *SI*, 13 July 1928; 22 May 1931; 3 July 1931; 10 July 1931.

54. Records, 8 September 1931, p. 356, *SI*, 11 September 1931; 2 October 1931; 6 November 1931; 11 November 1931; 22 July 1932.

CHAPTER FOUR (*Pages 65–80*)

1. Dist. Meet., 3 May 1915, pp. 202–205; 13 April 1917, pp. 226–29; 24 April 1923; pp. 288–89; 4 May 1926, p. 334; 20 December 1926, pp. 341–43; 24 October 1927, pp. 369–70.

Although until 1965 Scarsdale was formally divided into two school districts, it is necessary to discuss only the policies undertaken in district one, since these had a significant impact on the residents of the other district as well. District two included east Scarsdale—that is, the Quaker Ridge section—and a small part of the town of Mamaroneck. Until the years after World War II, district two's population was so small that a building on Griffen Avenue with only one main schoolroom fulfilled its needs, at least for the first eight grades. But even when the district opened an elementary school comparable in size to that of Scarsdale's other elementary schools, it still sent its students to the high school in district one. Hansen, *Scarsdale*, p. 25.

2. N. Y. State, Population Schedules, 1905, 1925; Arthur Zilversmit, "Progressive Education: Winnetka as a Case Study," (unpublished manuscript, 1972); interview with Roderick Stephens, a member of Scarsdale's school board in the 1920s who had formerly lived in Bronxville, New York, N.Y., 26 July 1972; recollections of Cleveland A. Dunn, *SI*, 3 May 1929; Russell statement, Bd. of Ed., 29 September 1924, p. 16.

The Winnetka school system under Superintendent Carleton Washburne and the Bronxville system under Willard W. Beatty both developed programs of progressive education in the 1920s. Indeed, the Winnetka Plan was probably the best known and most widely copied. Lawrence A. Cremin, *The Transformation of the School: Progressivism in American Education* (New York: Alfred A. Knopf, Inc., 1964), pp. 295–99.

3. Bd. of Ed., 24 May 1926, p. 210; Town Club Reports of the Committee on Education, 30 September 1926, p. 5 and 20 May 1937; School Report, 1928–29, p. 18.

4. Ralph Underhill, "The Scarsdale Application of the Dalton Plan of Individual Instruction," *School Review* 33 (Jan. 1925), pp. 48–49.

5. Ralph Underhill, "The Scarsdale Plan," *Journal of the National Education Association* 18 (Mar. 1929), p. 77; Ralph Underhill, *SI*, 24 November 1923.

6. Julius B. Maller, *School and Community: A Study of the Demographic and Economic Background of Education in the State of New York* (New York: McGraw Hill, 1938), pp. 77–78; Ralph Underhill, "The Scarsdale Plan," *School and Society* 23 (17 April 1926), p. 496.

7. Quotations from Underhill, "The Scarsdale Plan," *Journal of the National Education Association*, p. 77; interview with R. Stephens, 26 July 1972; N.Y. Census, 1925, *Population Schedules*; Underhill, "Scarsdale Application of the Dalton Plan," p. 48.

8. Committee report quoted in *SI*, 17 November 1923; Underhill, "The Scarsdale Plan," *Journal of the National Education Association*, p. 77.

9. *SI*, 25 June 1921; 17 September 1921; 4 February 1922; 3 November 1923; 10 November 1923; 17 November 1923; 1 December 1923; Bd. of Ed., 23 January 1922, p. 156.

10. Dixon Ryan Fox, Report of the Committee on Education, Town Club, 1927, p. 7; *NYT*, 5 January 1943, p. 19; Helen Parkhurst, *Education on the Dalton Plan* (London: G. Bell, 1922), pp. xvii, 15–19, 28–29, 113.

11. Fox, Report of the Committee on Education, p. 7. The members of the board were Orion H. Cheney, Philip W. Russell, Roderick Stephens, Grace L. Conger, and Ethel P. Howes. For biographical information on the men see *SI*, 20 January 1939; 29 August 1941; *NYT*, 18 January 1939, p. 19; 25 August 1941, p. 15; *Who's Who in New York*, 10th ed., (New York: Who's Who Publications, 1938), pp. 1064–65. On the women, the only source of information is N. Y. State, Population Schedules, Election District #1, pp. 3, 34.

12. Underhill, "Scarsdale Application of the Dalton Plan," pp. 49–50; *SI*, 24 November 1923; Bd. of Ed., 26 November 1923, p. 276.

13. *SI*, 15 December 1923; 26 January 1924; Underhill, "Scarsdale Application of the Dalton Plan," p. 52.

14. Editorials, *SI*, 25 June 1921; 5 September 1930; 4 September 1931.

15. *SI*, 1 December 1923; 8 December 1923; 15 December 1923.

16. Parkhurst, "Education on the Dalton Plan," pp. 24–25.

17. Editorial, *SI*, 24 November 1923.

18. *SI*, 19 January 1924; 26 January 1924; Bd. of Ed., 27 April 1925, pp. 86–87. See also the articles referred to throughout this chapter.

19. Bd. of Ed., 28 April 1924, p. 301; 23 February 1925, p. 69; *SI*, 19 January 1924. Although Parkhurst's book did not indicate on what a limited basis the Dalton schools had employed the plan, Evelyn Dewey's book, *The Dalton Plan* (New York: E. P. Dutton, 1922), made it clear. Apparently Underhill had not read Dewey's book.

20. Ralph Underhill, "The Dalton Plan in the Scarsdale Schools," *School and Society* 22 (25 September 1925), p. 337; Underhill, "Scarsdale Application of the Dalton Plan," pp. 52, 54–55; letter from Edward P. Smith, state specialist in history, comparing Scarsdale schools in spring 1924 with schools of 1927, Bd. of Ed., 28 February 1927, p. 299; reprint of Ralph Underhill, "The Experience of Scarsdale with Individual Instruction," *SI*, 8 May 1931.

21. *SI*, 8 December 1923; 15 December 1923; Underhill, "Scarsdale Application of the Dalton Plan," p. 54; Bd. of Ed., 28 April 1924, p. 301; *SI*, 27 September 1924.

22. Underhill, paraphrasing Parkhurst's view, "Scarsdale Application of the Dalton Plan," p. 54; Bd. of Ed., 28 April 1924, pp. 301–302.

23. Bd. of Ed., 8 April 1924, p. 302; 5 August 1924, pp. 3–4; 27 October 1924, p. 28; 13 February 1925, p. 68; Fox, Report of the Committee on Education, pp. 10–11.

24. *Ibid.*, p. 8.

25. *SI*, 19 January 1924; 5 April 1924; 19 April 1924; 3 May 1924.

26. The substance of Hawthorne's letter has been culled from references to it, since no copy survives. According to the reference librarian at the White Plains Public Library, the *Daily Reporter* is only available from 1925. The offices of the *White Plains Reporter Dispatch* do not store back issues for the early period.

27. Bd. of Ed., 14 November 1924, pp. 32–35; letter from Mary Hogg, *SI*, 22 November 1924.

28. Bd. of Ed., 14 November 1924, pp. 32–35; 28 November 1924, p. 36.

29. "The Experience of Scarsdale," *SI*, 8 May 1931; Bd. of Ed., 29 September 1924, p. 12; 26 January 1925, p. 53; School Report, 1924–25, p. 14; interview with Amelie Rothschild, former member of the Scarsdale school board, Hartsdale, N. Y., 19 August 1970; *SI*, 8 December 1923; Underhill quoted in editorial, "What the Scarsdale Plan Really Is," *SI*, 27 April 1928.

30. *SI*, 14 March 1925; "The Experience of Scarsdale," *SI*, 8 May 1931; Bd. of Ed., 22 December 1924, pp. 46–47; 26 January 1925, p. 54.

31. Underhill, "The Scarsdale Plan," *School and Society*, p. 496; School Report, 1925–26, pp. 13–14, 1926–27, p. 16; Bd. of Ed., 27 February 1929, p. 15; "The Experience of Scarsdale," *SI*, 8 May 1931.

32. *SI*, 16 December 1927.

33. Bd. of Ed., 25 June 1928, p. 112; School Report, 1928–29, pp. 17–18, 1929–30, p. 13.

34. School Report, 1928–29, pp. 17–18; Ralph Underhill, "The Scarsdale Plan," *Junior-Senior H.S. Clearing House* 5 (October 1930), p. 118; "The Experience of Scarsdale," *SI*, 8 May 1931.

35. "The Scarsdale Plan," *Junior-Senior H.S. Clearing House*, p. 118.

36. In 1919–20 the board of education budgeted a total of $110,440.00 for 625 students, or $176.71 per student. In 1929–30 the board budgeted $560,051.39 for 1,766 students, or $317.13 per student. School Report, 1918–19, p. 8; 1928–29, p. 7; Maller, *School and Community*, pp. 294–96, 326–28.

37. For the dispute with Maller, see Christopher Jencks, *In equality: A Reassessment of the Effect of Family and Schooling in America* (New York: Basic Books, 1972), pp. 148–49. On the teachers' backgrounds, see School Report, 1919–20, p. 4, 1929–30, pp. 3–4. In 1928 Scarsdale paid an average salary of $2,275.74 compared to Bronxville, $3,090.71; Mount Vernon, $2,833.87; New Rochelle, $2,678.18; White Plains, $2,594.00; Pelham, $2,421.40, and Mamaroneck, $2,329.74, Bd. of Ed., 23 April 1928, p. 88.

38. One indication of a strong educational program is the number of semifinalists a school has in the National Merit Scholarship competition. The five communities mentioned, along with Scarsdale, ranked among the top 25 schools of National Merit semifinalists from 1975 to 1978. *Exeter: Bulletin of Phillips Exeter Academy* 78 (November 1978), pp. 12–13.

39. Herbert J. Gans, *The Levittowners: Ways of Life and Politics in a New Suburban Community* (New York: Pantheon, 1967), p. 88.

CHAPTER FIVE *(Pages 81–109)*

1. TC Minutes, 13 October 1904, p. 2. In a study of the uses of leisure in Westchester County, a team of sociologists from Columbia University devoted several pages to Scarsdale's Town Club, which they referred to as "the Village Club of wealthy residential Suburb A." Their analysis of the club's influence corroborates my own impression. George

Notes

A. Lundberg *et al.*, *Leisure: A Suburban Study* (New York: Columbia University Press, 1934), pp. 163–68.

2. *SI*, 30 December 1932; Hansen, *Scarsdale*, pp. 108–109, 121–22; TC Minutes, 7 October 1904, pp. 1–2.

3. TC Minutes, 8 January 1914, p. 62; 14 September 1914, p. 67; 14 January 1915, p. 72; 11 December 1919, p. 143; 30 April 1921, p. 159; TC Yearbook, 1925, pp. 11–15 and 1933, pp. 11–16; *SI*, 3 March 1923. In 1930 the Town Club had a total of 378 members, while Scarsdale's population included 2,563 men aged 21 and over. TC Yearbook, 1930, pp. 11–15; U.S. Census, 1930, III, Part 2, p. 295.

4. TC Yearbook, 1931, pp. 3–5; Lundberg, *Leisure*, pp. 164–65.

5. Lundberg, *Lesiure*, p. 165.

6. *New York Herald*, 23 November 1919, sec. 8, p. 14; "Taking Scarsdale off the Market," *New Republic* 11 (2 June 1917), pp. 125–26.

7. Articles of Incorporation, reprinted in WC Yearbook, 1928–29, p. 2; *SI*, 15 November 1919; 6 May 1922; 2 June 1923; 27 March 1926; 9 July 1926; 10 June 1927; 5 July 1929; 28 August 1931.

8. WC Yearbook, 1929–30, pp. 3–4, 22; *SI*, 4 August 1933. The details of the description of "the Women's Club in Suburb A" fit the facts concerning Scarsdale's Woman's Club; see Lundberg, *Leisure*, pp. 146–57.

9. *SI*, 1 February 1929.

10. Lundberg, *Leisure*, p. 55.

11. Letter from Mary Fleming Orr, *SI*, 5 August 1927; cost of Rowsley, *SI*, 16 September 1927; Mayo and Mrs. A. W. Page, quoted in *SI*, 23 September 1927; final vote, *SI*, 21 October 1927. See also the description of Rowsley in a special section of the newspaper devoted to the fiftieth anniversary of the Woman's Club, *SI*, 29 November 1969.

12. WC Yearbook, 1932–33, p. 35 and 194–47, p. 34. Ruth Nash Chalmers, Woman's Club president from 1926 to 1927, *Inquirer* reporter from 1926 to 1930, and editor from 1930 to 1959, agreed with my analysis of the change in the club, but thought that the formation of the Factotums, which brought in "a Junior League influence," was also a factor. However, Susan Bennett, Woman's Club president from 1938 to 1940, resented my suggestion that the priorities of the club changed over time. Since Mrs. Bennett went on to say that the Woman's Club "might be akin to the DAR but not to the Colonial Dames," our differences might be the result of different perspectives. Interview with Mrs. Chalmers, Scarsdale, N.Y., 18 March 1971 and with Mrs. Bennett, also in Scarsdale, 2 September 1971.

13. For the fiscal year 1 April 1930 to 31 March 1931, the Scarsdale Woman's Club Publications, Inc., which published the *Inquirer*, yielded its sole owner a 228% dividend ($1,140.00) on $500 stock. WC Yearbook, 1931–32, pp. 24, 27–29.

14. Quoted from "Scarsdale (N.Y.) Inquirer Marks 21 years of Female Rule," *Newsweek* (25 November 1940), p. 47. See also *New York Herald*, 23 November 1919, sec. 8, p. 14, and *SI*, 18 November 1927; 8 February 1929; 21 June 1929; 6 February 1931; 20 November 1969.

15. Editorials, *SI*, 13 June 1930; 2 March 1928.

16. "A United Front," *SI*, 1 March 1929; see also chapter one of this work.

17. *SI*, 28 February 1917; 2 March 1928; 27 February 1931. See also *SI*, 7 September 1905.

18. See Appendix A. The information there is based on the following sources: the membership lists of the churches in Scarsdale; obituaries in the *New York Times* and *Scarsdale Inquirer*; the yearbooks of the Town Club and the Woman's Club; David Magowan, *The Scarsdale Golf Club, Inc., 1898–1948* (n.p., 1948); *Westchester County Social Record* (Newark: Reporter Publishing Co., 1931); *Who's Who in New York*, 5th–10th eds. (New York: Who's Who Publications, 1911, 1914, 1918, 1924, 1929, 1938).

19. As important as Protestant, Catholic, and Jewish divisions have been in Scarsdale, and although individuals have occasionally hazarded guesses on the relative strength of the three groups—see, for example, Alex Schoumatoff, *Westchester: Portrait of a County* (New York: Coward, McCann & Geoghagan, 1979), p. 180—there is no accurate way, given existing data, of measuring group identification. Total membership figures in the various churches do not answer the problem because Scarsdale's churches and, later, its synagogues attracted members from beyond the boundaries of the village and also because village residents attended churches and synagogues outside Scarsdale. Church registries are not always open to scholars, and mailing lists are rarely available for all religious groups in about the same year. Besides, many people may identify culturally with one or the other of the major religious groups without formally becoming members of a specific church or synagogue. One recourse is to base ethnoreligious identification on an individual's family name, or in cases of names common to all major groups, such as Smith, Ross, Miller, and Gordon, the individual's first name and the neighborhood in which he or she lives can be taken into account. In undertaking such an approach, I recognize that I may have made mistakes of categorization, but I hope that my errors of judgment were proportionately divided among the various groups and did not skew the totals for any one group. I based the figures for 1925 on the names of all heads of household listed in N.Y. State, Population Schedules for Scarsdale, 1925.

20. Lundberg, *Leisure*, p. 194.

21. *SI*, 22 February 1929; 1 March 1929; 28 February 1930; 13 February 1931; 21 March 1931.

22. For a discussion of the decline in political activity among women on the national level, see William H. Chafe, *The American Woman: Her Changing Social, Economic, and Political Roles, 1920–1970* (New York: Oxford University Press, 1974), pp. 25–47.

23. Dael Wolfle, *America's Resources of Specialized Talent* (New York: Harper & Brothers, 1954), p. 24, cited by Harold M. Hodges, Jr., *Social Stratification: Class in America* (Cambridge, Mass.: Schenkman Publishing Co., 1964), p. 140.

24. On Christie see *NYT*, 26 June 1934, p. 1; *SI*, 29 June 1934; on Pirnie see *NYT*, 25 February 1967, p. 27; *SI*, 2 March 1967.

25. For the role of successful leaders in enhancing the community's self-image, see the speech by George B. Clifton, Records, 22 March 1932, p. 103; interview with Harold H. Bennett, Scarsdale, N.Y., 2 September 1971; on Lavis see *SI*, 20 March 1931; 1 December 1950; *NYT*, 26 November 1950, p. 90; Hansen, *Scarsdale*, p. 204; on Bethell see the telephone company publications that are included as appendixes in Records (1915–16); on Hancock, see *NYT*, 26 September 1956, p. 33; *SI*, 28 September 1956; Hansen, *Scarsdale*, p. 208.

26. See Appendix A.

27. *SI*, 5 July 1924.

28. *SI*, 4 September 1931.

29. *SI*, 15 February 1929; 29 May 1926; 23 March 1928.

30. Letter from Herbert McKennis, Chairman, Democratic Town Committee, *SI*, 1 November 1929. See also *SI*, 19 August 1932; 16 September 1932.

31. McKennis, quoted in *SI*, 15 November 1929.

32. Joseph Carter and Robert E. Christie, Jr., Chairman, Republican Town Committee, *SI*, 8 November 1929.

33. In 1929, 2,765 Scarsdale residents were registered as Republicans and 668 as Democrats. In the fall elections of that year the two Republican candidates received 1,099 and 1,076 votes, and the Democratic candidates received 438 and 451 votes. *SI*, 1 March 1929; 8 November 1929; 28 February 1930.

34. *SI*, 21 February 1930.

35. *SI*, 28 February 1930.

36. Editorial, *SI*, 28 February 1930.

37. *SI*, 28 February 1930; 19 December 1930.

38. Editorial, *SI*, 9 December 1932; 27 February 1931.

39. *SI*, 27 February 1931; 20 March 1931.

40. *SI*, 9 December 1932; 13 January 1933; 24 March 1933.

41. Town Club, Report of the Nonpartisan Procedure Committee on Nonpartisan Systems of Comparable Communities, 19 October 1978, Appendixes C, F, G.

42. Millard Rothenberg, *SI*, 23 March 1967; U.S. Bureau of the Census, *Fifteenth Census, 1930, Population*, VI, pp. 13, 40, 901, 908, 933, 945; Mrs. Jacob E. Neahr, Records, 30 April 1925, p. 215.

43. *SI*, 29 December 1923; 12 January 1924; An. Rep., 1923–24, p. 7; C. Neal Barney, *SI*, 20 March 1926; Records, 17 May 1926, pp. 192–96; 25 November 1930, p. 400; *SI*, 5 December 1930; 19 December 1930.

44. *NYT*, 11 March 1927, p. 38; 5 May 1967, p. 39; *SI*, 11 May 1967; N.Y. State, Population Schedules, 1925.

45. Interview with Margaret M. Treacy, Scarsdale, N.Y., 16 August 1978. Mrs. Treacy said it was rumored that the Scarsdale Golf Club had a quota of Catholics and that it admitted only those Catholics who "fit in" at the club "in other ways." This suspicion paralleled a rumor that the Woman's Club had placed "a 10 percent quota" on Jewish membership. (This phrase slipped out in an interview with a former Woman's Club president who did not want to discuss the matter further.) While it is impossible to determine whether strict arithmetic quotas

existed, it is likely that the officers of the two clubs judged prospective members according to WASP standards of behavior and values.

46. See E. Digby Baltzell, *The Protestant Establishment: Aristocracy and Caste in America* (New York: Random House, 1964), pp. 212–14. A long-time Jewish resident, who was a member of the Woman's Club, the Scarsdale Garden Club, and the League of Women Voters, said she enjoyed "cordial but not intimate relations" with her Christian neighbors. She and her husband "never," in her words, "bore the brunt of prejudice" because they "never intruded" where they knew they were "not welcome." Interview with Irma Stein, Scarsdale, N.Y., 18 August 1970.

47. On the subject of where Jewish families lived in Scarsdale, see N.Y. State, Population Schedules, 1925. The names and addresses of eighty-one Scarsdale families were listed in the 10th Anniversary booklet of the White Plains Jewish Community Center (n.p., 1934) and in the notebook of the center's secretary. The other information contained in this paragraph is based on a number of confidential interviews.

48. *SI*, 21 March 1925; *NYT*, 14 January 1951, p. 85; Weinberg mentioned by Stephen Birmingham, *Our Crowd: The Great Jewish Families of New York* (New York: Dell, 1967), pp. 396–97, 412. Of the eighty-one families affiliated with the Jewish Community Center in 1934, fifteen women belonged to the Scarsdale Woman's Club and ten men belonged to the Town Club: WC Yearbook, 1934; TC Yearbook, 1934. Listings of local officials appear in the annual reports of the village board and the yearbooks of the Town Club. The board of education has a list of all past school board members for districts one and two.

49. N.Y. State, Population Schedules, 1925.

50. *Ibid.*

51. Economists from the U.S. Department of Labor argued that the positive attractions of industry (higher wages, greater freedom) were more important in limiting the number of servants than the immigration restriction acts. U.S. Department of Labor, Bureau of Labor Statistics, "Immigration Restriction and the 'Scarcity' of Domestic Servants," *Monthly Labor Review* 25 (July 1927), pp. 1–6.

52. According to economist George J. Stigler, full-time female servants in New York City earned an average of $625 in the year 1939. Ten years earlier the *Inquirer* had listed the average monthly wage in Scarsdale at $75 or $900 a year. Even allowing for the deflation of the 1930s, it would appear that employers had to pay a higher wage in Scarsdale. Stigler, *Domestic Servants in the United States, 1900–1940* (New York: Bureau of Economic Research, 1946), p. 41, and *SI*, 20 December 1929.

53. *SI*, 13 December 1929.

54. *SI*, 11 October 1929.

55. *SI*, 13 December 1929.

56. *SI*, 20 December 1929.

57. *Ibid.*

58. *Ibid.*

59. *Ibid.*

60. *SI*, 31 January 1930. Stigler was cautious in analyzing figures whose accuracy he found "questionable." Concerning the rise in wages, he said, "It is unsafe to say more than that the increase in weekly earnings was probably somewhat less and almost certainly no larger than in manufacturing." Stigler, *Domestic Servants*, pp. 12–13.

61. *SI*, 20 December 1929; 27 December 1929; 3 January 1930; 13 January 1923; 5 August 1927.

62. *SI*, 17 January 1930; 24 January 1930; 31 January 1930.

63. *Ibid.*

64. *SI*, 20 December 1929; 27 December 1929; Bd. of Ed., 25 April 1927, pp. 323–24; *SI*, 10 January 1930.

65. *SI*, 20 December 1929; 27 December 1929; 17 January 1930.

66. The 1925 census also indicated the presence in Scarsdale of four black heads of household who worked as laborers. The four families were the remnants of a small black population that had lived in Scarsdale, mainly near Saxon Woods Road, since the years before the Civil War. N.Y. State, Population Schedules, 1925; *SI*, 20 December 1929.

67. *SI*, September–November 1927; *SI*, 10 January 1930.

68. Pamphlet, "The Church of St. James the Less" (n.p., 1926), p. 6; *SI*, 3 October 1925; Bd. of Ed., 25 April 1927, pp. 323–24.

69. Letter from "Edgemont," *SI*, 17 January 1930; 20 December 1929.

CHAPTER SIX *(Pages 123–155)*

1. U. S. Bureau of the Census, *Historical Statistics of the United States, Colonial Times to 1970, Bicentennial Edition* (Washington, 1975), pt. 1, pp. 135, 224–25; general comments on the early effects of the depression in Scarsdale appear in *SI*, 14 November 1930; 25 September 1931; 1 January 1932; 2 September 1932.

2. An. Rep., 1925–26, p. 5; 1932–33, p. 11; 1929–30, p. 42; 1940–41, p. 11; U. S. Census, 1930, *Population, III*, pt. 2, p. 295; U. S. Census, 1940, *Population, II*, pt. 5, p. 114; *SI*, 21 July 1939; *NYT*, 24 April 1932, p. 10; 20 November 1932, sec. 10, p. 1; 8 April 1934, sec. 11, p. 1.

3. *SI*, 12 December 1930; 1 April 1932; 27 January 1933.

4. *SI*, 27 January 1933.

5. *SI*, 26 January 1934, 27 April 1934; 18 October 1935.

6. *SI*, 18 October 1935.

7. N. Y. State, Temporary Emergency Relief Administration, "Emergency Relief in the State of New York: Statutes, Regulations, Opinions, and Interpretations of Counsel" (Albany, November 1934), pp. 11, 93; An. Rep., 1935–36, pp. 12, 23, 27; Hurdman and Cranstoun, Public Accountants, Report to the Mayor and Common Council of the City of White Plains, 24 April 1936, pp. 2, 9; Annual Report of the City Auditor for the City of New Rochelle for the Year 1935, pp. 2, 35, 60–61.

8. The proportion (2,024 divided by 30) is based on the number of households listed in U. S. Bureau of the Census, *Fifteenth Census, 1930, Population*, VI, p. 901, divided by the largest number of households in any single year listed as receiving home relief, An. Rep., 1936, p. 24; *NYT*, 2 November 1935, p. 2; Records, 22 March 1932, p. 106; *SI*, 17 January 1933; 3 February 1933; 17 February 1933; 1 December 1933; 15 December 1933.

9. For a perceptive introduction to Hoover's administration, see Carl N. Degler, "The Ordeal of Herbert Hoover," *The Yale Review* (Summer 1963), pp. 563–83.

10. See cartoon on Scarsdale's high taxes, *SI*, 26 September 1925; and more serious discussion, *SI*, 20 March 1926.

11. *SI*, 25 March 1932; 27 January 1933; 3 March 1933.

12. *SI*, 7 April 1933.

13. *SI*, 21 April 1933; 7 April 1933; 14 April 1933; 28 April 1933; *NYT*, 29 April 1933, p. 15; Records, 25 April 1933, pp. 87–91; 26 April 1933, pp. 100–102.

14. In the early forties the budget declined below the 1939–40 figure. Then, in 1945–46, it shot up to $995,563.24 and, in 1946–47, to $1,116,975; School Rep., 1929–1947.

15. Bd. of Ed., 27 June 1932, pp. 79–80; 12 October 1932, p. 120; 31 October 1932, pp. 143–44; *SI*, 29 April 1932.

16. Roderick Stephens, *SI*, 21 February 1920; Bd. of Ed., 23 April 1928, p. 88; 28 May 1928, p. 96; 24 September 1928, p. 139; *SI*, 8 March 1929; School Rep., 1931–32, p. 14; Bd. of Ed., 23 May 1932, p. 69; *SI*, 29 April 1932; 6 May 1932; 10 February 1933; 10 March 1933; Bd. of Ed., 6 February 1933, pp. 193–95; 6 March 1933, p. 208.

17. *SI*, 10 November 1904; 31 August 1912; 9 November 1912; 15 November 1916; 11 November 1932; *NYT*, 11 November 1932, p. 8; John Morton Blum *et al.*, *The National Experience*, 3rd ed. (New York: Harcourt Brace Jovanovich, 1973), p. 847. The vote for Hoover in Scarsdale ran well ahead of the vote for him in other New York suburbs. Hoover barely won Westchester County with 51 percent of the vote. He received 54.8 percent of the vote in Nassau County and 55.5 percent in Suffolk. *NYT*, 10 November 1932, p. 6.

18. William E. Leuchtenburg, *Franklin D. Roosevelt and the New Deal* (New York: Harper & Row, 1963), pp. 39, 42–43.

19. *SI*, 10 March 1933; 17 March 1933; Leuchtenburg, *Franklin Roosevelt*, pp. 43–44.

20. *SI*, 4 August 1933; 11 August 1933; 18 August 1933.

21. *SI*, 25 August 1933; 1 September 1933.

22. *SI*, 18 August 1933; 25 August 1933; 12 January 1934.

23. Leuchtenburg, *Franklin Roosevelt*, p. 145; *SI*, 24 May 1935; 31 May 1935.

24. *SI*, 6 July 1934; 29 June 1934; 17 August 1934; 29 March 1935; 22 March 1935; *NYT*, 8 July 1934, secs. 10 and 11, p. 1; 10 August 1934, p. 2; 16 September 1934, sec. 11, p. 1.

25. *SI*, 30 June 1933; Records, 11 July 1933, p. 153.

26. *SI*, 6 October 1933.

27. *SI*, 7 July 1933.

28. Records, 23 September 1933, appendix to p. 171; 30 September 1933, pp. 174–77; *SI*, 7 December 1934.

29. *SI*, 22 December 1939. It should be noted that the PWA did build a new post office in Scarsdale during the 1930s, but this was a federal government decision, not a local government decision. *SI*, 21 August 1936; 16 April 1937.

30. *SI*, 6 July 1934; 21 June 1935.

31. *SI*, 9 October 1936; 23 October 1936; 6 November 1936; Blum, *National Experience*, p. 847; *NYT*, 5 November 1936, p. 3. Of all the municipalities in Westchester County, the voters in Scarsdale gave Roosevelt the lowest percentage of their ballots; *NYT*, 5 November 1936, p. 8.

32. Leuchtenburg, *Franklin Roosevelt*, pp. 232–39; letter from William T. Brewster, *SI*, 16 July 1937.

33. *SI*, 19 February 1937; 26 February 1937.

34. *SI*, 14 October 1938.

35. Records, 25 July 1939, pp. 262–64; 14 November 1939, pp. 319–20; *SI*, 8 December 1939.

36. Two of the three residents quoted did not identify themselves by name; *SI*, 8 December 1939; 15 December 1939. As William Walker Orr noted, an application for WPA funds from the village government in behalf of the Girl Scouts was probably illegal, since a Girl Scout house was technically not a public building.

37. *SI*, 29 March 1940.

38. Dist. Meet., 1 March 1937, p. 111; *SI*, 12 February 1937; 5 March 1937.

39. Editorial, *SI*, 30 April 1937; Records, 28 February 1938, p. 56.

40. *SI*, 15 January 1939; 16 April 1937.

41. See in particular the petition signed by 298 property owners, Records, 27 April 1937, pp. 100–102; *SI*, 30 April 1937; *NYT*, 10 May 1937, p. 9.

42. Records, 11 May 1937, pp. 142–43; *SI*, 14 May 1937; 10 December 1937; *NYT*, 10 December 1937, p. 48; 14 December 1937, p. 6.

43. *SI*, 24 December 1937–11 March 1938.

44. *SI*, 11 March 1938.

45. *SI*, 17 December 1937.

46. *SI*, 17 December 1937; 11 March 1938.

47. Letter from I. W. Glasel, *SI*, 17 December 1937; letter from F. L., *SI*, 10 January 1936.

48. *SI*, 4 March 1938; 18 March 1938; Records, 22 March 1938, pp. 96–97.

49. Letter from Fred Lavis, *SI*, 7 January 1938.

50. *SI*, 1 December 1939; 22 March 1940; 12 January 1940; 2 February 1940.

51. *SI*, 5 July 1940; 14 June 1940; 21 June 1940.

52. *SI*, 26 July 1940; 1 November 1940; Willkie advertisement, *SI*, 2 August 1940; election results, *SI*, 8 November 1940; *NYT*, 6 November 1940, pp. 6–7; Blum, *National Experience*, p. 847; editorial, *SI*, 20 December 1940.

53. *SI*, 7 June 1935; 3 August 1934; 14 June 1940.

54. *SI*, 17 January 1941; 11 July 1941.

55. *SI*, 14 November 1941; 31 October 1941; 28 November 1941.

56. Editorial, *SI*, 12 December 1941; 3 July 1942; 9 January 1942; 30 January 1942; 19 December 1941; 29 May 1942; 19 June 1942; 26 December 1941; 16 January 1942.

57. *SI*, 30 January 1942; 21 August 1942; 10 April 1942; 11 December 1942. In May 1942 the village board passed a blackout and air raid ordinance detailing the authority of policemen, firemen, and air raid wardens; prohibiting unauthorized warning or all-clear signals; and providing penalties for the use of lights during blackouts. Records, 12 May 1942, pp. 141–45.

58. *SI*, 22 May 1942; 15 October 1943; Records, 15 October 1943, p. 215.

59. *SI*, 6 February 1942; 8 May 1942; 15 May 1942; 1 January 1943; 9 April 1943; 17 December 1943. For a lively discussion of wartime shortages and their impact, see Richard R. Lingeman, *Don't You Know There's a War On?* (New York: G. P. Putnam's Son, Capricorn Books,1976), pp. 234–70.

60. *SI*, 13 February 1942; 15 May 1942; 1 January 1943.

61. *SI*, 2 January 1942; 8 May 1942; 15 January 1943; 26 June 1942; 13 March 1942; 10 September 1943; 5 January 1945.

62. *SI*, 10 April 1942; 13 November 1942; 20 November 1942.

63. *SI*, 1 January 1943.

64. *SI*, 26 February 1943; 5 March 1943; 17 March 1944; 2 March 1945; 5 November 1943; 10 November 1944; 9 November 1945.

65. The $17,500,000 figure represents the rounded total of the amounts raised in the eight bond drives from early 1942 through the end of 1945. *SI*, 10 July 1942; 7 May 1943; 1 October 1943; 18 February 1944; 7 July 1944; 15 December 1944; 29 June 1945; 14 December 1945.

66. *SI*, 20 February 1942; 3 April 1942; 12 June 1942; 19 June 1942; 3 July 1942; 10 July 1942.

67. *SI*, 9 April 1943.

68. *SI*, 16 April 1943; 23 April 1943; 7 May 1943; 28 May 1943; 4 June 1943.

69. *SI*, 1 October 1943; 18 February 1944; 7 July 1944; 15 December 1944; 6 May 1945; 29 June 1945.

70. *SI*, 26 May 1944; 2 June 1944; 9 June 1944.

71. The wartime relationship between industry and government is discussed in John Morton Blum, *V Was for Victory* (New York: Harcourt Brace Jovanovich, 1976), pp. 117–24 and Lingeman, *Don't You Know*, pp. 107–11.

72. The only lists that exist of Scarsdale servicemen and women are either too exclusive (naming only former students of Scarsdale High School and leaving out those residents who attended private or parochial schools) or too inclusive (naming not only current residents of the village but also those whose families had moved away from Scarsdale and others who lived outside the village limits but within the Scarsdale postal district). Obviously it would not be appropriate to use such lists as the

basis for comparing the proportion of residents of the village of Scarsdale who served in the armed forces to the proportion of servicemen and women in other communities. The figures listed here come from an all-inclusive list that appears on the Scarsdale war memorial. In addition, thirty-three women served in the Red Cross, and nine men joined the American Field Service.

73. The names of those who died are listed on the Scarsdale war memorial; see also *SI*, 22 December 1944; 22 September 1944; 18 February 1944; 31 March 1944.

74. Stories on Newkirk appeared in *SI*, 23 January 1942; 6 February 1942; 27 March 1942; 22 May 1942; 20 November 1942; 1 January 1943; 6 May 1949.

75. Stories on Szaniawski appeared in *SI*, 23 July 1943; 2 June 1944; 7 July 1944; 8 September 1944; 2 March 1945; 11 May 1945; 15 June 1945.

76. *SI*, 5 November 1943; 10 May 1946; 27 November 1942; 2 January 1942; 31 July 1942; An. Rep., 1944–45, pp. 47–49; 1945–46, pp. 53–54.

77. *SI*, 19 February 1943; 30 April 1943; Records, 10 November 1942, pp. 287–89; 8 December 1942, pp. 316–17; 29 December 1942, p. 322.

78. *SI*, 19 February 1943; 30 April 1943; Records, 23 February 1943, p. 36; 27 April 1943, pp. 93–100.

79. *SI*, 19 April 1943; 13 August 1943; 31 December 1943; 30 June 1944; Records, 27 April 1943, pp. 97–98; 9 May 1944, pp. 159–60; 27 June 1944, pp. 215–16.

80. An. Rep., 1947–48, p. 11; *SI*, 27 June 1947; 12 September 1947.

81. These statements were made by Dr. Russell E. Auman, pastor of the Redeemer Lutheran Church, at ceremonies marking the dedication of the temporary honor roll, *SI*, 9 July 1943.

82. *SI*, 25 September 1942; 18 December 1942, 21 May 1943.

83. *SI*, 10 November 1944; Blum, *National Experience*, p. 847.

84. Editorial and letters signed "A Resident of the Community" and "A Republican," *SI*, 20 April 1945.

85. *SI*, 17 August 1945.

CHAPTER SEVEN (*Pages 157–186*)

1. U.S. Bureau of the Census, *Nineteenth Census, 1970*, vol. 1, pt. 34, sec. 1, p. 19. The Census Bureau's official advance count for 1980 is 17,650. See copy of table 1: persons by Race and Spanish Origin and Housing Unit Counts, village clerk's file.

2. U.S. Bureau of the Census, *Eighteenth Census, 1960*, vol. 1, pt. 34, pp. 311 and 228; vol. 1, pt. 1, p. 286.

3. U.S. Bureau of the Census, *Eighteenth Census, 1960*, vol. 1, pt. 15, p. 344; vol. 1, pt. 6, p. 361; vol. 1, pt. 32, p. 255; vol. 1, pt. 37, p. 327; vol. 1, pt. 24, p. 261.

4. The first set of percentages is based on adding the numbers listed under the categories of professional, technical, and kindred workers; farmers and farm managers; and managers, officials, and proprietors, excluding farm workers. These members were added first for Scarsdale, then for New York State, and finally for the New York Standard Metropolitan Statistical Area, divided by the total number of employed men over 14 years old—4,604 for Scarsdale, 4,330,216 for New York State, and 2,842,283 for the New York SMSA. The second set of percentages includes all the numbers listed in the categories craftsmen, foremen, and kindred workers; operatives and kindred workers; private household workers; other service workers; farm laborers and farm foremen; and laborers, excluding farm and mine workers. These totals were again divided by the number of employed men in Scarsdale, in the state as a whole and the New York SMSA, U.S. Bureau of the Census, *Eighteenth Census, 1960*, vol. 1, pt. 34, pp. 223, 271, and 283.

5. *SI*, 2 April 1948.

6. Stories about Wilson appeared in *SI*, 25 September 1942; 1 September 1944; 13 December 1946; 21 October 1949; 18 August 1950; 22 December 1950; 23 February 1951; 25 January 1957; 8 February 1957; 16 March 1961; 6 January 1972. N.B.: Scarsdale's Charles Edward Wilson should not be confused with Charles Erwin Wilson, the president of General Motors, who became Eisenhower's secretary of defense. For summaries of the careers of the two Charles E. Wilsons, see *Who's Who in America*, vol. 28, 1954–55 (Chicago: Marquis–Who's Who), p. 2888.

7. *SI*, 7 June 1957; 26 January 1967; *Who's Who in America*, vol. 31, 1960–61, p. 1811.

8. On Rusk, see *SI*, 20 September 1955; 15 December 1960; *Who's Who in America*, vol. 28, 1954–55, p. 28. On Gardner, see *SI*, 28 January 1955; 9 July 1964; 29 July 1965; *Who's Who in America*, vol. 28, 1954–55, p. 958.

9. On Meyer, see *SI*, 27 February 1942; 25 January 1952; 12 August 1955; *Who's Who in America*, vol. 23, 1944–45, p. 1454. On H. Rusk, see *SI*, 13 April 1951; 15 December 1960; 5 March 1970; *Who's Who in America*, vol. 28, 1954–55, p. 2316. On Hogate, see *SI*, 7 February 1941; 14 February 1947; *Who's Who in America*, vol. 21, 1940–41, p. 1274.

10. *SI*, 5 November 1948; 7 November 1952; 9 November 1956; 10 November 1960. The influx of Catholics and Jews into Scarsdale is discussed in chapter eight of this work.

11. The description of "a Scarsdale Galahad" comes from the introduction to the song "I'll Know," music and lyrics by Frank Loesser. The statements from the Greensboro and Richwood newspapers were quoted in *SI*, 28 October 1949; 7 August 1953. See also Howard Rushmore, "The Class Struggle in Suburbia," *American Mercury*, November 1953, p. 43.

12. Letter signed "A Thirty-Year Resident—The Last Two Homeless," *SI*, 10 October 1947 and editorial, 23 November 1945. Additional letters on the subject appeared in *SI*, 18 October 1946; 18 April 1947; 25 April 1947; and 21 November 1947.

13. For the Beckerman case, see *SI*, 23 November and 30 November 1945. After granting the variance in that case, the board of appeals denied at least one other petition for a two-family house, *SI*, 26 April 1946. In October 1944 the board of trustees rejected a plan to shift twenty-six acres of land, known as the Crane estate, from the Residence A to the Residence C zones. The shift would have permitted Mr. and Mrs. Miller McClintock to build forty-four two-story buildings containing a total of 280 apartment units. The McClintocks said they wanted to provide housing for the married children of local property holders and "especially for the returning veterans of the war." Records, 26 September 1944, pp. 248–49 and 10 October 1944, pp. 257–62; *SI*, 29 September 1944; 13 October 1944.

14. The homeowners who signed the petition lived in the vicinity of the Crossway, Carthage Road, and the eastern end of Heathcote Road, Records, 24 October 1944, pp. 275–77. Although for a time Scarsdale's zoning ordinance was the most restrictive in New York State, in more than twenty years the village board had made only a few changes in its provisions. In 1935 the board distinguished between a Business A zone, which excluded gasoline stations and lunch wagons, and a Business B zone, which permitted such uses. In 1944 the board limited the circumstances under which a private school, hospital, or similar facility could be established in the village. Records, 25 June 1935, pp. 179–93; An. Rep., 1944–45, p. 12.

15. Records, 10 October 1944, pp. 265–66; *SI*, 15 November 1946.

16. Records, 4 March 1947, pp. 61–62, 67–68.

17. Records, 4 March 1947, pp. 58, 62, 64, 65, 71; *SI*, 15 November 1946.

18. Records, 4 March 1947, pp. 72–75; 11 March 1947, pp. 85–102; 9 May 1961, pp. 228–31; *SI*, 31 January 1947; 7 March 1947; 14 March 1947; 30 March 1961; 11 May 1961. See article, "No Substandard Areas for Scarsdale, New York," *American City*, August 1947, p. 7.

19. Plan. Comm., 17 June 1946, pp. 104–106 and 3 October 1949, pp. 161–62; Building Permit #4036, issued 21 September 1949, reissued 2 December 1949, in files of building inspector.

20. Elting represented a group of over 125 property owners in East Scarsdale. His letter to the village board appears in Records, 8 November 1949, pp. 293–94. See also Records, 10 October 1949, pp. 268–72; 25 October 1949, pp. 280–83; 8 November 1949, pp. 289–90; *SI*, 28 October 1949; 11 November 1949.

21. *SI*, 28 October 1949; 11 November 1949; 18 November 1949.

22. Records, 15 November 1949, pp. 304–308; *SI*, 18 November 1949; 25 November 1949; *Herald Tribune*, 17 November 1949.

23. *SI*, 25 November 1949; 2 December 1949; 9 December 1949.

24. *SI*, 2 December 1949; 17 February 1950; 30 December 1949; 13 January 1950.

25. *SI*, 16 December 1949; 3 February 1950. A number of similar requests appear in Records, 22 November 1949, pp. 314–15; 13 December 1949, pp. 326–27.

26. Records, 25 April 1950, pp. 152–55; *SI*, 7 April 1950.

27. For a sample of public opinion on the look-alike law, see the comments by John E. F. Wood, Benjamin Smith, and Edwin de Lima, Records, 25 April 1950, pp. 116–18; *SI*, 28 April 1950. For a discussion of the efforts of a mass-production builder and the clientele those efforts attracted, see Gans, *The Levittowners*, pp. 3–43.

28. These additions brought the number of one-family houses to 4,576, in 1960, apartment houses to 9, business buildings with apartments to 5, and business buildings to 34. An. Rep., 1949–50, p. 11, and 1959–60, p. 9; *SI*, 28 February 1958; 28 March 1958; 18 April 1958.

29. *SI*, 17 December 1937; 7 November 1958; *NYT*, 28 September 1962, p. 35; *SI*, 12 January 1967; William L. Foley, "Citizens on the Alert," *Recreation*, January 1964, pp. 14–15. In 1960 the village owned 177.988 acres, in 1980 it owned 222.277 acres. An. Rep., 1959–60, p. 8, and 1979–80, p. 17. For the number of residents who signed away the development rights on their lots, see the file, "Development Rights Open Space Preservation" in the village assessor's office.

30. *SI*, 28 May 1948; 18 June 1948; 31 March 1950; 9 July 1954. The records of the village board contain numerous references to the community's parking problem for virtually every year of the period from 1945 to 1975.

31. An. Rep., 1948–49, p. 11; *SI*, 13 February 1953; 15 June 1954.

32. *SI*, 6 April 1956; 26 September 1958.

33. *SI*, 29 June 1956; 24 October 1963.

34. Statements by Mrs. Simon Breines, Friends of the Scarsdale Parks, and Mrs. David Rumsey, quoted in, *SI*, 29 June 1956; 28 September 1956; 23 November 1956; 12 September 1958; and 24 October 1963.

35. Statements quoted by merchant Mary Rothman in her letter, *SI*, 31 October 1963. See also Records, 22 October 1963, pp. 406–408.

36. The trustees backed down from the plans for the Chase Road parking lot in November 1963, but did not formally abandon them until ten years later. Records, 26 November 1963, pp. 461–62; Records, 13 November 1973, pp. 287–92. For a proparking-lot view, see the letter from George M. Waugh, Jr., *SI*, 9 May 1963. For Mrs. Rumsey's antiparking-lot statement, see *SI*, 29 June 1956.

37. On train station-park dispute, see *SI*, 12 March 1964; 16 April 1964; 30 April 1964; 22 October 1964; 29 October 1964. On the Freightway decision, see *SI*, 12 March 1964; 15 October 1970; 24 December 1970; 15 July 1971; Records, 13 July 1971, pp. 200–203. Proposals for placing a multilevel parking facility at Freightway went back to at least 1956, but the trustees had long opposed the idea because of the expense of such construction, the inconvenience of the location, and the impact the garage would have on the already extremely congested traffic conditions on Garth Road and on the Popham Road bridge. *SI*, 21 September 1956, 28 November 1963.

38. *SI*, 25 July 1974; 1 August 1974.

39. *SI*, 11 April 1941; 8 March 1946; *NYT*, 15 April 1947, p. 17; "Scarsdale's $1,066,000 Question," *American City*, June 1947, p. 109.

40. *SI*, 8 March 1946.

41. *SI*, 22 March 1946; 29 March 1946. For further endorsements of the pay-as-you-go plan, see *SI*, 5 April 1946; 19 April 1946; 12 December 1948; 17 December 1948. For dissenting views, see the letters of Fred Lavis and Gaius Merwin, *SI*, 12 April 1946, and the statements of George B. Clifton, *SI*, 30 April 1948, 15 October 1948.

42. The trustees passed a resolution formally adopting pay-as-you-go financing, Records, 26 March 1946, pp. 80–82. With regard to reserves, they set aside a low of $25,000 in fiscal 1947–48 and a high of $306,800 in fiscal 1962–63. The figure for major capital expenditures comes from totaling the amounts listed in the summary of general fund operations under the headings "Capital Outlays—Major Improvements" and "Capital Outlays—Capital Reserves" minus the capital reserve balance of $1,140,168.53 on 31 March 1965. The figures for bonded indebtedness appear in the bond charts for 31 March 1946 and 31 May 1965. See the section "Taxation and Finance" for each Annual Report from 1945–46 to 1964–65. Also, for a discussion of specific projects undertaken, see the "Village Manager's Statement" in each Annual Report.

43. An. Rep., 1944–45, pp. 7, 9; 1964–65, pp. 7, 10. The average assessment was obtained by dividing the total assessed valuation for each year by the number of taxable properties (houses, apartment buildings, business buildings, and clubs) in Scarsdale at the time.

44. For the inflation rate, see the table on Consumer Price Indexes, U.S. Bureau of the Census, *Historical Statistics of the United States, Colonial Times to 1970, Bicentennial Edition*, pt. 1, p. 210. For state comptroller Arthur Levitt's findings, see *SI*, 15 January 1964.

45. Report of the taxation and finance committee, quoted in *SI*, 16 April 1954; Donald H. Ogilvy letter, *SI*, 16 May 1958; John Snyder, quoted in *SI*, 25 March 1965.

46. Records, 23 May 1967, pp. 151–54; 27 June 1967, pp. 198–99; 22 August 1967, pp. 235–37; *SI*, 22 June 1967; 24 August 1967; 14 March 1968. The drive for a swimming pool dated back to the end of World War II. See "Scarsdale Wants a Swimming Pool," *American City*, September 1946, p. 132, and *SI*, 27 May 1949; 16 December 1949; 17 March 1950; 30 June 1950; 12 February 1954; 22 April 1955; 13 February 1959; An. Rep., 1965–66, p. 13.

47. *SI*, 25 April 1958. For other allusions to Scarsdale's lack of experimentation in the postwar era, see Sybil Conrad, *SI*, 20 February 1959; 20 March 1959.

48. Arthur Zilversmit points to this national trend at the end of his article, "The Failure of Progressive Education, 1920–1940," in *Schooling and Society*, ed. Lawrence Stone (Baltimore: Johns Hopkins University Press, 1976), pp. 252–63.

49. *The Education Index* lists a total of 43 articles on education in Scarsdale for the years 1930 to 1965. The articles alluded to in the text are Irene Allen Fiske, "The Guidance Program in a Suburban Community in the East," *National Elementary Principal*, July 1940, pp. 313–19; George E. Raab, "The Class Group: Social Setting for Learning," *Elementary School Journal*, December 1958, pp. 150–53; and Archibald B. Shaw, "Scarsdale Schools Get Full-Time Use," *School Executive*, April 1948, pp. 35–37.

50. Stories about Nelson appeared in *SI*, 10 February 1933; 26 December 1947; 30 November 1951; 24 October 1952; 6 March 1953; 11 September 1953; 17 December 1954. Nelson was the one local educator to receive the Scarsdale Bowl award, *SI*, 18 January 1952. For articles on Shaw, see *SI*, 9 December 1949; 15 May 1959; 20 December 1962; 15 July 1965. For articles on Howe, see *SI*, 11 December 1959; 30 April 1964; 23 December 1965; 23 July 1970.

51. Editorial, *SI*, 11 January 1962.

52. Enrollments from Bd. of Ed., 3 July 1945, p. 302 and 14 June 1965, p. 206. Quotation from Gaius Merwin, *SI*, 12 April 1946. Although the voters passed nine different bond issues from 1945 to 1965, in 1962 they defeated a proposal for an addition to the high school that included an indoor swimming pool by a vote of 1,381 to 2,254. The proposition later passed, without the pool, by a vote of 2,189 to 1,219. Dist. Meet., 7 May 1946; 16 April 1951; 19 November 1951; 25 February 1953; 28 October 1954; 21 November 1955; 6 July 1957; 24 February 1958; 1 December 1962; 16 November 1963. In addition, the voters in district two, which included East Scarsdale and a small part of Mamaroneck, sold their original school on Griffen Avenue and built the Quaker Ridge School, in 1946–47, for $600,000. Because of the rapid growth of the population of the district, they built two additions to the school in the 1950s that cost $400,000 and $960,000. Education and School Budget Committee of the Town Club, "The Scarsdale Schools," 1959, p. 118.

53. For articles on the Heathcote School, see *SI*, 2 November 1951; Archibald B. Shaw and Lawrence B. Perkins, "Planning an Elementary School," *School Executive*, July 1954, pp. 58–64; and George E. Raab, "Facilities for the Elementary School Science Program," *Science Teacher*, February 1960, pp. 25–29. For articles on the house plan at the Scarsdale Junior High School and the new library and audiovisual facilities at the Scarsdale High School, see Walter E. Fogg, "Scarsdale Plan is Flexible and Relaxed," *Nation's Schools*, June 1961, pp. 66–68; Stan Leggett, "Upgrading Existing School Facilities," *Architectural Record*, February 1963, pp. 163–65; and James L. Theodores, "A New, But Much Used, Multi-Media Center," *American School and University*, April 1966, pp. 28–30. The Quaker Ridge School in district two was also innovative. See "Community Needs Served by New Suburban School," *American School Board Journal*, June 1949, pp. 41–44.

54. Ogilvy letter, *SI*, 6 February 1953; school vote, Dist. Meet., 19 November 1951; "Cluster of Classrooms," *Life*, 15 November 1954, pp. 73–74, 77–78; "Heathcote: A Pioneering School in Plan and Atmosphere," *Architectural Forum*, July 1954, pp. 98–107; John De Wolf, speaking to the Arthur Manor Association, *SI*, 22 January 1954.

55. Bd. of Ed., 3 July 1945, p. 299; 14 June 1965, p. 206; An. Rep., 1944–45, p. 7; 1964–65, p. 10; *SI*, 5 February 1954; 9 May 1958; views of John M. Franz, *SI*, 13 February 1953.

56. Town Club Committee Report, as analyzed and quoted in *SI*, 23 May 1947 and *NYT*, 24 May 1947, p. 56. Supt. Vernon G. Smith harshly criticized the report, *NYT*, 29 May 1947, p. 23.

57. Education and School Budget Committee of the Town Club, "The Scarsdale Schools," 1959, pp. i, iii; *SI*, 27 February 1959; 6 March 1959; 20 March 1959.

58. See discussion in letters' columns, *SI*, 6 June 1947; 13 June 1947; 24 April 1959. For the reaction in the schools, see Bd. of Ed., 9 June 1947, p. 441; 3 March 1959, p. 193; 9 March 1959, p. 200; 19 March 1959, p. 205; 23 March 1959, p. 209. For references to the 1947 report in the press, see "Lower Learning," *Newsweek*, 2 June 1947, p. 82, and Farnsworth Crowder, "Educational Strait Jackets," *Survey Graphic*, November 1947, p. 619.

59. The direct quotations are from letters written by Ellis H. Carson and R.D.K., *SI*, 17 December 1948; 7 January 1949; 14 January 1949; Elbert Gross, "The Scarsdale Controversy: 1948–1954" (Ph.D. dissertation, Columbia University, 1958), pp. 65 and 68.

60. Interestingly the 1948 HUAC investigations had implicated two Scarsdale residents, Lauchlin Currie of Gaylor Road, an expert in international economics who had served as a wartime adviser to President Roosevelt, and Laurence Duggan of Walworth Avenue, the president of the Institute of International Education and a former state department official. While Currie appeared before the committee to deny the charges against him, Duggan never made a public statement on the subject. Ten days after questioning by agents of the F.B.I., Duggan fell, jumped, or was pushed to his death from the sixteenth floor of a mid-Manhattan building. Nevertheless, there seemed to be no connection between the charges made against Currie and Duggan and the accusations against the school board. *SI*, 6 August 1948; 20 August 1948; 24 December 1948; Walter Goodman, *The Committee* (Baltimore: Penguin Books, 1969), pp. 246, 251–53, 267–69.

61. Richard Hofstadter, *The Paranoid Style in American Politics and Other Essays* (New York: Alfred A. Knopf, Inc., 1965).

62. For a summary of the anticommunists' charges see the account of their 27 March 1952 meeting, *SI*, 4 April 1952 and the chapter, "The Scarsdale School Battle," in William C. Kernan, *My Road to Certainty* (New York: D. McKay Co., 1953), pp. 164–88.

63. Report of the Committee on Educational Policies and Teaching Staff, Bd. of Ed., 7 November 1949, insert following p. 82; *SI*, 11 November 1949; 6 April 1956.

64. Quotations from Treacy and Dohrenwend, *SI*, 16 September 1949; 7 October 1949; 11 November 1949; 27 January 1950; 10 February 1950; 10 March 1950; 7 April 1950; Bd. of Ed., 12 September 1949, pp. 41–42; 3 October 1949, pp. 64–66; 7 November 1949, pp. 82–84; 9 January 1950, p. 135; 6 February 1950, p. 144; 6 March 1950, p. 156; 3 April 1950, p. 177. For background on Fast, see Goodman, *The Committee*, pp. 177, 181, 392, 414.

65. *SI*, 14 October 1949; 11 November 1949; 7 April 1950.

66. Report of the Committee on Educational Policies and Teaching Staff, Bd. of Ed., 7 November 1949, insert following p. 82; 6 March 1950, pp. 156–57; *SI*, 11 November 1949; 10 March 1950.

67. *SI*, 10 February 1950; 7 April 1950.

68. Statement of board, Bd. of Ed., 9 May 1950, pp. 196–97; *SI*, 7 April 1950; 5 May 1950; 12 May 1950.

69. *SI*, 12 May 1950; Bd. of Ed., 9 May 1950, pp. 197–98. See also the Report on the Course "Studies in American Life," Bd. of Ed., 5 June 1950, attachment B to p. 224.

70. Letter from Ruth D. Kellogg, *SI*, 12 May 1950.

71. Bd. of Ed., 5 June 1950, pp. 220–21; *SI*, 9 June 1950; 23 June 1950. The individuals listed in the text as members of the Committee of Ten were identified as such at the June 19 meeting, where they were photographed by the *Inquirer* at a table reserved for Dohrenwend's followers. The membership of the committee was not static, however. Just eight months earlier several different names had appeared on a letter from the committee that was printed in the newspaper. These were Ellis H. Carson, Sylvan Gotshal, Oscar Halecki, Henry G. Koch, Henry C. Link, and Thomas E. O'Donnell, along with Dohrenwend, Kernan, and Schaumber (in other words, nine people signed themselves as the Committee of Ten), *SI*, 14 October 1949. Of course, during the controversy other individuals such as Cyril S. Treacy and James R. Meehan also promoted the anticommunist cause. For more on committee members and sympathizers, see Gross, "The Scarsdale Controversy," pp. 65–68.

72. *SI*, 23 June 1950.

73. Bd. of Ed., 5 July 1950, pp. 18–19 and attachment F to p. 29; *SI*, 7 July 1950.

74. *SI*, 16 February 1950; 15 April 1950; 7 July 1950.

75. Before printing excerpts from McConahay's speech, the *Inquirer*, fearful of being implicated in libel, obtained a written release from Superintendent Shaw, *SI*, 22 September 1950; 13 October 1950; Bd. of Ed., 14 September 1950, pp. 47–48; 9 October 1950, p. 77. It should be mentioned that, after September 1950, the board spent considerable time answering communications written by members of the Citizens' Committee and that, beginning in September 1953 it seemed to allow some discussion of the issue in public meetings. However, neither the written exchanges nor the later verbal exchanges received much attention in the press. See Bd. of Ed., 6 November 1950, p. 98; 5 February 1951, p. 194; 5 March 1951, p. 214; 2 April 1951, p. 247; 4 October 1951, p. 65; 14 September 1953, p. 69; 5 October 1953, p. 111; 2 November 1953, p. 146; 7 December 1953, p. 180; 4 January 1954, p. 226; 1 February 1954, p. 257; 29 March 1954, p. 328; 3 May 1954, p. 376; 4 May 1954, p. 395; 16 June 1954, p. 439; 28 June 1954, p. 443.

76. *SI*, 21 April 1950; 5 January 1951; 6 April 1951; 20 April 1951; 7 December 1951; Howard Rushmore, "The Class Struggle in Suburbia," *American Mercury*, November 1953, pp. 43–46; William C. Kernan, "Communist Infiltration of Scarsdale Public Schools," *Catholic World*, August 1952, pp. 339–45; Kernan, "Snake in Suburbia's Garden," *Catholic World*, October 1954, pp. 16–23.

77. *SI*, 27 April 1951; 4 May 1951; 4 April 1952.

78. *SI*, 4 April 1952; Gross, "The Scarsdale Controversy," p. 129. After writing an article, "The Scarsdale Story," for the *Humanist* mag-

Notes

azine, Gould himself came under attack from the Citizens' Committee, see *SI*, 8 May 1953, and Bd. of Ed., 5 October 1953, p. 112.

79. *SI*, 4 April 1952; *NYT*, 5 April 1952, p. 5 and 10 April 1952, p. 5.

80. *SI*, 4 April 1952; 11 April 1952; 25 April 1952; 2 May 1952.

81. Dist. Meet., 6 May 1952; *SI*, 9 May 1952; *NYT*, 7 May 1952, p. 29; "Scarsdale's Victory," *Nation*, 17 May 1952, pp. 464–65. See also "No Fuss or Feathers," *Library Journal*, 1 June 1952, p. 948, and Eleanor Finney, "Five Cities on the Spot: Scarsdale, New York," *Saturday Review*, 7 March 1952, p. 19.

82. *SI*, 12 December 1952, 24 April 1953; 1 May 1953.

83. For the committee's view of this episode, see Kernan, "Snake in Suburbia's Garden," pp. 16–23.

84. Bd. of Ed., 3 May 1954, p. 376; 4 May 1954, p. 395; 16 June 1954, p. 439; 28 June 1954, p. 443; 6 July 1954, pp. 12–13; *SI*, 9 July 1954.

85. *SI*, 16 July 1954; 23 July 1954; 30 July 1954; 6 August 1954; 20 August 1954. The board of education did conduct written communications with Dohrenwend and some of his associates, but these received no public attention. Bd. of Ed., 8 September 1954; 1 November 1954, p. 134; 10 November 1954, pp. 158–59; 1 December 1954, p. 161; 6 December 1954, p. 174; 14 December 1954, p. 195; 3 January 1955, p. 205; 1 June 1955, p. 343; 7 November 1955, p. 125.

The public would not hear from the members of the Citizens' Committee again until 1962, when Constance Dohrenwend and Gertrude Wetzel went to court to try to prevent the use of the high school auditorium for a concert to benefit the Freedom Riders. They charged that some of the performers (Ossie Davis, Ruby Dee, and Pete Seeger) as well as the intended benefactors were communist sympathizers and subversives. The state supreme court found that the school board was legally entitled to rent the auditorium for the concert. A few weeks later a lawyer representing Dohrenwend, Wetzel, and Robert Fitzpatrick revealed that a member of the school board, Samuel J. Duboff, had signed a petition for three Communist Party candidates in 1940. Though Duboff admitted he had signed the petition, he denied "the implication that I am a communist and have infiltrated the board." With obvious community support, Duboff retained his position on the board of education and, indeed, was renominated and re-elected. *SI*, 15 March 1962; 22 March 1962; 12 April 1962; 19 April 1962; 21 February 1963; 9 May 1963; *NYT*, 10 April 1962, p. 88; 13 April 1962, p. 23; 19 April 1962, p. 24.

86 Robert Griffith, *The Politics of Fear: Joseph R. McCarthy and the Senate* (Lexington, Ky.: University Press of Kentucky, 1970).

87. At a time when Catholics composed about 20 percent of the local population, they made up an important part of the Scarsdale Citizens' Committee. Otto E. Dohrenwend, I. Herbert Schaumber, Cyril S. Treacy, James R. Meehan, Thomas E. O'Donnell, Andrew P. McLaughlin, Edward A. Wetzel, Robert J. Fitzpatrick, and Oscar Halecki—all were Catholics. William C. Kernan, the assistant rector at the Episcopal Church, converted to Catholicism in 1952. A number of other Catholics

wrote letters to the *Inquirer* and appeared at public meetings in support of the anticommunist cause. Moreover, relatively few identifiable Catholics spoke in support of the school board or signed the petition that appeared in the *Inquirer* on 2 May 1952.

88. Quoted by Philip Carret, from 1 March 1953 issue of *The Firing Line*, in *SI*, 1 May 1953.

89. It is difficult to prove conclusively that there was or was not an anti-Semitic aspect to the controversy, since the whole area of Christian-Jewish relations is a subject most well-informed individuals are reluctant to address in interviews. Still, it is clear that at least one Jew, Sylvan Gotshal, actively supported Dohrenwend, at least for a time. It is also clear that the Town Club report on the controversy, while accepting the Citizens' Committee's claim that its members represented "all three of the principal religious groups in Scarsdale," stated, "Even so, such a controversy as this tends to arouse latent religious bigotry." Finally, it is interesting that the American Jewish Committee saw fit to distribute the Town Club report, which exonerated the board of education and most of the individuals attacked, and which criticized the tactics of the Citizens' Committee. Town Club report, quoted in Gross, "The Scarsdale Controversy," pp. 193, 68; *Education Index*, June 1953–May 1955, p. 1100.

90. Ruth D. Kellogg, *SI*, 12 May 1950; Patrick Candido, *SI*, 4 April 1952.

CHAPTER EIGHT (*Pages 187–215*)

1. For a perceptive analysis of the significance of Scarsdale's reaching a population "plateau," see the speech by John S. Snyder, former president of the board of education in school district one, *SI*, 18 March and 25 March 1965.

2. These percentages are based on a random sample of the names listed in the Scarsdale Telephone Directories for 1940 and 1960, and the Scarsdale Handi-Book for 1980–81. The author was careful to exclude people whose residences were not located within the village limits. For a discussion of the difficulties of analyzing the ethnoreligious composition of a community like Scarsdale, see note 19, chapter five, above.

3. Letter from Cynthia Bunker, *SI*, 11 February 1949; editorial, *SI*, 15 November 1962; statement by Mrs. Robert Linnett, *SI*, 1 April 1965. For additional allusions to Christian-Jewish relations, see editorial, *SI*, 17 February 1956; editorial, 19 December 1963, letter by Robert S. Hackett, *SI*, 23 January 1964.

4. *SI*, 12 January 1961; *NYT*, 13 January 1961, p. 1.

5. *Ibid*.

6. *NYT*, 14 January 1961, p. 1; 15 January 1961, p. 64; 16 January 1961, p. 24; 24 January 1961, p. 1; statement by Rabbi David Greenberg, and editorial, *SI*, 12 January 1961; statement by Rev. Walter G. Hed, and letter by Raymond J. Blair, *SI*, 19 January 1961; letter by Sylvia

M. Halpern, 26 January 1961. References to the Holly Ball incident have appeared in Baltzell, *The Protestant Establishment*, pp. 359–61, and J. Robert Moskin, *Morality in America* (New York: Random House, 1966), pp. 229, 232.

7. The quotation is from the resolution establishing the human relations committee, Records, 27 January 1964, pp. 38–40; 23 March 1965, pp. 115–17, 126; *SI*, 21 September 1961; 16 January 1964; 11 April 1968.

On the crèche dispute, see *SI*, 5 October 1961; 12 October 1961; Records, 23 October 1962, pp. 405–405a; 15 January 1963, p. 1; 26 November 1963, p. 460; *SI*, 5 December 1974; *SI*, 30 November 1978; 29 November 1979; 11 December 1980.

8. *SI*, 5 November 1948; 7 November 1952; 9 November 1956; 10 November 1960; 5 November 1964; 7 November 1968; 9 November 1972.

Although, in 1976 and 1980, the Republican presidential candidates, like Nixon in 1972, received a slim majority of the local vote, it was clear that Scarsdale was not solidly in either party's camp. In 1976, 49.47 percent of Scarsdale's voters favored the Democratic candidate, Jimmy Carter, while 50.53 percent chose the Republican, Gerald Ford. Four years later, Carter received less than 34 percent of the local return; the independent candidate, John Anderson, received nearly 14 percent; Republican Ronald Reagan, 51 percent, and various other candidates the remaining 1 percent. *SI*, 4 November 1976; 6 November 1980.

9. *SI*, 11 July 1952; 6 September 1957. Although critics of the nonpartisan system were few in number in the 1930s, forties, and fifties, interestingly the strongest critics were staunch Republicans who believed the system gave too much representation to Democrats. *SI*, 23 February 1945; 31 January 1947; 28 February 1948.

10. *SI*, 14 February 1963; 28 February 1963; 21 March 1963; 13 February 1964; 20 February 1964; 4 February 1965. The demands actually dated back to a report drawn up by a Democratic committee chaired by Dean Rusk and Theodore Tannenwald, Jr., *SI*, 13 November 1959.

11. *SI*, 9 April 1964.

12. *SI*, 25 June 1962. Koblitz was reacting to statements made by former trustee and mayor, Harold L. Smith, *SI*, 18 January 1962.

13. *SI*, 28 January 1965; 19 January 1967; 6 April 1967; 11 January 1968; 9 January 1969; 16 October 1969.

14. *SI*, 19 January 1967; 23 February 1967; 16 March 1967.

15. *SI*, 26 January 1967; 16 February 1967.

16. *SI*, 13 February 1967; 2 March 1967; 9 March 1967; 16 March 1967; 23 March 1967.

17. *SI*, 29 February 1968; 21 March 1968.

18. This analysis stems from a broad understanding of the circumstances of the 1970 election. *SI* describes the events without setting them in context. *SI*, 29 January 1970; 26 February 1970; 19 March 1970.

19. *SI*, 1 February 1979; 31 May 1979; 24 January 1980; 19 June 1980; 29 January 1981; 19 March 1981.

20. *SI*, 22 January 1981; 26 February 1981; 5 March 1981; 12 March 1981. Interestingly, an article written on the occasion of the Town Club's seventy-fifth anniversary speaks glowingly of the "democratizing" of the nonpartisan system. *SI*, 20 September 1979.

21. See the comments by Rita H. Satz, Malcolm A. MacIntyre, and John S. Snyder for three examples of the "Scarsdale is or is not an island" metaphor, Records, 26 December 1963, p. 487; 14 May 1968, p. 152; *SI*, 18 March 1965; 25 March 1965. An *SI* editorial on 11 January 1968, stated, "The expression that Scarsdale is not an island has become a cliché, but it is true that this community cannot hide from the profound changes taking place in our country, nor, we think, does it wish to."

22. Quoted in *SI*, 3 February 1966.

23. *SI*, 23 November 1961; 29 March 1962; 7 June 1962.

24. *SI*, 11 November 1965; 18 November 1965; 28 April 1966.

25. Records, 23 March 1965, pp. 115–17, 126; 8 June 1965, p. 245; 13 July 1965, p. 295; 8 November 1966, pp. 311–12; 22 November 1966, pp. 327, 331; 10 December 1968, pp. 354–58; 11 February 1968, pp. 37–47; *SI*, 24 November 1966; 12 December 1968; 13 February 1969.

26. Editorial, *SI*, 14 April 1966.

27. *SI*, 18 November 1965.

28. See the discussions of zoning in chapters two and seven of this work, and *SI*, 28 June 1962; 25 February 1965; Records, 23 February 1965, pp. 64–73.

29. Records, 9 April 1968, p. 128; 23 April 1968, pp. 139–140; *SI*, 11 April 1968; 25 April 1968; 28 November 1968.

30. Records, 13 August 1968, pp. 248–50; 22 October 1968, pp. 319–20; 10 December 1968, pp. 352–53; *SI*, 20 June 1968; 15 August 1968; 24 October 1968.

31. Records, 8 October 1968, pp. 301–302; *SI*, 10 October 1968.

32. *SI*, 10 October 1968; statement by Carol Stix, *SI*, 6 February 1969.

33. Letters by Joseph Arthur Cohen and Lionel M. Kaufman, *SI*, 5 December 1968, and statement by Mrs. Martin J. Brennan, Records, 26 November 1968, pp. 343–44.

34. Records, 8 October 1968, pp. 314–16; *SI*, 17 October 1968; *NYT*, 18 October 1968, p. 24.

35. Records, 10 December 1968, pp. 350–51; *SI*, 12 December 1968; 17 July 1969; 2 July 1970; *NYT*, 19 July 1981, sec. 11, pp. 1, 8.

36. Letters by Joseph Arthur Cohen and Jack Haig Murdick, *SI*, 24 December 1968.

37. In 1960 the census distinguished only between white and nonwhite heads of household. Since the author knows that several Asian families lived in Scarsdale at this time, the number of black heads of household was smaller than the number of nonwhite heads of household, twenty. U. S. Bureau of the Census, *Eighteenth Census, 1960*, vol. 1, pt. 34, p. 110; Advance Counts, 1980 Census, table 1, "Persons by Race and Spanish Origin," village clerk's file; *SI*, 18 June 1981; *NYT*, 19 July 1981, sec. 11, pp. 1, 8.

38. *SI*, 14 August 1969; 20 August 1970; 11 March 1971; 29 April 1971; 13 May 1971; 10 January 1974; 7 February 1974; 14 February 1974; 28 March 1974.

39. *SI*, 24 July 1969; 25 September 1969; 20 November 1969; 29 January 1970; 23 May 1974; 29 August 1974; 15 January 1976. At the end of 1981, two proposals that would require a change in Scarsdale's zoning were still pending; one for cluster-housing, at a site on Post Road in South Scarsdale (see *SI*, 7 January 1980; 20 March 1980; 12 June 1980), and one for an eight-story apartment complex with professional offices and a two-level parking garage, on village-owned land near the railroad tracks (see *SI*, 30 August 1979; 27 March 1980; 17 July 1980; 18 January 1981; 14 May 1981; 4 June 1981; 3 September 1981).

40. *SI*, 26 August 1965.

41. Bd. of Ed., 10 June 1968, pp. 213, 219; *RD*, 11 June 1968.

42. The other members of the board during Thompson's tenure as president were George F. James, Murray Steyer, Samuel J. Duboff, Frederick P. Rose, J. Walter Severinghaus, Leonard F. Howard, Anita Pickering, Margaret Madison, Nora Simon, and Betty Menke; Union Free School District No. 1, Announcement of Annual Meeting of All Qualified Voters, 2 May 1967; *SI*, 3 March 1966; Bd. of Ed., 8 January 1968, p. 118; *SI*, 4 March 1971; personal communication from the administrative offices of the Scarsdale Public Schools, 5 February 1982.

43. The Summer Cooperative Project was also known as the Scarsdale-Mount Vernon Summer School Project and the Urban-Suburban Schools Cooperative Educational Project. Bd. of Ed., 9 January 1967, p. 140; 6 February 1967, p. 152; 7 May 1967, p. 223; 11 December 1967, p. 108; 8 January 1968, p. 122; *SI*, 9 February 1967; 11 May 1967; 14 December 1967.

44. *SI*, 18 January 1968.

45. Bd. of Ed., 11 March 1968, pp. 144–45; *SI*, 14 March 1968.

46. Statement on Title III Application, Bd. of Ed., 11 March 1968, pp. 144, 153.

47. *SI*, 9 May 1968, 1 August 1968; Bd. of Ed., 13 May 1968, p.189; 9 September 1968, p. 45; 9 December 1968, p. 138; Sarah Lawrence College, Institute for Community Studies, "An Evaluation of the Urban-Suburban Cooperative Educational Project funded by Title III, Elementary and Secondary Education Act of 1965," 1 December 1968, p. 44; Bd. of Ed., 9 December 1968, pp. 137–39; 14 April 1969, p. 201, and appendix to p. 213; 12 May 1969, p. 232 and appendix to p. 236; *SI*, 24 December 1968; 3 April 1969; 15 May 1969.

48. U. S. Department of Health, Education, and Welfare, Office of Education, *Equality of Educational Opportunity*, 1966 (usually referred to as the Coleman Report after its principal author, James S. Coleman); U. S. Commission on Civil Rights, *Racial Isolation in the Public Schools*, 1967.

49. *SI*, 21 April 1966; 2 November 1967; Emery, "Memo from Scarsdale: A New Role for Suburban Schools," *Look*, 2 April 1968, p. 18.

50. Materials on all three of these projects were among those collected by the P-T Council Study Group on Scarsdale's Urban responsibility

and later contributed to the Scarsdale Public Library. See, in particular, "Metco: A Report to the Carnegie Corporation," 18 December 1968.

51. *SI*, 25 August 1966.

52. *SI*, 28 December 1967; *NYT*, 18 February 1968, p. 51; Study Group on Urban Responsibility, Scarsdale Council of PTAs, "A Time for Commitment to Interracial Education in Scarsdale," 29 February 1968; *SI*, 21 March 1968.

53. Editorial, Traub letter, and Fink statement, *SI*, 21 March 1968; letter from seniors, *SI*, 28 March 1968.

54. Letters from Jack Murdich and Joseph Ballinger, *SI*, 28 March 1968; letter from Sheldon Gerber, and statement of Harry B. Gilbert, *SI*, 21 February 1968.

55. Lloyd Sand, *SI*, 17 October 1968; Dorothy Singer, *SI*, 11 January 1968.

56. Statement of Judy Poole, and letter from Mrs. Marvin S. Traub, *SI*, 21 March 1968; letter from Irene and Stanley Frankel, *SI*, 27 November 1969; statement of Roger Seasonwein, *SI*, 21 March 1968.

57. Hubert Horan, *SI*, 17 October 1968, and Howard B. and Janet M. Demb, *SI*, 21 November 1968.

58. *SI*, 21 March 1968; Bd. of Ed., 10 June 1968, pp. 213, 219; *RD*, 11 June 1968.

59. *SI*, 9 May 1968; 10 October 1968; Dist. Meet., 7 May 1968.

60. *SI*, 6 June 1968; 10 September 1968; 17 October 1968; 24 October 1968.

61. Dorothy B. Gordon, the nonpartisan candidate, defeated Lenore Sofia, the CFR candidate, by a vote of 2,772 to 1,615. In addition, there were thirteen write-in votes for various candidates. *SI*, 13 March 1969; 20 March 1969; Bd. of Ed., 10 March 1969, pp. 186, 194; 13 October 1969, *SI*, 19 June 1969.

62. *SI*, 30 October 1969; 6 November 1969; 13 November 1969; 20 November 1969; 27 November 1969; 4 December 1969; *NYT*, 3 December 1969, p. 32.

63. *SI*, 20 November 1969.

64. Bd. of Ed., 8 December 1969, pp. 87–88, and appendix to p. 93; *SI*, 11 December 1969; *NYT*, 9 December 1969, p. 87.

65. Statements by Matthew Smith and Max Hansen, *RD*, 23 January 1970; *SI*, 12 March 1970; *NYT*, 13 March 1970, p. 23.

66. Letter by Raymond Davies, *SI*, 20 November 1969; letter by Cooper D. Ponton, *SI*, 14 May 1970; *NYT*, 24 May 1970, p. 71; *SI*, 11 June 1970; letters by Ann H. DelGaudio and Jack D. Samuels, *SI*, 25 June 1970; *SI*, 2 July 1970; Bd. of Ed., 4 June 1970, p. 184; 25 June 1970, p. 200.

67. *SI*, 17 August 1970; 17 September 1970; 8 October 1970; 14 January 1971; quotation from letter by Mrs. Sabino Rodriguez, Jr., *SI*,7 January 1971; 27 May 1971.

68. For antiwar activities of Scarsdale High School students, see *SI*, 23 March 1967; 9 October 1969; 23 October 1969; 14 May 1969; see also letter from C. Galante, accusing Scarsdale's schools of radicalizing the students, *SI*, 14 May 1970, and letter by L. O. Dorfman, suggesting the presence of "subversives" in the schools, *SI*, 21 May 1970.

69. *NYT*, 15 August 1969, pp. 1, 6.

70. *SI*, 21 August 1969; editorial, "Vietnam in Scarsdale," *NYT*, 16 August 1969, p. 26.

71. "Revolution in the Twentieth Century" was a half-credit, elective course, open to upperclassmen at Scarsdale High School. The six revolutions it examined included three communist (Russian, Chinese, and Cuban) and three noncommunist (Turkish, Mexican, and Egyptian). The course focused on the causes, character, and consequences of these revolutions. Any discussion of guerrilla warfare was ancillary to these themes. Stephen Kling, by the way, was a Ford Foundation fellow with degrees from Carleton and Yale. He had studied Russian at Columbia, had investigated social development at first hand in India and Egypt, and had served as an officer in the air force under General William C. Westmoreland. *SI*, 21 August 1969; 28 August 1969; letter from Mrs. William G. Fallon, *SI*, 21 August 1969.

72. *SI*, 1 April 1965; 20 January 1966; 28 December 1967; 11 January 1968; 29 February 1968; 20 June 1968; 4 June 1970.

73. Among the letters supporting the war effort, one of the most emotional was written by village trustee Richard W. Darrow, as a tribute to Tom Dean, a Scarsdale youth who was critically wounded in Vietnam and survived two months before dying. Said Darrow: "His story . . . provides a vivid contrast with some of those we read of, young men turning their backs on their country's needs, responsibilities, and commitments in a world that can't be wished to peace in the face of enemy forces who don't want peace. . . . I wouldn't trade one Tommy Dean for a whole army of Dr. Spocks, William Sloan Coffins, and their misled followers." *SI*, 18 January 1968.

74. *SI*, 16 February 1967.

75. Letter from Donald H. Ogilvy, *SI*, 23 February 1967; letter from five couples (Marquesee, Brown, Wadler, Handman, Fujimoto) and Gloria S. Karp, *SI*, 2 March 1967.

76. Letters from Ernest S. Black and Charles S. Pachner, Town Club Statement, *SI*, 9 March 1967.

77. Letters from Ferguson, Feldman, and editorial, *SI*, 9 March 1967; letter from Harold L. and Edith Friedman, *SI*, 23 March 1967.

78. *SI*, 11 May 1967; 4 May 1967. The presentation of a glass eagle to the secretary of state proved to be unwittingly symbolic.

79. *New York Post* column, reprinted in *SI*, 18 May 1967.

80. *SI*, 23 March 1967.

81. *SI*, 11 January 1968; 21 November 1963; 18 March 1965.

82. *Time*, 12 October 1970, p. 50.

83. Kenneth Keniston, "You Have to Grow Up in Scarsdale," *NYT Magazine*, 27 April 1969, p. 128. Reprinted in *Youth and Dissent: The Rise of a New Opposition* (New York: Harcourt Brace Jovanovich, 1971).

84. Letter from Dick Immerman, Becky Jones, Jon Leland, Judy Poole, Alan Snitow, and Neil Westreid, *SI*, 8 May 1969.

85. Letter from Steven E. Tisch, *SI*, 7 May 1970. For other examples of references to Scarsdale, see the script for the Broadway play, "Butterflies Are Free," by Leonard Gershe (New York: Random House, 1969), pp. 11, 89–90, 100; and Irving Kristol, "The Young Are Trying

to Tell Us Something About Scarsdale," *Fortune*, August 1971, pp. 173–74.

86. Thompson gave these views in a speech, after receiving the Scarsdale Bowl Award. *SI*, 13 January 1972.

EPILOGUE (*Pages 217–221*)

1. The diet book was, of course, *The Complete Scarsdale Medical Diet*, which, from the time of its publication to the end of 1981, had sold several hundred thousand copies, and the more famous of the two murders was that of the book's author Dr. Herman Tarnower, who practiced medicine in the village. Tarnower's murder and the subsequent trial of Jean Harris, his lover for fourteen years, were prime topics of media attention from March 1980 to March 1981. The publicity this brought to Scarsdale caused resentment among village residents. As Mayor Grady Jensen remarked, "She lived in Virginia, he lived in Harrison, the case was being tried in White Plains, and the entire affair had almost nothing to do with Scarsdale," *NYT*, 2 March 1981, sec. 2, pp. 1, 5.

The second murder involved two Yale undergraduates. In July 1977, Bonnie Garland was beaten to death with a hammer in her parents' Scarsdale home. A year later her former boyfriend Richard Herrin was found guilty of first-degree manslaughter. For more on the case, see J. Kornbluth, "Fatal Romance at Yale," *New York Times Magazine*, 7 May 1978, pp. 44–45.

2. An. Rep., 1980–81, p. 9. The average assessment was obtained by dividing the total assessed valuation in the village by the number of taxable properties. For community response to recent budgets, see *SI*, 26 April 1979; 21 May 1981.

3. Under citizen pressure, the village board rejected a proposal from the heirs of George G. Allen to build cluster-housing condominiums on his 25-acre estate; *SI*, 23 May 1974; 29 August 1974; 15 January 1976. They also rejected a proposal submitted by the Polera Corporation to build an eight-story apartment complex with professional offices and a two-level parking garage on village-owned land near the railroad tracks; *SI*, 30 August 1979; 27 March 1980; 17 July 1980; 18 January 1981; 14 May 1981; 4 June 1981; 3 September 1981; 24 December 1981; 28 January 1982. On the auditorium issue, see *SI*, 1 February 1979; 5 April 1979.

4. *SI*, 15 June 1978; 6 July 1978; 7 December 1978; 22 February 1979; 15 March 1979; 5 April 1979; 28 June 1979; 27 December 1979.

5. *NYT*, 24 June 1978, pp. 1, 24.

6. *SI*, 8 February 1979; 10 May 1979; 28 August 1980; 19 February 1981; 7 January 1982; 28 January 1982; 15 July 1982.

7. *SI*, 31 May 1979; 7 January 1980; 14 June 1980; 4 September 1980; 20 November 1980; 15 January 1981; 19 March 1981; 14 January 1982; 18 March 1982.

8. *SI*, 5 October 1961; 12 October 1961; Records, 23 October 1962, pp. 405–405a; 15 January 1963, p. 1; 26 November 1963, p. 460; *SI*,

5 December 1974; *SI*, 30 November 1978; 29 November 1979; 11 December 1980; 12 November 1981; 19 November 1981; 26 November 1981; 3 December 1981; 20 May 1982; 27 May 1982.

9. *SI*, 4 November 1971; 15 January 1981; 8 August 1971; 13 July 1978; 24 October 1974; 23 October 1981. The exclusion of women from the Town Club had long been a source of criticism; see letter from Robert J. Koblitz, *SI*, 28 May 1964; letter from three women, *SI*, 10 June 1964; *SI*, 4 November 1974; *NYT*, 12 February 1973, p. 29; 24 May 1977, p. 39; 28 October 1977, p. 17; 29 October 1977, p. 27.

10. *Newsweek*, 9 June 1980, pp. 48, 50.

Bibliographic Note

The principal sources for this study, in the approximate order of their importance, are the local newspaper, village and school board records, state and federal census records, deeds and subdivision maps, the real estate news and other items in the *New York Times*, the records of clubs and religious groups, interviews, special studies concerning Scarsdale, and general works. The weekly newspaper, the *Scarsdale Inquirer*, is the one source that provides information and opinions on all the topics discussed in this history. Available except for brief periods from 1901 to the present, the *Inquirer* has operated under a number of owners whose editorial attitudes have varied. For example, the boosterism of a real estate agent colored the reporting from 1902 to 1909, and the desire of the Woman's Club to minimize controversy affected the tone of the paper from 1919 to 1959. Still, the *Inquirer* is a good source, accurate in its factual content and reflective of opinion within the community.

The official records of the village and school boards are also indispensable. Neatly typed and indexed, the records of the meetings of the village board of trustees document the actions taken by the trustees and usually indicate some of the reasons for their actions. The village board has also published an annual report, which contains information regarding the budget and other statistics. The records of the meetings of the board of education and its annual reports provide similar information for that body. The town board minutes are less helpful. They are available for the years 1911 to 1915, but are missing for the entire period between 1864 and 1910.

The state and federal census records constitute the major source of information concerning the social structure of the

271

community. The population schedules (the census takers' hand-written listings of every member of every household, often with data regarding each individual's age, sex, race, place of birth, occupation, and family relationship) are available at the Mormon Genealogical Library, in Salt Lake City, for every federal census but one up to 1900 and for the three New York State censuses of 1905, 1915, and 1925. For similar information on more recent decades the scholar must resort to the published federal census records which, especially for a small community like Scarsdale, summarize only a part of the information collected by the census takers.

The deeds and subdivision maps filed in the land records division of the Westchester County clerk's office provide data regarding the previous place of residence of buyers of property in Scarsdale and the restrictions on the use of land in the various subdivisions. The real estate advertisements in the *New York Times* supplement the information contained in the deeds and subdi-vision maps with examples of how the developers of the various subdivisions addressed their appeals to different groups of pro-spective buyers.

The information available from the various clubs and religious groups is so uneven as to prevent a thorough study of these dimensions of community life. The records available for the Town Club do not reflect that organization's importance, at least in the first four decades of its history. The minutes of the club's meetings are extremely brief, and available only for the years 1904 to 1922. Yearbooks are available from 1925 on, but they only list the rules and the names of members. Most of the reports issued by committees of the club in the 1920s and early thirties have been lost, although those for most recent decades are available at the Town Club's office. The Woman's Club yearbooks are a rich source of information. For every year, beginning in 1924, they summarize the activities of the club, list the names of members, and detail the club's financial situation. The only source available regarding the history of the Scarsdale Golf Club is a booklet commemorating the club's fiftieth anniversary. Un-fortunately the club does not have any membership lists from the years before World War II. The unwillingness of some religious groups to release the names of their members prevented a close analysis of where in Scarsdale the members of the various churches resided. Although none of the churches and synagogues have samples of sermons from decades past, each has a pamphlet history, a few of which are particularly helpful.

An attempt has been made to fill in gaps in the written record by interviewing a number of individuals, most of whom were active in village affairs thirty to fifty years ago. Nearly every one of these interviews has provided a core of information not available elsewhere.

In addition to those sources available only in Scarsdale, White Plains, or at specialized genealogical libraries, there are a number of published writings about the village. The majority of these are articles written about specific topics, such as Scarsdale's wartime farm, its experimental waste disposal plant, the application of the Dalton Plan in the public schools, and the dynamics of the anticommunist crusade. There are also two histories of the village, Harry Hansen's *Scarsdale: From Colonial Manor to Modern Community* (New York: Harper & Brothers, 1954) and Diana Reische's *Of Colonists and Commuters: A History of Scarsdale* (Scarsdale: Junior League of Scarsdale, 1976). Written, respectively, in conjunction with the Town Club and the Junior League, these works take the celebratory tone of many local histories. While Hansen's book is more detailed, Reische's book, which is intended for seventh-grade students, is rich in illustrations and anecdotes. Neither work contains much analysis. *Leisure: A Suburban Study* (New York: Columbia University Press, 1934) by George A. Lundberg, Mirra Komarovsky, and Mary Alice McInerny is a more interesting source. Focusing on leisure institutions in Scarsdale and other Westchester suburbs in the early thirties, it provides a contemporary sociological insight, particularly into the workings of the Town Club and the Woman's Club.

An extensive body of literature concerning suburbia has arisen since World War II. Generally these works fall into two schools. Some writers, for instance, Sylvia Fava, speak of "a suburban way of life." Others, including Bennett Berger and Herbert Gans, argue that the culture of a particular suburb depends on the social class of its residents. Clearly the present study lends substantiation to the latter point of view. However, because of the differences in methodology between historians, on the one hand, and sociologists and cultural anthropologists, on the other, the points of comparison between this and most other community studies are few. For example, *Crestwood Heights* (New York: Basic Books, 1956), the study of an upper-middle-class suburb of Toronto, is based on interviews and observations conducted over a five-year period. The authors, John R. Seeley, R. Alexander Sims, and Elizabeth W. Loosley, discuss their subjects' intimate concerns regarding such topics as family, school, career, and club. They pay no attention to public issues such as municipal services and zoning.

One book that aims to bridge the gap between the sociological literature on suburbia and the historian's methodology is Zane L. Miller's *Suburb: Neighborhood and Community in Forest Park, Ohio, 1935–1976* (Knoxville: University of Tennessee, 1981). Miller does an excellent job of examining Forest Park within the context of changes in metropolitan Cincinnati and the broader American society. But since Forest Park, which began as a New Deal "greenbelt" town and has since developed many "urban" problems, is not Scarsdale, readers will turn to it largely for reasons different from those that might inspire a reading of the present study.

For background information on the issues discussed in the present history, a number of works are helpful. They include E. Digby Baltzell, *The Protestant Establishment* (New York: Random House, 1964); Lawrence A. Cremin, *The Transformation of the School* (New York: Alfred A. Knopf, Inc., 1961); and Seymour Toll, *The Zoned American* (New York: Grossman Publishers, 1969). For other sources consult the notes listed for each chapter.

Index

Index

Index

Index

282